PILOT
OF
FORTUNE

Frank H. Jerdone

With a foreword by Senator Barry M. Goldwater

VANTAGE PRESS
New York / Washington / Atlanta
Los Angeles / Chicago

Published by Vantage Press, Inc.
516 West 34th Street, New York, New York 10001

Manufactured in the United States of America
ISBN: 0-533-06861-4

Library of Congress Catalog Card No.: 85-91348

To Clare with love

Contents

Foreword

Having been a licensed pilot myself for fifty-seven years and having enjoyed the art or act of flying immensely during that time, I know exactly what Frank Jerdone has gone through in putting together this very interesting book about his lifetime of flying. Often people have asked me to relate some interesting remembrance of flying and, you know, it is the most difficult thing in the world. Even with the thousands of hours I have in the air, I have to sit and think a long time before I can come up with something that might be even partly interesting.

The facts of Frank's life, what he did to get into flying, are pretty much typical of the old pilot. In fact, as all of us grow older—and some of us are not even around now—younger pilots will be in the same fix. Frank has been a pilot a little bit longer than I have, but he got into it pretty much the same way that all of us got into it. We watched someone fly and we thought, *Wouldn't that be interesting and wouldn't it be wonderful if I could do the same thing?* The first thing you know, off we go and learn how to fly.

The fact that Mr. Jerdone established the first airline in Nicaragua, he was the second pilot hired by Eastern Air Transport, and he participated in establishing Eastern's Miami-Atlanta route is just indicative of the type of information contained in this book.

It is a real honor and pleasure for me to have been asked by Frank to write a short foreward for his book, and I can assure anyone interested in flying, whether he be a pilot or not, that he will find this book an extremely interesting account of a man who has devoted his life to flying. There are many hundreds of thousands of pilots in this country, and, hopefully, some of them will start putting down what they remember about their experiences in the air before they become completely forgotten by that particular pilot.

I do recommend the reading of this book. It is interesting not just from a pilot's standpoint, but from the standpoint of an American who still has great faith in the ability of an American to do anything he sets out to do and the ability of America to produce the equipment needed to accomplish those desires.

—SENATOR BARRY M. GOLDWATER

Preface

The scene of my early childhood was the farm of my paternal grandparents in Orange County, Virginia. The estate, known as Bloomsbury, was one of the oldest in the Commonwealth of Virginia. The house was built in 1722 by the original owner, James Taylor, Jr., a great-grandfather of the twelfth president of the United States, Zachary Taylor. Bloomsbury was acquired by an ancestor, Francis Jerdone, in 1843 and remained in the Jerdone family until as recently as 1964.

I often walked to the top of Jerdone Mountain, a rise of land situated some distance from the house. Here I would sit and view the countryside below. From this vantage point, horizons seemed far away, but I sensed that an immense world that I very much wanted to explore lay beyond.

In later years, I was to travel far beyond those horizons to many distant lands. When I became a man and revisited the scenes of my childhood, those far horizons seemed small in comparison.

I was born on October 5, 1903. The Wright brothers, at Kill Devil Hill, North Carolina, made their historic first flight on December 17, 1903. Therefore I am exactly two months and fourteen days older than powered flight. I can remember when, at the age of six, I was taken to visit an aunt in Washington, D.C. Standing on the balcony of her apartment on Meridian Hill overlooking the Potomac and Fort Meyer, Virginia, I witnessed one of the first demonstration flights to the United States Army by the Wright brothers. This, of course, was 1909, and I really don't know why this event has remained so vividly in my memory.

Perhaps at even this tender age there was born in my subconscious mind an overwhelming interest in aviation that only manifested itself during the First World War. I was an avid reader of the exploits of Nungesser, Lufbury, Bishop, and Rickenbacker. Two years too young for that war, I had to be content in living through the air battles vicariously through those great fliers.

Now, in the late years of my life, walking slowly down the winding corridors of time, I seem to hear the muted sound of engines droning overhead, long echoes of the flight.

Pilot of Fortune

Chapter 1   Annapolis

The spring of 1920 found me living in a farmhouse high on a hill overlooking the Severn River at Annapolis. My companions were two pilots who owned a flying boat with which they eked out a precarious living flying from a little beach on the Severn just below our farmhouse.

Howard French and Charlie Boylan were as disparate types as one could imagine. Howard French was an ex–army air service lieutenant. He wore a waxed mustache, which he was inordinately proud of and with which he was constantly fiddling. His attire consisted of army breeches and highly polished boots, and he usually wore a white shirt, which was always spotlessly clean. He was a very fastidious guy.

Charlie Boylan was the antithesis of Howard. Charlie had been a navy-enlisted pilot trained by the French, and practically all of his flying had been overseas on French flying boats. Charlie was a tough Irishman with hardly a fourth-grade education. I often wondered how he qualified for flight training. But Charlie was a superb pilot, far superior to French. He was also a good instructor, but when you made a mistake you could hear his cuss words above the roar of the engine.

I don't remember how I learned of these two pilots and their flying boat. I had saved up a little money working at odd jobs and had conned my grandfather into advancing me the balance of my "tuition" demanded by Charlie and Howard. However, in addition I was to act as a general handyman around the airplane, sort of a "flunky" to do the dirty work. In return for all this, I was to be taught to fly. That is, I was to receive flying instruction to the point where these two pilots considered me qualified to solo the airplane. Nothing was said about my actually soloing this boat, and later I could understand why. These two weren't about to let any student take their airplane up alone, thereby risking their only means of livelihood.

Beached alongside of us on the Severn was a Curtiss "F" boat, owned by Ewing Easter of Baltimore. Ewing was, like Howard French, an ex–army flyer. And he too, like French, wore boots and breeches. It seemed that 'most every army pilot I ran across wore these same boots and breeches, and I often wondered if they wore this attire to make them stand out from us ordinary folks or if they just couldnt't afford anything else.

Ewing was a handsome chap. He very much resembled Ronald Coleman, and a lot of people mistook him for the famous movie actor. Ewing and I became very good friends, and in the years to come he was to prove of great help to me. But more of that later.

During the summer of 1920, we did a modest passenger business from our base on the Severn River. In addition to this we would fly over to Betterton, Oxford, Cambridge, and Saint Michael's, thereby covering most of the eastern shore of Maryland. On these short flights, Charlie (who did most of the flying) would let me handle the controls and any mistakes I made would be rewarded with a blow on the wrists. However, in this fashion I did learn to keep the plane straight and level and make shallow turns. Finally, the summer came to an end and we all went our separate ways. I never saw Charlie Boylan again. I heard later that he was killed flying for some rumrunners off the New Jersey coast. Howard French I was to meet in later years both in California and Florida. As I write this, I have just learned that Howard died in Miami at the age of ninety.

After my summer's stint as an apprentice pilot at Annapolis, I returned to Washington and holed up in my Aunt Kitty's apartment on Columbia Road. Whenever I was out of a job and broke (which was frequently the case in those days), Aunt Kitty would provide me with room and board. As I had no parents of my own, Kitty was more like a mother to me than an aunt. She provided a place I could call home. I used her apartment as sort of a base of operations, a mailing address, and a place to receive phone calls.

When I left for Washington, I had no idea what I would do next. Continuing my flying training seemed impossible. I had no money and no job. The future looked bleak indeed. One day Kitty mentioned that my father had been a good friend of Col. E. Lester Jones, who at that time was head of the Coast and Geodetic Survey. It occurred to me that possibly through the influence of this important government official I might get a job. Of course, I had no idea what kind of a job, for I was not qualified for anything in particular. I finally got up nerve enough to call Colonel Jones for an appointment. When I appeared in Colonel Jones's office, he greeted me cordially, asked me to be seated, and mentioned something about having known my father well. He asked me what I had been doing, and I told him of my brief flying experience at Annapolis.

Colonel Jones suggested the possibility of my entering the army air service as a flying cadet. This idea had never occurred to me. I knew nothing of any postwar training program that the army was conducting at that time. The colonel then told me that Gen. "Billy" Mitchell, who at that time commanded the army air service, was a friend of his and that he would be glad to give me a letter to General Mitchell.

A few days later, I appeared at the office of the commanding general of the army air service in the old munitions building on Constitution Avenue. Almost immediately a secretary ushered me into the general's office. Meeting such a famous person face to face was an awesome experience for a kid barely nineteen years old. However, the general soon put me at ease. He arose from his desk, shook my hand, and greeted me cordially. He asked me a few questions, such as how did I like flying, did I want to become an army pilot and air-reserve officer, et cetera. He then got up from his desk and said, "Let's go down to Personnel." He led me down a long corridor. We entered an office marked "Personnel," and he introduced me to a Major somebody and said, "I want you to start processing this man for flying cadet training."

After filling out endless forms and finally passing a very rigid physical examination, I was told to go home and await orders to proceed to Carlstrom Field, Arcadia, Florida, for pilot training. There was a long wait of about two months, but finally my orders came through. I was to report to the Commanding Officer, Primary Flying School, Carlstrom Field, Florida, on January 1, 1922. The routine of army life was indeed strange to me. The strict discipline was especially galling at first, but I soon became adapted to this new life. As a matter of fact, this army discipline was just what I needed, for all of my young life I had been allowed too much freedom.

Our day began at 5:45. We had calisthenics and breakfast and then were on the flight line at 7:00. Our mornings were devoted to flying, our afternoons to ground school. We were taught theory of flight, engine maintenance, navigation, radio (Morse Code), military law, et cetera. Saturday's drill was in the morning, and after an inspection we were off duty for the weekend. We would visit the town of Arcadia, where we soon became acquainted with some of the local girls. I had the good fortune to meet a very attractive young lady by the name of Alberta Bennett. I don't recall just how I happened to meet Alberta, but we became good friends, and I usually had a date with her on Saturday evenings. Her father and mother were very kind to me and often invited me to Sunday dinner. To a youngster such as I, far from home in strange military surroundings, the Bennetts' hospitality was much appreciated. Somehow the memory of Alberta has been with me off and on throughout the years. I wonder, Alberta, how life has treated you. I hope that fate has been kind to you.

At the time of my tour of duty at Carlstrom, the army was still using the World War I training plane the Curtiss JN4d, known throughout the service as the Jenny. However, these airplanes were equipped with the 150 H.P. Hispano Suiza engine instead of the old Curtiss 90 H.P. OX5 engine. This was a two-place biplane; the instructor sat in the front seat, the student in the rear. My instructor, Lt. Frederick I. Patrick, was a man I never could understand. He seemed to hate the very idea of teaching cadets to fly. I got the impression, which I am sure was correct, that he was afraid some cadet would kill him, perhaps in panic freezing the controls while in a spin. In fact, often Lieutenant Patrick made the remark, "You're going to kill me yet," when I made some mistake that inevitably brought on a fit of anger. He would then grab the controls away from me and dive the airplane toward the ground and land. There was no explanation, no remark of any kind. He would just walk away.

This went on for about four months. I soon realized, of course, that I was getting nowhere with Lieutenant Patrick. I simply had to be assigned a new instructor, one whose temperament and method of instructing were more compatible with my personality.

I finally got up nerve enough to take the initiative and request a new instructor. So one afternoon just before reporting for ground school, I appeared at the office of Lt. Julian S. Haddon, officer in charge of flying. Haddon was of medium height and stocky build and had a rather swarthy complexion. (He was part Cherokee.) He had the reputation of being a hard-boiled officer and especially rough on flying cadets. After knocking, I entered the office, saluted, and said, "Sir, Cadet Jerdone requests permission to speak with the lieutenant." He nodded, and I proceeded. "Sir, I am having some difficulty with my instructor, Lieutenant Patrick."

"What seems to be the trouble?"

"Well, it's probably a personality clash. Anyway, I'm not getting anywhere, and I'm afraid he is going to wash me out for lack of inherent flying ability." Ah, that phrase "lack of inherent flying ability" covered a broad field indeed. It didn't necessarily mean what it said. If an instructor didn't like you or thought you were not good officer material, he would report you to the base commander as "lacking inherent flying ability."

Haddon gave me a hard look. "What do you propose to do about it?"

"Sir, I request that I be assigned to another instructor."

"Lieutenant Patrick is a good instructor."

4

"No doubt, but he is not good for me. I'm not learning how to fly."

"What makes you think you could do better with another instructor?"

"Sir, I feel that I could do very well with an instructor who would be more interested in teaching me to fly than Lieutenant Patrick is."

Haddon gave me an even harder look. "Jerdone, your request for another instructor is denied. You will continue with Lieutenant Patrick."

Now the old army air service, at the time of which I speak, had adopted a rather peculiar policy regarding the training of student pilots, officers and cadets alike. Simply stated, it meant that once a student had been discharged for lack of flying ability, he could not at any time in the future reapply for pilot training. There was no second chance. But if he failed in his ground-school studies and was discharged for that reason, he could at any time in the future once again apply for pilot training. I had somehow heard of this strange policy, and although it was not to be found in army regulations, nevertheless it was strictly adhered to by the Office of Chief of Air Service and by the staff of both primary and advanced flying schools.

Now, I knew that I was not going to last very much longer with Lieutenant Patrick. I was also determined not to be kicked out of the air service for lack of flying ability, for even then I had some vague notion of getting back in the army air service at some future date and getting my pilot's wings.

I now began "flunking" my ground-school subjects. As the examinations came up, I would turn in papers with all the wrong answers. Very soon I received orders to report to the "benzine board." This was a name we cadets had given the board of officers headed by Maj. Ralph Royce, the base commander.

Standing stiffly at attention before this imposing group of officers that had been especially convened to determine the fate of one lowly cadet, I could sense that the major and the other officers (with the exception of Lieutenant Patrick) were somehow reluctant to wash me out.

Major Royce asked, "What seems to be your difficulty with your school work?"

"The subjects are too technical," I replied. "I have trouble understanding what they are all about."

"Don't you want to continue your training?"

"No, sir."

The major looked bewildered. There was a long silence, then finally the order, "Dismissed."

5

About a week later, I received orders relieving me from flying training. I was no long a flying cadet. I was out of the army—once again a civilian—but I had not been kicked out for "lack of flying ability."

"Cadet Jerdone, having failed to meet academic requirements, is hereby relieved from duty."

Chapter 2   Savannah

Once again I was adrift in a sea of uncertainty. I had so soon rejoined the ranks of the unemployed. As I walked the streets of Arcadia, a wave of anxiety came over me. I was alone in a strange land and a little bit frightened. I was even afraid to call Alberta and tell her of my "failure."

But youth is resilient. Worry, depression, and anxiety strike only a passing blow. Optimism is a youth's "stock in trade." Tomorrow everything will be all right again. So it was that a few days later through a mutual friend I met Sam Taylor, also a former flying cadet, but now a barnstormer with his own airplane.

Sam had, for a few hundred dollars, purchased from the government a Standard J.1 training plane of World War I vintage. This plane was powered with the standard OX5 engine, and it differed from the Jenny in that it carried two passengers in the front seat. Sam had taken delivery of the plane at Dorr Field, which was adjacent to Carlstrom, but then was being used only as a storage base for surplus equipment. Sam explained to me that he wanted to head north, carrying passengers on short hops from the beaches of Florida and continuing as far as Savannah, where he would operate throughout the summer. He said that after assembling and flight testing the airplane, he had very little money left. I took this as a subtle invitation to put up some operating capital and thereby become a sort of partner in this flying venture.

I had managed to save up a few hundred dollars from my meager cadet pay, so I timidly suggested that I join him (with my few hundred dollars) in his barnstorming venture. The optimism of youth again! I felt almost euphoria compared with the dejection of yesterday. Sam was as eager to have me aboard as I was to join him, for he would now be able to carry out his plans and I would be able to eat regularly for a while at least.

One day in the latter part of May 1922, Sam and I took off in the Standard, now named *Betsy* in honor of some girl friend of Sam's, and headed for the beaches of central and northern Florida. We paused briefly at such places as New Smyrna, Daytona, and Jacksonville, and at each stop our passenger business, at five dollars per passenger for about a five-minute flight, brought in enough money to pay our gasoline, hotel, and food bills and we would still have something left over.

From 3,000 feet we were now approaching Savannah, which was faintly visible under a light smoke haze. The 90 H.P. OX5 engine purred smoothly, pushing our old Standard a good 70 miles per hour. We dropped down to a thousand feet, circled over the river and docks where ocean going frieghters were loading and discharging their cargoes, then headed back over the city toward Daffin Park. Sam, flying from the rear seat, spotted the small open field and came in low over the trees to a smooth landing on the green turf.

Our arrival in Savannah, we thought, offered promise of busy flying days ahead, but we had not reckoned with the economic facts of that year of 1922. The market for cotton, which was Savannah's lifeblood, had hit a record low. This was a depression year, and people didn't have money to spend on pleasure, especially airplane flights, as Sam and I soon found out.

Flying the beaches of Florida had proven fairly profitable, and now as the taxi took us into town, our enthusiasm for the future increased with every mile the meter ticked over.

Checking into the Savannah Hotel, we felt the burden of our affluence. Little did we know that very soon the scene would change from the luxury of this hotel to the drab bareness of a second-rate rooming house. But then we were very young and optimism was our stock in trade.

Sitting on a bench in Daffin Park, sipping a soft drink, Sam and I discussed our financial plight. There was a common saying among pilots of those days that the only danger in flying was starving to death. Now as we sat there contemplating our misfortunes, that old adage kept running through my mind, for we were fast approaching the time when we would have to postpone a few meals.

Suddenly a shadow appeared before us. Looking up, we were a little startled to see a man standing in front of us. We had been so preoccupied with our thoughts that we hadn't heard him approach. Now he looked down at us and asked, "That your airplane over there on the field?"

He was short and fat, with a huge paunch, and he badly needed a shave.

Sam nodded and admitted that the airplane belonged to us.

"I'm with the carnival," the man continued. "I run the high-wire concession, and I gotta do something to stir up business."

We could sympathize with him there; we needed some business, too.

"Is that the wire stretched across the lake on two poles about thirty feet high?" I asked.

"Yeah, that's it," the man said. "Tell you what," he went on. "I'll give you guys ten bucks to fly over the lake tonight; I figure it might help business."

Sam, looking belligerent, spoke up. Sam was short and sandy-haired with a freckled face, and he weighed about 130 pounds. But Sam had a temper and sometimes made little effort to control it. "You crazy?" he barked. "Risk our airplane and my neck for ten bucks? Nothing doing."

"Make it fifteen," I said, trying to salvage something out of the deal.

The man hesitated; for a long moment he looked at his feet. Sam gave me a dirty look, but said nothing. I thought of that little patch of grass surrounded by tall trees that we euphemistically referred to as a flying field. It was tough flying out of it in daytime. At night with no lights, it could be dangerous.

Finally the man looked up. "Okay, you guys win. The show starts at eight. Better take off at seven-thirty and fly around until five minutes to eight." He added, "And be sure you fly low."

Digging deep into his pocket, he came up with two dirty five-dollar bills and five ones. Dropping them into my lap, he turned on his heel and abruptly walked away.

The problem of lights for Sam to land by—he would fly the plane for he was much more experienced than I—worried us both. The simplest plan would be to have an automobile stationed at each end of the field and at a prearranged signal from Sam, the drivers would turn on their headlights, marking the boundaries of the field. He would still have to feel his way down to the ground, but with luck, I was confident he would land safely.

Now the problem was to find two automobiles. I remembered seeing the young man who ran the hot-dog stand drive up one day in a Model T Ford. Maybe he had a friend who also owned a car. I walked over to the stand and explained my problem to the young man, who told me to call him Jim. It turned out that he had a friend who owned a Maxwell and would be glad to help. I gave Jim two dollars and cautioned him to be ready promptly at 7:30.

Sam took off at the appointed time and circled the area around the lake at about 200 feet. The boys with their cars had arrived on time, eager to play their part in this night-flying drama.

Very soon, cars came pouring into the park from all directions. Remember, this was 1922 and airplanes were not a very common sight, especially buzzing around at night over an amusement park.

Bright searchlights played upon the tight-wire walker as he picked his way across the lake, balancing himself with a long pole. A band started playing a loud, discordant tune, competing with the noise of the plane low overhead. People were crowding the ticket booth. Our friend with the paunch and beard was doing all right.

At a few minutes before eight, Sam came around low over the trees and gunned the engine three times. This was the signal for the boys to turn on their headlights. Now that he could see where the field was, Sam glided in to a perfect landing. Sam was an excellent pilot, and in later years he became an outstanding airline captain.

Not long after the episode of the night flight, we read in the paper that an insurance company had scheduled a convention to be held at the Tybee (now Savannah) beach. The article stated that the affair would continue for five days and about 500 people were expected to attend. This was the opportunity for which we had been waiting. Now we thought we were really in business. With the few dollars we had left from the night flight, we gassed up the airplane and flew down to Tybee, landing on the beach at low tide. It was late in the afternoon, and we had time for only three flights at five dollars per passenger before it became too dark to see to fly.

We were staking down the plane for the night when a young couple stopped by and engaged us in conversation. After a few minutes, they introduced themselves—Jim and Geri Wrightson. We talked awhile longer, mostly about the airplane. They both seemed quite interested in flying. Jim said that they were entertaining some friends at their cottage on the beach and asked if we would care to join them. (In those days, people were very hospitable to young barnstorming pilots.) We were grateful for the invitation and said so. Jim and Geri were a likable couple; he was tall and handsome, and Geri was a very pretty blond with amazingly bright blue eyes.

The party at the Wrightsons' continued until the early hours of the morning. After the last guest left, Jim insisted that Sam and I spend the night with them. He probably guessed that we had no place to sleep anyway.

It was after eight when we awoke. The sun was glaring through our bedroom window, warm and bright. After dressing hurriedly, we went into the living room, where Jim greeted us with cups of hot coffee. He said that Geri had gone up the beach to get some groceries for breakfast. We sat shooting the breeze and drinking coffee, and after a while Geri came running into the house excited and out of breath. After she had calmed down a bit, she said, "Your plane's a wreck. There was a storm last night, and the wind blew quite hard. It must have lifted your plane into the air and rolled it over and over!" Sam and I had slept soundly, quite unaware of any storm.

For a moment neither of us said anything. We were too stunned to comprehend fully what Geri had been saying. Then suddenly we were out of the cottage and running up the beach. Geri had not been exaggerating. The plane was a total wreck, a mass of twisted wires, torn fabric, and splintered wood.

The engine was all that was worth salvaging. With some tools Sam and I borrowed from a nearby garage, we spent the rest of the day cutting the wings from the fuselage. We dragged them down to the water's edge; the tide would take them out to sea, where they would slowly sink. We found a man who owned a mule and hired him to drag what was left of the fuselage (with motor intact) up on a sand dune, safe from the tide.

Sam and I said good-bye to our new friends, the Wrightsons, and boarded a trolley back to Savannah. After wandering around town for a week, trying unsuccessfully to find jobs, we discovered that we had less than a dollar between us and no place to sleep. (Our landlady had locked us out of our room for nonpayment of rent.)

Passing by Colonial Cemetery, which is situated in the heart of downtown Savannah, one night, we turned in at the entrance and looked around. Just inside the gate, in a corner of the cemetery, were two graves close together, covered with flat concrete slabs. Tired and sleepy, we were both hit by the same idea. Well, why not? It was a place to lie down and rest anyway.

"Sam," I said, "you take one, and I'll take the other." I soon fell asleep despite the cold, hard slab. I awoke with the sun shining brightly. It was morning and people were walking along the street on their way to work. It took a few moments to get fully awake. My body was stiff and sore. Looking around, I was startled to discover Sam missing. His hat was lying beside the grave, but Sam had disappeared.

I picked up his hat and walked down Bull Street to Congress and into the Savannah Hotel, thinking that perhaps Sam had wandered into the lobby and fallen asleep in one of the easy chairs. But except for a sleeping porter, the lobby was empty. I walked around downtown Savannah, looking for Sam. After about an hour or more of searching in the hot sun, I turned up Bull Street to Nunnally's (where Walgreen's now stands) and went in and ordered a cold drink. It was the custom then for young men to stand in front of Nunnally's and watch the girls go by. It was the meeting place for the younger crowd in downtown Savannah.

I had been sitting at the counter for perhaps twenty minutes when Sam walked in. At first, I was a little startled and then much relieved to see him standing there with a sheepish grin on his freckled face.

"Where the devil have you been?" I asked.

"In jail," he replied, in an almost apologetic tone.

"Why? What, for heaven's name, did they charge you with?"

"Desecrating the dead."

"Good Lord, I've never heard that one before. How did you get out?"

"I talked my way out. The judge was a pretty good sort. He said he'd dismiss the charges if I promised not to sleep on any more graves. I promised."

"Why didn't the cop get me, too? I was right next to you."

"I wondered about that, but I didn't dare say anything for fear he'd go back and get you, too."

"Well, thanks, old pal, but I still don't understand it. Anyway," I added, "wait till the afternoon paper comes out. I can just see it now, front page, too: 'Prominent Pilot Arrested—Charged with Desecrating the Dead.' "

Shortly after the graveyard incident, Sam and I split up. He told me one day that a bootlegger had offered him a job—something about flying out to sea and looking for rum boats.

I went back to Tybee. (Sleeping on the beach would be preferable to sleeping on the cold, hard grave in the cemetery.) A few days later, a flying boat landed in the water and taxied up to the beach. As I waded out to take his bow line, I recognized the pilot—Ewing Easter, my old friend of the Annapolis days. He was on his way home from Florida, so I hitchhiked a ride, and in a few days I was back home at my Aunt Kitty's in Washington.

Chapter 3 San Antonio

I had not been back in Washington long when I decided to apply for a commission as second lieutenant in the air-service reserve. My eligibility for the commission was based on a regulation permitting anyone having commercial flying experience to apply for a reserve commission. I completed ponderous paperwork and the writing of a cover letter stating why I thought I was qualified to become an army air-reserve officer. And of course there was the inevitable physical examination. About three months later, I received a communication from the War Department informing me that I had met all requirements.

I was jubilant on receiving this good news. The army had instituted a new training program whereby reserve and national-guard officers would be given a four-months' course at the Primary Flying School, Brooks Field, San Antonio, Texas. (Carlstrom had been abandoned and the school transferred to Brooks.) Upon graduation from this four-months' course, the officer would receive a rating of junior airplane pilot. Of course, this was not the prestigious airplane pilot's rating one would receive if he had graduated from the Advanced Flying School at Kelly Field. However, it was a pilot rating; you could wear the coveted wings and pilot army aircraft.

In those days, the air service resembled a stepchild to the army. Funds for training pilots and even for gasoline to fly the planes were very limited. I knew that while I was eligible for this training, there would be literally hundreds of applicants, and my chances would be slim indeed. Nevertheless, my application was submitted almost immediately after I received my commission.

In the fall of 1923, I received orders to report to Brooks Field, Texas, for flying training. My class, which would consist of student officers, regular, reserve, and national guard, would start November 1. Old Lady Luck was indeed smiling on me. It looked like I just might attain what I had started out to get in the first place.

13

I arrived at Brooks Field late in the afternoon, reported to the adjutant who was still on duty at headquarters, and was assigned a room in Bachelor Officers' Quarters. I had just stepped out of the shower and was preparing to shave when who should walk in but my old adversary, Lt. Julian B. Haddon? He looked at me with an enigmatic grin.

"Well, I see you're back with us."

"That's right," I replied.

"I see your status has changed—an officer now! Congratulations!"

"Thanks. I've been lucky so far."

I would learn that in the two years since I had left Carlstrom as a washed-out cadet, the administration had changed very little. But confronting Lieutenant Haddon had really unnerved me. Somehow, I had not even considered the possibility of Lieutenant Haddon's being stationed at Brooks, and he still had his old job as officer in charge of flying. Now my appearance at Brooks, two years after I had been discharged as a lowly cadet at Carlstrom, as a student officer was an open invitation for Haddon to see that I failed here also. Being the insensitive guy that he was, he would probably delight in showing off his authority over me once again.

My first day at Brooks was not a promising beginning. My chances of graduating and getting my wings seemed slim indeed. I might just as well pack my bags and catch the first train back home.

At the beginning of flying training, Old Lady Luck smiled on me once again. I had been assigned to Lt. Bob Ashley's class for flying instruction. Bob and I had been classmates at Carlstrom, but unlike me, he had finished primary training and gone on to Kelly and graduated with his airplane pilot's rating. In addition, he had passed the examination for regular army and was now stationed at Brooks as a flying instructor. This was a real break for me, for Bob and I had been friends when we were cadets. Furthermore, he was a very good pilot and an excellent instructor. I was to have no difficulty from here on out. Even Lieutenant Haddon failed to interfere with my progress.

Now this class of 1924–25 was composed of reserve, national-guard, and regular-army officers. Most of the regulars were recent West Point graduates who had elected the air corps as their branch of service. Some, such as Lt. Thomas D. White, Lt. Nat Twining and Lt. Hoyt Vandenburg, were destined to become famous generals in World War II. White, Twining, and Vandenburg were at various times chiefs of staff of the United States Air Force.

In those days, there existed in the officer corps of the army some caste distinction between officers of different backgrounds. West Point

14

graduates were the elite of the army. Next came regular officers, who for the most part had obtained their commissions by having graduated from the various technical schools affiliated with ROTC units. The low man on the totem pole was, of course, the reserve officer.

In spite of this so-called caste system, I want to say unequivocally that I, as a Johnny-come-lately reserve, was treated with the utmost courtesy, consideration, and camaraderie. I was at no time made to feel inferior to any other officer of the air corps. In fact, Lieutenants White, Twining, and Vandenburg, along with other West Pointers such as Lt. K. J. Gregg, Lt. Carl Crane, and others, became very good friends of mine.

Our weekends in San Antonio always proved interesting. I found this old historical town, with its Alamo, flower-banked river winding through the center of town, and two distinguished hotels, the St. Anthony and the Gunther, fascinating. The mild winter climate (except when the northers blew) was much to my liking. There was always dancing on the St. Anthony roof on Saturday nights. Of course, the pretty Texas girls enhanced our pleasure.

One Saturday afternoon, K. J. Gregg and I were strolling down the street in San Antonio when we came upon a long line of people queued up for we knew not what. At first I thought they were waiting to get into a movie theater, but there was no theater in that vicinity. Anyway, just out of curiosity Gregg and I fell in line with all the rest. We shuffled slowly forward and finally came to the entrance of a churchyard in which there was a bier bearing a casket. As we passed by, we recognized the corpse of Samuel Gompers, the founder of the American labor movement, who had died while attending a convention in San Antonio.

The four months at Brooks passed rapidly. Under Bob Ashley's tutelage, I had no trouble with my flying, and I easily passed all groundschool subjects. So it was that I was graduated from the Air Corps Primary Flying School, and in a very formal ceremony the commanding officer pinned upon my blouse the wings of a junior airplane pilot.

I said good-bye to all those great friends I had made in so short a time and embarked on the long train ride back to Washington. There were no airlines in those days.

Again I was back at Aunt Kitty's without work. There were very few commercial flying jobs open in those days, and of course I was a very inexperienced pilot with not nearly enough flying time to qualify for any pilot job. Reserve officers with pilots' ratings at that time were allowed to pilot "army Jennies" around the area surrounding Washington—no cross-countries, only local flights. I took advantage of this opportunity, and at least twice a week I went out to Bolling Field and flew a Jenny around the Virginia and Maryland countryside. This at least kept me in practice, and besides, it was fun.

Through a friend of mine at headquarters in the munitions building, I learned that the air corps was going to accept applications from a limited number of reserve officers for extended active duty (one year) at Langley Field, Virginia. My friend seemed to think that if I got my application in right away I would have a good chance of being selected. Of course, I lost no time applying. A month passed by and one day, to my amazement, I received orders to report to the commanding officer, Second Bombardment Group, Langley Field. I was amazed, because I, frankly, had no idea that I would be accepted. I was qualified all right, but I was still low man on the totem pole. Old Lady Luck was still with me.

The Second Bombardment Group was one of three elite groups of the army air corps. The First Pursuit Group at Selfridge Field, Michigan, the Third Attack Group at Barksdale Field, Louisiana, and the Second Bombardment Group comprised the three tactical units of the air corps. The rest of the air corps was made up of observation and service squadrons. The aircraft of the Second Bombardment Group, Martin bombers and DeHaviland 4Bs, were used by General Mitchell to sink the *Osfriesland* off the Virginia Capes, thereby proving the vulnerability of naval vessels to air attack. Even so, the army and navy brass remained unconvinced as to the efficacy of air power over surface craft. General Mitchell was an ardent advocate of the superiority of air power over surface warfare. He predicted, and correctly, the important role the airplane was to play in future wars. Even at that time, he warned of the Japanese attack on Pearl Harbor. In his crusade for a superior air force, the general was publicly critical of his superiors, the old-line admirals and generals who took such a fractious view of the upstart air service. For his vigorous efforts to persuade his superiors and Congress that the defense of this country depended upon an adequate air force, he was subsequently court-martialed and forced out of the service.

The court-martial of Billy Mitchell received worldwide attention. The newspapers carried headlines and front-page publicity throughout the length of the trial. In later years, a major motion picture based on the court-martial was produced, with Gary Cooper playing the part of Gen. Billy Mitchell.

Langley Field, at the time I reported for duty, was the only "permanent" air-corps post in the country. All of the buildings, including the officers' quarters, both married and bachelor, headquarters building, school buildings, et cetera, were of modern construction, stucco with red tile roofs. The lawns were well kept; the streets were paved, with concrete sidewalks running throughout the area. This contrasted greatly with all other air corps stations, which had been built hastily during World War I. The buildings were of wood, heated for the most part with coal-buring stoves, and the roofs leaked. Langley was truly the Waldorf-Astoria of the air corps.

I was assigned quarters in Dodd Hall, the Bachelor Officers' Quarters. As a lieutenant, I rated two rooms, which were adequately furnished, and an enlisted man to make my bed, clean the rooms, and even shine my boots. (In the British army, these enlisted men were known as batmen.) This, of course, was the "Old Army." Today, officers have no such perquisites. The army has become a more democratic institution.

The quarters across the hall from me were occupied by Lt. Les Tower, a reserve officer from Montana. Les was a tall, rather gawky-looking chap with sandy hair. He looked as if he had just come off the range, which, indeed, he had. Les and I took an immediate liking to each other and were good friends throughout our tour of duty. Les and I were to meet some years later in Seattle, where he was chief test pilot for Boeing. I was saddened to learn later that he had been killed demonstrating the first B-17 bomber to the air corps at McCook Field, Ohio.

Also down the hall a few doors was Cadet Bernard "Bunk" Bridgett. Bunk was one of several cadets who had been assigned to active duty on "cadet status" although they were reserve second lieutenants, with airplane-pilot rating. At that time, the air corps had only sufficient funds for a limited number of officers to be placed on active duty. As the cadet pay was merely seventy-five dollars per month, they could afford to place a few men on duty as flying cadets. Bunk and others had been willing to accept this "demotion" in order to build up flying time on various types of aircraft. Bunk and I are sure some of the others resented having to serve under other second lieutenants, such as me. Bunk was later to get his revenge. He became a regular-army officer, and during part of World War II he was *my* commanding officer.

The Second Bombardment Group at that time was under the command of Maj. Louis Brereton. The group was composed of the Ninety-sixth Squadron, commanded by Maj. Willis Hale, the Twentieth by Capt. Charles "Chink" Rust, and the Eleventh by Lt. Ken Walker. I was assigned to Lieutenant Walker's Eleventh Squadron as engineering officer. This meant that I would be responsible for keeping the aircraft in flying condition. Each squadron was equipped with the Martin bomber (MBS-1), which was powered with two 450 H.P. Liberty engines. The Martin was a huge biplane capable of carrying a 2,000-pound bomb. It was the air corps' largest tactical aircraft in operation at that time.

Each flying officer was assigned his own personal plane for which he was entirely responsible. It was with considerable pride that when I approached my airplane one morning, I saw painted on the side of the cockpit these words:

Lt. Jerdone—Pilot
Sergeant McKenna—Crew Chief

"Red" McKenna was one of the best. His sole responsibility was to keep our aircraft operational at all times. We enjoyed a very fine relationship, for "Red" took great pride in keeping the airplane in as near perfect condition as possible.

Our daily routine consisted of much flying—cross-country flights (navigation training) and simulated raids on naval vessels as far as 150 miles at sea. This delighted us all, for that was what we were there for: to pile up flying time.

Unless we had other duties, we were allowed "cross-country" flights to Washington or New York almost every weekend. These flights also came under the heading of "navigational training," although of course we flew over the same course so often that we could almost fly the route with one eye closed. Every river, stream, railroad, and farmhouse became as familiar to us as the fingers on our hands.

My weekends were usually spent at Aunt Kitty's, and I would almost always bring along another officer friend. Carl Ben Eilson (the first pilot to fly in Alaska), Les Tower from Montana, and Mike Brady from Florida were frequent guests at Aunt Kitty's. I was usually successful in arranging a party for Saturday night and getting a date for myself and whomever I had brought home with me. This was not difficult to do, for Washington always seemed to have a surplus of women and I was on home grounds.

The esprit de corps of the group was of the highest. Every month we would give a group dinner at one of the nearby resorts such as Virginia or Buckroe Beach. These were Prohibition days, and theoretically liquor was not allowed on the post. But in preparation for our monthly dinners, two or three airplanes were dispatched to Washington to bring back "refreshments" for the party. Upon landing at Bolling Field, we were met by the bootlegger, who would drive out to the airplane and deliver aboard quite a few gallon tins of pure alcohol.

Upon arriving back at Langley, we were met by the officer of the day and escorted, along with the alcohol, to our quarters. Alcohol mixed with ginger ale was indeed a potent drink. Needless to say, everyone had a high old time at the dinner. I never did know who it was that made all the elaborate arrangements for flying booze down from Washington, and I wasn't a bit curious to find out.

As time passed, I became more and more proficient at piloting the various types of aircraft that were available at Langley. My cross-country navigation had improved, and I felt confident in attempting a flight to almost any destination. Several months had passed when one day I received orders promoting me from second to first lieutenant. I was really amazed at this good fortune. It was almost unheard of for a reserve officer to receive a promotion while on extended active duty. I lost no time exchanging my gold bars for those of silver.

About a month after I received my promotion, another happy surprise awaited me. In my morning's mail was a copy of the latest *Air Corps Regulations*. Underscored in paragraph 3 was the following line: "1st Lt. Frank H. Jerdone is hereby rated Airplane Pilot." Now this was cause for jubilation. I had come full circle. I had finally achieved the goal I had set out for in the first place. True, I had followed a circuitous route and had, so to speak, come in through the back door. But here I was, a first lieutenant air-corps reserve, with the rating of airplane pilot. No longer would I be burdened with that word *junior* attached to my rating.

It was April 1926. My tour at Langley was coming to an end. It had been a wonderful year, and now as I look back from the vantage point of so many years, I believe it was probably the happiest year of my life.

Tomorrow I would be leaving this active life once again to face an uncertain future. As I sat in my quarters contemplating what the future had in store for me, Dave Behnke walked in. Dave was from Chicago, and he reminded me very much of a jovial ward politician. In later years he became an air-mail pilot and was one of the founders of the Air Line Pilots Association.

"Dave," I said, "what are you going to do when you leave here?"

"Well, you know," he replied, "there are so few jobs in commercial aviation that we hardly stand a chance."

"I know that, but flying is all we know. Just what alternatives are there?"

Dave sat there staring at me. "I'm going back to Chicago," he said, "to climb the highest hill and offer myself up as a sacrifice to the gods." And with a grin he got up to leave.

"Well, Dave, I'm going back to Washington, and as there are no high hills around there, I am not going to offer myself as a sacrifice to anything.

"But," I added, "somehow I'm going to keep on flying. It's *in* me. I can *feel* nothing else."

Chapter 4   Washington

From the end of World War 1 through the spring of 1926, the aviation industry was kept alive primarily by the efforts of barnstorming pilots flying army surplus airplanes. In May of 1918, the Post Office Department in cooperation with the War Department inaugurated airmail service between Washington and New York. This route, originally flown by army pilots in military aircraft, was in September 1920 expanded into a transcontinental route from New York to San Francisco. At this time, the operation became the sole responsibility of the Post Office Department, and consequently the War Department ceased to be involved. This ambitious effort by the Post Office Department gave tremendous impetus to the fledgling aviation industry.

For some years prior to 1926, the industry had, with the exception of barnstorming pilots, worked actively for federal regulations. As a consequence, Congress enacted the Air Commerce Act of 1926, and in May of that year President Coolidge signed it into law. This legislative act served as the basis for the future development of commercial aviation in America.

The Air Commerce Act of May 1926, as it was then known, provided for the licensing of pilots and mechanics; for establishing, operating, and maintaining aids to air navigation; for arranging for research and development to improve such aids; for issuing airworthiness certificates for aircraft; and for investigating accidents. The act stated that the secretary of commerce would be responsible for implementing and enforcing the provisions of the act.

Having recently been discharged from the military and without a job, I found the news of this new legislation of vital interest. I knew that the implementation of this law would require the services of those persons possessing a background in aviation technology, including pilots, mechanics, engineers, and scientists.

The newspapers of that day gave considerable space to the enactment of this new legislation, and soon after reading about it, I appeared one day at the information desk of the Department of Commerce, which was located on H Street, just off Pennsylvania Avenue. I was directed to the office of a Mr. Ernest Jones, who upon my entrance greeted me warmly and asked me to be seated. He seemed glad to have someone to talk to, for it was evident that he had very little work to occupy his time. Jones said that someone in the secretary's office had appointed him a sort of one-man information center, but he had very little information to give out to people such as I, looking for a job.

Jones was a man approaching middle age of pleasing personality and seemed genuinely interested as I related to him the highlights of my aviation experience. When I finally got up to leave, he asked me to keep in touch, as something might open up very soon. Apparently, I was the first and only person who had approached him for a job.

After about two months of haunting Jones's office and phoning him almost every other day, I was getting a little discouraged when one day the phone rang and it was Jones on the line, "Hello," he said. "I have good news for you."

"That's fine," I replied. "A job?"

"Yeah, a good one, too!"

I was now so excited I could hardly hold the receiver.

"How soon can you get down to my office?"

"I'll be there in fifteen minutes," I replied.

As I entered his office, almost breathless from hurrying, Jones held out his hand.

"Congratulations! Your perseverance has paid off." He seemed almost as excited as I was.

Jones explained that a research division was to be organized within the Bureau of Standards, which was a component of the Department of Commerce. The bureau was to conduct tests on radio beacons that had been installed at College Park, Maryland. This work would, of course, require the services of a pilot and airplane. The Post Office Department had agreed to turn over to the Bureau of Standards an airmail D.H. for use in this experimental project. Jones said that I was to leave the following day for Hadley Field, New Brunswick, New Jersey, which was the eastern terminus of the transcontinental airmail service. There I would take delivery of the airplane and fly it to College Park.

I arrived at Hadley Field as scheduled and introduced myself to the field manager, who ordered a couple of mechanics to roll the airplane out of the hangar and gas it up. While I had had considerable time on army D.H.s, the airmail version was of a very different configuration. The army aircraft was a two-seater observation plane equipped with a 400 H.P. Liberty engine. The pilot flew from the front seat with an observer in the rear. The airmail version was also powered with a Liberty engine, but the fuselage had been entirely rebuilt of plywood with a single-pilot cockpit far aft near the tail. All of the forward section of the airplane consisted solely of mail compartments.

I strapped on my parachute and climbed into the cockpit; a mechanic swung the propellor; the engine coughed a few times, then settled into a smooth, muted idle. I let the engine idle for a few minutes to warm up, then opened the throttle full out and checked both magnetos. She sounded beautiful, so I taxied out into the wind and took off. The takeoff run was extremely short; the airplane, being light, did some steep turns, and headed on a course to Washington. The plane handled very nicely; it was much easier flying it than the army D.H.s I had been used to. After about two hours of flying, I spotted the black cinder runway of College Park dead ahead. I circled the field and then came in for a smooth landing, my first with this type of aircraft.

On August 11, 1926, William P. MacCracken, Jr., a Chicago lawyer and a former World War I army pilot, took office as assistant secretary of commerce for aeronautics. He became the first head of the Aeronautics Branch, which was created in the Department of Commerce by Secretary Herbert Hoover to carry out the provisions of the Air Commerce Act of 1926.

From the time of MacCracken's taking office, the organization of the Aeronautics Branch proceeded rapidly. Initially there were three main units making up the Aeronautics Branch. They were the Air Regulation Division; the Airways Division, organized within the Bureau of Lighthouses; and the Research Division, within the Bureau of Standards.

From the very beginning, I realized that the tests that we were supposed to conduct from the air on radio beacons would be impossible with the type of aircraft assigned to the bureau. In the first place, with the D.H. being a single-seat airplane, there was obviously no way to carry a technician and the necessary electronics equipment with which he would be required to conduct his experiments. Also, working with these scientists was going to be difficult at best, for they had no understanding whatsoever of aircraft operation. And I, of course, had absolutely no knowledge of what they were trying to do.

The only way out of this impasse that I could think of was to obtain an airplane suitable for our needs or have the one we now had modified for our special requirements. I decided to call on Dr. Dellinger, the scientist in charge of our project to explain to him what we were up against. Dr. Dellinger listened attentively while I explained the impossibility of conducting any air work that was vital to the development of the radio beacon. I suggested that he grant me permission to consult with Mr. MacCracken as to the possibility of getting the army to convert our airplane back to the conventional two-seater. I felt that this was the only feasible action to pursue, for I was almost certain that the army would not let us have another airplane.

Having obtained Dr. Dellinger's consent, I called on Mr. MacCracken at his office in the Department of Commerce building on H Street, in downtown Washington. I found MacCracken to be an affable person, easy to talk to, and being a pilot, he understood perfectly my predicament. I didn't know it then, of course, but this initial meeting was going to prove to be the beginning of a very close relationship between the assistant secretary and myself.

I suggested to Mr. MacCracken that he contact General Gilmore, the chief of the Material Command, and request authority to have our aircraft rebuilt at their repair facility at McCook Field, Dayton, Ohio. Without hesitation, MacCracken picked up the phone and in two minutes he had General Gilmore on the line. MacCracken then and there made an appointment for me to see the general and tell him in detail what I wanted done.

My interview with General Gilmore was brief and to the point. I could see that the General was somewhat puzzled as to how to handle a young upstart such as I who dared approach him with such an unusual request. However, MacCracken had paved the way, for not even an air-corps general dared to ignore an assistant secretary of commerce. The interview ended with instructions for me to fly the airplane to McCook Field, where the necessary work would be accomplished.

On a hot, humid day in August, I took off from College Park and headed up the Potomac River, over Cumberland, Maryland, across the Alleghenies, and over the flatlands of Ohio into Dayton. McCook Field was situated within the city limits of Dayton. It was a small field, and the approaches from all directions necessitated coming in over houses and various industrial buildings. As I neared the field, I saw a huge billboard that warned in letters three feet high: "This Field Is Small— Use It All." Heeding this advice, I landed, taxied up to a hangar, and turned the airplane over to the army. In six weeks, I would return to McCook (by train) and fly the converted plane back to College Park.

I was delighted with my *new* airplane. The work done on the plane had in no way detracted from its flying qualities. Back at College Park, all sorts of electronic equipment was installed in the rear cockpit, transceivers for communication with the ground personnel, a beacon receiver for testing the radio beam, an intercom for conversation between pilot and engineer, and other necessary instruments.

So at last we entered into a daily routine; flying beacon tests in the morning, the afternoons devoted mainly to research and modification of equipment on the part of the engineers and scientists. This left me free to do mostly as I pleased. On our morning flights, very often the technician in the rear seat and I would get into a heated argument over some technicality and our language would become, to say the least, quite abusive. We must have been operating on the same frequency as that of some broadcast stations in Washington, for one day MacCracken called me in and told me in no uncertain terms to cut out the profanity on the air. It seems that he had received numerous complaints about the foul language from people listening to news broadcasts.

One day there landed at College Park an S.E.5-type airplane. This was a British fighter plane of World War I vintage. It so happened that I had flown this type of plane while stationed at Langley Field and found it a beautiful flying airplane. The pilot taxied up to the one hangar, cut his engine, and climbed out of the cockpit. I was the only one around, so he came up, extended his hand, and said, "I'm Charlie Collyer."

"Glad to know you, Charlie," I replied.

"I'm with the Skywriting Corporation of America, and I will be here for some time writing *Bond Bread* over Washington."

"I'm flying that D.H. over there for the Bureau of Standards, and we are conducting tests on radio beacons."

"That sounds interesting," replied Charlie. "I would like to hear more about what you are doing. By the way, I've rented an old house on the edge of town. Why don't you come over and have a drink with me this evening?"

"I'll be glad to. What time? About six?"

"Fine," said Charlie. "See you then."

Charlie Collyer (I was to learn that his formal name was C. B. D. Collyer and he was sometimes known as Alphabetical Charlie) had been a pioneer airmail pilot, having flown various segments of the transcontinental route. He was now the only American pilot serving with the Skywriting Corporation of America, a British organization founded by a Major Savage, formerly of the Royal Flying Corps. Major Savage had perfected a method of forming letters in the sky with smoke emitted from the plane's exhaust stacks. The fuel used was lube oil, but apparently some ingredient, which was patented, was emitted along with the smoke to bind the letters together long enough to be read as one or several words. This had proved a very effective advertising medium. Major Savage had just completed a million-dollar contract with the American Tobacco Company for writing *"Lucky Strike"* in the skies over most large American cities.

I arrived at Charlie's house a little after six. He greeted me warmly and introduced me to a young man named Jim Read, who he said was a cousin of his. Jim was an advance man for the company and also a sort of errand boy for Charlie. After a couple of drinks, two good-looking girls arrived, coeds from the University of Maryland. After several more rounds of drinks (Charlie's capacity for alcoholic beverages was amazing, even though he was of slight build and medium height), I decided I had to go home. The party was still going strong at midnight, but I had a long drive home, and I knew that if I stayed any longer I wouldn't be able to make it home. I thanked Charlie for his hospitality, said good night to the girls, and left. This was the first of many parties at Charlie's house.

One day while on some business down at the Department of Commerce, MacCracken called me into his office and said, "Frank, Charlie Collyer was in this morning, and he paid you a fine compliment."

"What was that?" I asked.

"He said that he had witnessed some of the finest D.H. flying by one Frank Jerdone that he had ever seen."

"Coming from Charlie Collyer, that *is* a great compliment indeed. Thanks for telling me," I replied.

There was, at the time of which I write, a certain distinction among pilots regarding the ability to fly certain types of aircraft. From a military viewpoint, the fighter pilot, or rather the *pursuit* pilot, as he was then called, was the elite of the air corps. Then came the bomber pilot, and this category included the pilot of the DeHaviland 4B, and the least prestigious of the lot was the pilot of the low-powered training plane. Now the D.H. was considered a somewhat tricky airplane to fly, if not a little dangerous. It was a heavy, single-engined airplane, and the Liberty engine was not as reliable as some other engines of that day. Consequently, if the pilot was making a steep climb after takeoff (known as a chandelle) and the engine quit in this extreme steep-climb attitude, the airplane would stall, fall off into the beginning of a spin, and crash. Thus pilots who were qualified on D.H.s were considered a cut above the ordinary.

Now Charlie Collyer was an old, experienced D.H. pilot, having flown them in the First World War and later in the Airmail Service. Compared to him, I was a johnny-come-lately, so his remark to MacCracken regarding my flying I considered then, and still do, the finest compliment I have ever received.

26

Charlie, a native of Amelia County, Virginia, was to attain even greater fame in the coming year when, accompanied by John Henry Mears, he circled the globe in twenty-three days, thus establishing a new world record.

It was now the middle of December 1926, and I was becoming bored with the routine of flying for the Bureau of Standards. In the first place, I was working alone; there were no other pilots involved in this project. I felt very much a stranger, an outsider, for the fraternity of scientists was a closed order as far as I was concerned. Then, too, I had learned that the inspection service of the Aeronautics Branch would start operating after January 1, 1927. This would require the services of qualified pilots, and I had heard that a few had already been hired. The more I thought about it, the more I wanted to become one of the first pilot-inspectors in this new branch of service.

I made an appointment with Mr. MacCracken, explained to him my reasons for wanting to leave the bureau assignment and become an inspector, and requested that he transfer me from my present duties to the inspection service. MacCracken understood my reasons and agreed to approve my transfer. He warned me, however, that I would have to take a reduction in salary, but as I was being paid what I considered a magnificent salary, I was not adverse to a reduction in pay for the privilege of being one of the first pilots forming the nucleous of this service.

Chapter 5 **Washington, New York, and Quebec**

In January of 1927, I reported for duty at the office of the Inspection Section of the Aeronautics Branch of the Department of Commerce. I was introduced to Ralph Lockwood, a former Royal Flying Corps officer and later one of the two civilian test pilots for the army air corps at McCook Field, who had been appointed chief inspector. In addition, there were four others recently hired as inspectors present. I was the fifth. They were, as I recall, Bob Gast of Louisville, Kentucky, Walter Jones of New Jersey, Parker "Shorty" Cramer of Clarion, Pennsylvania, and Scott Breingan of Philadelphia.

For the first few weeks, we just hung around the office helping Ralph draft regulations, devising inspection forms, and doing other routine office work. Finally, led by Ralph, we all went out into the field to *learn* how to inspect.

Our first stop was Ludington Field, Philadelphia, operated by Bob Hewitt for the owners, the Ludington Brothers. We inspected various airplanes for licensing and gave written examinations to pilots and mechanics. At this early beginning, we were not required to ride with a pilot for his flight test. We merely told him to go up and make three landings, which we studiously observed, and if the landings were not too bad, we granted him his license. A little later, we were, of course, required to ride with the pilot in a dual-controlled airplane.

After a couple of weeks of this "practice" licensing, we moved on to Roosevelt Field, Long Island. In spite of the reluctance of some of the pilots to having to be licensed, we got along very well, and I, for one, found a good friend in Bob Hewitt.

We arrived at Roosevelt Field shortly after Lindbergh's flight and found a tremendous amount of activity. Stimulated by Lindbergh's dramatic success, others were preparing for transoceanic flights. There was Rene Fonck, Clarence Chamberlin, Admiral Byrd, George Halde-

Commercial Pilot's License Number 5

man, Ruth Elder, and others, all hoping to achieve fame and fortune by being the first to fly the oceans to various points in Europe.

George Haldeman and Ruth Elder had come up from Florida with a Stinson monoplane with which they hoped to fly to Paris. Of course, Ruth would be the first woman to attempt to fly the Atlantic, and as such she would receive a tremendous amount of publicity, even though the flight was doomed to failure. She and George had to ditch in the Atlantic 2,600 miles out, due to a broken oil line. Fortunately they were picked up by a tanker off the Azores.

One day Ralph came to me and said, "Ruth Elder wants a private pilot's license. She has obtained a Waco 9 that's dual-controlled, and I told her I would have an inspector ride with her this afternoon. Would you like the job?"

"I sure would," I replied. Ruth was a very pretty girl.

"By the way, why do you want me to ride with her? Don't you think she can fly?"

Ralph gave me a crooked grin and said, "I'm not too sure."

Ruth's Waco was on the line, ready to go. She was sitting in the rear seat, and I climbed into the front.

The first group of inspectors hired by the Aeronautics Branch of the U.S.

"The traffic on this field is very heavy, so I'll take the plane over to Mitchell and let you make some landings," I said. At that time Mitchell, an army field, would, as there was little activity there, allow civilian aircraft to practice landings, because Roosevelt was a smaller field and most of the time very crowded.

I took off and climbed to 3,000 feet over Mitchell. I signaled to Ruth to take the controls and make a few fairly steep turns. Her air work was a little sloppy, but not too bad. After about ten minutes of this, I decided that she was not dangerous, so I cut the throttle and shouted, "Go ahead and land." We were directly over the field, and she didn't seem to know which way to head for her approach into the wind.

"You land this way," I said, pointing in the direction from which the wind was blowing. She nodded and flew almost to Long Beach on the ocean before turning into the wind for an extraordinarily long approach to the field. She finally landed wheels first, bounced a few feet, and rolled to a stop.

"Okay," I said. "Now take off and make another landing." This time she repeated her first performance, but her landing was on three points. Not bad. But by this time I had decided that this girl had never soloed an airplane. When the airplane stopped rolling, I climbed out of the cockpit and said, "Okay. Now take off and make three landings. You're on your own." I had decided to call her bluff and really expected her to protest at going up alone, but she fooled me. Her first landing was rough, her second, she hit wheels first and bounced, but her third was perfect. I walked over to the plane and said, "Congratulations. You did just fine." I got in the plane and flew it back to Roosevelt. As I taxied up to the line, crowds of people, mostly reporters, surrounded the plane. I shut off the engine and climbed down before Ruth got out.

A reporter came up to me and asked, "Did she pass her flight test?"

"Yes, indeed," I replied.

"Aw, she can't fly. You gave her a license just because she's a pretty girl."

Well that burned me up! After all, I was a government official, and I wasn't about to be giving out pilot's licenses to pretty girls who couldn't fly. Ruth was still in the cockpit. I walked over to her and said, "These guys think you can't fly, that I am granting you a license because you are a pretty girl. Now listen," I continued, "do you think you can take this thing off and land it safely in front of this crowd of people?"

She nodded. "Sure, I'll do it." She smiled confidently.

I thought, *This girl's got what it takes.*

I spun the prop and as she taxied out for the takeoff, it suddenly occurred to me that I was taking one hell of a chance. I was asking too much of this girl. What if she made a bad landing, maybe cracking up? . . .

The takeoff was smooth and professional. She climbed to about a thousand feet, circled the field, turned back into the wind for that inevitable long approach, and made a perfect landing. She taxied up to where I was standing and shut off the engine. I helped her out of the cockpit.

"Congratulations!" I said. "That was a perfect landing. Now there will be no more questions about your qualifications for a pilot's license." And I added, "Thanks a lot."

As I write this, I have before me a clipping from the obituary column of the *Washington Star* announcing the death of pilot Ruth Elder. It is datelined "San Francisco (AP)," and I quote in part:

Ruth Elder, dubbed the "Miss America of the Air" after a failed attempt to be the first woman to fly the Atlantic, will be cremated and her ashes scattered over San Francisco Bay. Elder, 74, died in her sleep Sunday in her downtown San Francisco apartment. Her husband of 21 years, Ralph F. King, said there would be no funeral services.

In the half century that followed her abortive flight in 1927 the flamboyant beauty made movies, hobnobbed with royalty, married and divorced six times, made a lot of money and spent it all.

For Elder, her dramatic failure meant instant stardom. She was received by European royalty, went on tour and made two silent movies with Richard Dix and Hoot Gibson. She lunched with President Calvin Coolidge, and she boosted her bank account to $250,000. "The money slipped through my fingers and soon there was nothing," she said in an interview years later.

She acquired six husbands, including New York socialite Walter Camp, Jr. She divorced them all—including six-times married Ralph King, a retired Hollywood cameraman. They later remarried, and he was her husband when she died.

Our brief stint at Roosevelt Field came to an end, and we returned to Washington. In the meantime, Clarence M. Young, a lawyer from Des Moines, Iowa, who had learned to fly in World War I and served as a pilot on the Italian front, had been appointed the first director of aeronautics.

At this time, the Bureau of Standards had completed its work on radio beacons that required the use of an airplane. Mr. Young had remarked that he would have need of an airplane in the near future. I suggested to him that we transfer the old D.H. from College Park to Bolling Field, where it would be convenient for his use. Also, at this time our pilot personnel was expanding rapidly and a new regulation requiring that all new pilots be checked out as to their flying ability was soon to be enforced. I pointed out to Clarence that the D.H. could, as it was dual-controlled, be used for this purpose also. Clarence okayed my suggestion, so one day I flew the airplane from College Park to Bolling, where it would be based permanently.

For some reason, probably the good send-off Charlie Collyer had given me, McCracken appointed me a sort of unofficial check pilot to check out all new pilots coming into the department. I felt highly complimented, but also a little silly when such old-time D.H. pilots as Charlie Stanton, Monty Mouton, Parker Cramer, and others who had pioneered the first air-mail service, reported to me for a check ride. Charlie Stanton, one of the very first of the Post Office Department pilots, reported to me one day for a "check." Feeling kind of foolish, I said to Charlie, "I'll take her around once and make a landing. After that, you can have her." I knew Charlie hadn't flown for some time, and I wanted to give him an opportunity to get the feel of the airplane again. However, after a few turns at 2,000 feet, I thought, *What's the use of fooling around with this guy? He knows a lot more than I do.* So I motioned him to go in and land. Of course, he did just fine, and I got out of the airplane and said, "It's all yours." Charlie never got over my change of mind, and every time we would meet in the years to come, he would tell me about the incident, with embellishments. Charlie was later to become administrator of the Civil Aviation Administration (CAA).

I shall never forget the time Monty Mouton reported for his "check" ride. (In all these instances, I use the word *check* euphemistically.) Monty had flown the first San Francisco–Reno segment of the transcontinental air mail and was another old-timer of whom I stood in awe. This was my first meeting with Monty, and I was duly impressed with his impeccable attire. He wore an elegantly tailored sport jacket, well-fitting riding breeches encased in highly polished custom-made boots, and a white shirt with dark-blue tie, and to cap it all off he was constantly twirling a waxed mustache. Now before climbing aboard the airplane, I was amazed to see him pull on a pair of expensive pigskin gloves, don a custom-made helmet, and meticulously adjust his goggles. But in spite of all this fastidiousness, Monty was a very likable chap and a superb pilot.

Clarence Young made frequent use of the airplane, and I was

pressed into service as a sort of an instructor–check pilot. On our first flight together, I took the plane up, did a few turns, and made a couple of landings. I crawled out of the rear seat and said, "Go ahead, Clarence. She's all yours."

But Clarence just sat there. "Get back in here, Frank," he said. For some reason known only to Clarence, I could never get him to fly the airplane alone.

For several months, I had to accompany Clarence on flights to Philadelphia, New York, Norfolk, Baltimore, and Atlantic City. These flights always occurred on Saturdays or Sundays, for of course during the week Clarence was occupied with his duties as director of aeronautics. On most of these trips we would arrive at our destination just before noon and would be met by some friend of Clarence's who would take us to lunch. I knew he liked to impress his friends, so I would always ride in the rear seat, allowing Clarence to occupy the front (pilot's) seat. For the most part, I enjoyed these weekend excursions, and I had no objection to helping boost Clarence's stature in the eyes of his friends.

One day Clarence called me in and asked me to go to Farmingdale, Long Island, and take delivery of a Fairchild monoplane that the department had purchased recently and fly it to Washington. This airplane was, I believe, the second or third cabin aircraft built. All previous aircraft were open-cockpit types. I arrived at Farmingdale to find this brand-new airplane gassed and ready for my flight to Washington. I had flown once before in a cabin-type airplane. It was a Stinson biplane, I believe the first cabin-type built in this country. This Fairchild, however, was an entirely different type of aircraft. In the first place, it was equipped with a Pratt and Whitney 450 H.P. engine, twice the power of the Stinson. Also, its configuration was different from that of any airplane I had ever seen. The fuslage, instead of being square, was triangular, and the pilot sat with his legs almost wrapped around the engine. However, the plane proved easy to fly and I had no difficulty on the flight down to Washington.

The day after my arrival at Bolling Field with the new Fairchild, MacCracken called me into his office. He asked, "How do you like the new Fairchild?"

"Fine," I replied. "She handles very nicely."

"That's good. I want you to take this airplane and leave tomorrow for Pittsburgh, where you will pick up a Monsieur Bokonowski, the French minister of commerce, industries, and aviation. The minister is a guest of Secretary of Commerce Hoover, and we have been asked to fly him on a tour of the eastern states and parts of Canada. This is a very important person, so be careful. Don't take any chances."

"By the way," he added. "I'll be attending a bar-association meeting in Buffalo, and if you need to you can get in touch with me there." MacCracken at that time was secretary of the American Bar Association.

The next morning as I was warming up the engine preparing to take off for Pittsburgh, a tall, rather good-looking young man approached the airplane and motioned that he wanted to talk with me. I shut off the engine and got out of the airplane. The young man shook hands and said, "I'm J. B. Alexander from Los Angeles. I have been east for a couple of weeks on some business for Howard Hughes. I hear you're going to Pittsburgh, and I'd like to bum a ride."

"Sorry, but I'm not allowed to carry passengers. This is a government airplane."

"Whom do I have to see to get permission to go with you?" J. B. asked. (He had already asked me to call him J. B.)

"In this case," I replied, "you will have to see Mr. MacCracken, assistant secretary of commerce."

"What time are you leaving?" he asked.

"Right after lunch, 2 o'clock at the latest."

In a little over an hour, he was back with a note signed by MacCracken authorizing me to carry one J. B. Alexander to Pittsburgh. *This guy,* I thought, *has a lot of clout. The Hughes association probably did it.*

For some reason, which I do not now remember, I decided to go to Philadelphia, spend the night, and get an early start the next morning for Pittsburgh. We landed at Ludington Field about 5 o'clock and were met by Bob Hewitt. Bob suggested that we stay overnight at his home, as he had plenty of room, and anyway, he lived close to the airport.

After a jolly evening over drinks, we took off early for Pittsburgh. A little past Chambersburg, we ran into bad weather. The ceiling dropped lower and lower until we started flying through scud. We were following the highway that now forms the Pennsylvania Turnpike. I shouted to J. B., who was sitting directly behind me, to fasten his seat belt; I was going to have to land. There was no going ahead, and the weather had closed in behind me. I saw an open field off to the side of the highway that looked fairly smooth, so I throttled back and went in to land. Fortunately we got away with the forced landing in good shape. The field was adequate, and no damage came to the airplane. But we had just made it. Visibility was now zero.

After about two hours, the weather improved somewhat. The clouds had lifted and the ceiling was now about 500 feet. We took off and continued following the highway. It was "touch and go"; we were not only following the highway directionally, but, also the contours up and down. We finally cleared the last mountain range, and below us lay Ligonier. We couldn't see the town itself, but I caught a glimpse directly below us of a circle in the middle of a field. That was about all I could see, but I knew it was the airfield for Ligonier. I dropped down low over the field. In order to land, I had to fly straight away from the field and make a blind turn in the fog back toward the white circle I had seen and land. It was a hairy procedure, but luck was with me.

Later that afternoon, the weather cleared and we flew on to Bettis Field near Pittsburgh. There J. B. left me to proceed by train to the West Coast. He thanked me profusely for the ride. I wondered at the time if he very much regretted going to the trouble to get permission to accompany me on this flight. But that was not the last of J. B. I was to see a lot of him in the years to come.

I learned from Barr Peet, the field manager at Bettis, that Monsieur Bokonowski had gone on to Buffalo the night before. I was a day late arriving in Pittsburgh, and he probably was not inclined to wait around for some unpredictable aviator.

The next morning, I flew on to Buffalo. MacCracken had left word for me at the airport that he wanted to see me and gave the address of the auditorium where the bar association was having its meeting. Later that morning, I entered this huge, cathedral-like hall where sat several hundred lawyers. MacCracken saw me as I came through the door and motioned me up to where he sat on the podium. He asked me about the flight, and I explained my troubles with the weather that had caused my delay in arriving at Pittsburgh. He nodded understandingly. He said that Bokonowski had proceeded to Quebec and that I was to continue my flight the next day, meet with the minister at the Chateau Frontenac, where he was staying, and fly him to New York. This had developed into a game, like chasing the fox, only I was covering a lot of territory trying to catch up with the French minister— Pittsburgh, Buffalo, and now Quebec, where I could only hope finally to meet with the elusive minister.

As I walked through the lobby of my hotel, who should I run into but an old friend, Jack Little, who, I learned, was flying the mail from Cleveland to Buffalo? I hadn't seen Jack for several years, so our meeting seemed to call for a little celebration. We made the rounds of Buffalo speakeasies and finally returned to our hotel in the early hours of the morning. I left a call for 6 o'clock, knowing I would feel lousy after so little sleep.

At the airport, I inquired as to the location of the field at Quebec and was told to land on the Plains of Abraham, also known as Chateau

Frontenac Heights. This field, I was told, would be easy to find as it lay on the banks of the Saint Lawrence River, just outside the city of Quebec. I estimated my flying time at five hours and forty minutes nonstop with sufficient fuel in reserve. Even so, in those days this was considered quite a long flight. I had never been over the course before, and the only map I had was that of the eastern U.S. states and Canada as far as Quebec. I don't recall where I got this map, but it was cut out of a school geography book.

I left Buffalo and followed the southern shore of Lake Ontario and picked up the Saint Lawrence River north of Watertown, New York.

This was a very easy course to fly. All I had to do now was follow the Saint Lawrence to Montreal and thence on to Quebec. I arrived in Quebec at my estimated time and came in over some high cliffs overlooking the river. I was now directly over what should have been the flying field, but all I saw was what looked like a city park; crowds of people were milling around the "park," and I assumed some sort of celebration was taking place. I thought as I circled overhead that if necessary, I could land in this place. Still I saw no sign of anything that resembled a flying field. I started flying in ever-widening circles, hunting the elusive field. After about fifteen minutes of this, I decided that I was not going to find an airfield. By this time, I was running low on fuel, and it behooved me to find a place to land. About five miles north of the "park," I spotted a hay field that looked adequate, so I landed with no trouble and taxied up to a fence that ran parallel to a country road. I had no sooner shut off the engine when two motorcycle cops roared up. I got out of the airplane and walked over to the fence.

One of the cops said, "You're supposed to land back there on the Plains of Abraham."

"You mean that place that looks like a city park?"

"Yeah, that's it," he replied.

"But I thought it was a city park," I added.

"Well, it's really the flying field for Quebec, but occasionally we have outdoor gatherings there."

I took off and in a couple of minutes I was back over the river. As I came in low over the river, I noticed that the police had cleared a path for me and were holding back the spectators. As I was nearing the end of my landing roll, the crowds broke loose from the police line and surged directly in front of me. I had to cut the switch and jam on the brakes to keep from running over some people and perhaps decapitating someone with the propellor. Two police on motorcycles appeared immediately and cleared a line for me to taxi to the end of the field. The cops helped me stake down the plane for the night and promised to keep a guard on it all night.

A limousine appeared from somewhere, and with a motorcycle escort I was driven to the Chateau Frontenac Hotel. I found the lobby crowded with men and women in evening clothes. Over in one corner I spotted a small group of men in white tie and tails with ribbons across their shirtfronts. These, I thought, were the diplomats, so I started over in their direction. As I approached, one of the men came forward and inquired if I were the pilot for Monsieur Bokonowski. I acknowledged that I was, and he introduced himself as the minister's secretary. He was very cordial and taking me by the arm, led me to where stood a tall, handsome man whom I instinctively knew to be the minister.

The minister greeted me effusively, and said in perfect English, "You must join us at the banquet this evening."

Now, I would be as far out of place joining that group for dinner as anyone could possibly imagine. I was dirty and tired and had a hangover. I had started to mumble objections to the minister when the secretary interrupted and led me to the elevators. Going up in the elevator, I said, "Please get me out of this. I'm tired, worn out, dirty, and have no clothes to change into."

"I understand," he said with a smile and proceeded to lead me to my room. I had been in my room barely five minutes when a bunch of French newspapermen arrived carrying bottles of cognac. They made themselves right at home and started pouring drinks for everyone. Now I needed a drink all right, but not nearly as many as I eventually consumed during the evening. I don't know how long the party lasted. I do know that we had no dinner.

The next thing I knew, Monsieur Bokonowski himself was standing over me trying to shake me awake. He laughed and said it was time to get up. I, for one, did not feel like laughing. I felt terrible, both physically and mentally. It was fortunate for me that the minister was a good sport. I could easily imagine the minister reporting this episode to MacCracken, who was a Scotch Presbyterian and a teetotaler who would fail to see any humor in my escapade.

After hurriedly gulping down some orange juice, toast, and coffee, we were, the three of us, the minister, the secretary, and myself, driven out to the airport. To my amazement, crowds of people were still lining the field. I wondered if they had been there all night. Sure enough, there was a police guard standing over the airplane. We all got aboard and I started the engine, warmed it up, and started to take off. The wind had shifted 180 degrees during the night, and my takeoff would be over the Saint Lawrence. I opened the throttle and was about halfway down the field when the crowds broke loose, surging in front of me, and I had to repeat the performance of the day before. I made two more attempts to get off, each time having to cut the engine and jam on the brakes. On the third attempt, I finally was airborne and headed on a direct course to Boston.

This route lay over some rugged country, over the Green Mountains of Vermont and the White Mountains of New Hampshire. Still flying by that eastern states map, we continued on our course to Boston, going over the water to land on a cinder runway at the location where Logan Airport now stands.

We had an excellent dinner at the Ritz Carlton Hotel and went to bed early. While at dinner, I asked the minister what all the crowds had been milling around the airfield at Quebec for. He said that he had heard that Admiral Byrd had been expected to arrive there about the time I showed up. So that was it! They had thought I was Admiral Byrd. No wonder the police had difficulty controlling that enthusiastic bunch of people.

The next morning, we flew without incident to Roosevelt Field, Long Island. Both the minister and his secretary thanked me profusely for the flight. The minister said, "I have a parting gift for you." He handed me a handsome photograph of himself with the words "With my heartfelt thanks" inscribed over his signature. I have managed to keep this photograph all through the years, and I still cherish it very much. I have often wondered, though, were his "heartfelt thanks" meant for me or was he thanking God that he ended the flight all in one piece?

Chapter 6   Kansas City

My work, so far, with the Aeronautics Branch had been extremely interesting and a lot of fun. I had been associated with some very fine people—many with a background of great accomplishment and not a few who were celebrities in their own right. But now the time had come for me to go out into the field and license pilots and aircraft, the job for which I had been hired in the first place.

My first assignment was Kansas City, and I would be the first inspector west of the Mississippi. Thus it was that on a hot, humid morning in July, Scotty Bringan, who was to be my assistant, and I arrived at Richards Field to assume our routine duties.

Richards Field was the center of all flying activity in that area. It was also a division point on National Air Transport's Chicago-Dallas route. My and Scotty's arrival failed to stimulate any enthusiasm on the part of the operators, nor, for that matter, those officials of National Air Transport. They remained hostile to any government regulations, and our reception was somewhat chilly, to say the least.

I first entered the NAT's office and introduced myself and Scotty to E. P. Lott, the division operations manager. Lott was a tall, blond young man of medium weight and totally lacking in humor. He grudgingly acknowledged my introduction, but had nothing further to say. There were a couple of pilots lounging around the office, and I was soon to learn that they considered Lott a Mr. Scrooge. His initials, E. P., they informed me, stood for "Everything Perfect."

I foresaw a difficult job ahead in selling these people on the idea of being licensed by a government agency. But I also knew that first, I had to sell myself. To make matters worse, Scotty, at dinner that evening at the President Hotel, where we had taken rooms, had some startling news for me. We were enjoying our meal with some casual conversation when abruptly Scotty said, "Frank, you know I can't fly."

"What do you mean, you can't fly?" I thought he was trying to be funny.

"I mean just that; I never learned to fly."

"Well how in the hell did you get this job?"

"I was a mechanic in the Royal Flying Corps during the war. And, after coming to this country, I continued working as a mechanic at various flying fields."

"Who hired you and where were you hired?" I asked. Scotty had, of course, already been hired when I came to work with the bureau.

"It was at Philadelphia. Bob Hewitt recommended me to Ralph Lockwood."

"Didn't Ralph know you couldn't fly?"

"He never asked me."

I could halfway understand it now. Bob didn't know that one of the requirements for the job as inspector was that one had to be a good pilot. Bob, knowing that Scotty was a good mechanic, thought he would be an asset to the department inspecting airplanes for licensing, which indeed he would. And Ralph merely assumed that Scotty was a pilot and accepted Bob's recommendation.

Unfortunately, I had introduced Scotty as a fellow inspector. If I had known beforehand that Scotty couldn't fly, I would have introduced him as a mechanic whose sole duty was to inspect the airplane for licensing. This would have been quite credible. But as I had informed them that Scotty was another inspector, they of course assumed that he was a pilot.

"All right, Scotty. I'll do my best to cover up for you, but it's going to take some doing."

For the next couple of days, we just hung around the field. We made no attempt to impose any authority on these people. We kept our mouths shut and only answered questions when we were asked. I was waiting for them to come to me.

When I arrived on the field one morning (this about the third day), Ben Gregory, a pilot who owned a Laird Swallow, came up to me and hesitatingly asked if I would like to fly his airplane. Now, I thought, this guy has got guts. I knew his airplane was his sole means of livelihood. Asking a perfect stranger, whom he had no reason to have any confidence in anyway, to fly his airplane could, I thought, only be the result of extreme curiosity. He and the others really wanted to know if I could actually fly an airplane, and the only way they knew to find out was to ask me to fly theirs.

I thanked Ben and acknowledged that I would be delighted to fly his airplane. I had never flown a Swallow before, but I knew that I would have no difficulty, for I had flown similar airplanes equipped with the 90 H.P. OX5 engine. So, I climbed into the cockpit, Ben swung the propellor, and I taxied down to the end of the field, turned into the wind, and took off. I climbed up to 2,000 feet, made steep turns and a stall, and came in to a three-point landing.

"It's a nice airplane, Ben; I enjoyed flying it. Thanks a lot."

Well, that broke the ice. I hadn't had time to walk off the field before Tex Lagrone came up and asked, "Would you like to fly my Waco 9?"

"Yes indeed, Tex. I would like to very much."

"When you are through flying, let Scotty take up," Tex added.

"Well, Tex," I said, "there's no use wasting your gas. Scotty can ride with me, and we can both fly the airplane."

Tex seemed to get the point; he was not averse to saving gasoline.

"Okay," he said. "That's a good idea."

I motioned to Scotty to get into the front seat, Tex swung the prop, the engine started, and after a few minutes of warm-up, I taxied out onto the field and took off. I stayed up this time for about twenty minutes. I wanted to give Tex the impression that I was giving Scotty, too, ample time to try out the airplane. I came in for a good landing, taxied up to where Tex was standing, and cut the engine. "Thanks, Tex," I said. "This airplane handles very nicely."

"How did you like it, Scotty?" Tex asked.

"Fine," replied Scotty. "I enjoyed flying it."

Well, I thought, *we got away with that, at least for the time being.*

From that day on, all the pilots on Richards Field were our friends. Even E. P. acknowledged my existence. Some of the married pilots invited Scotty and me to their homes for dinner. Some of the bachelors would take us out to a restaurant or speakeasy for an evening of fun.

Scotty and I continued our work of licensing pilots, airplanes, and mechanics at Richards Field. I let Scotty handle the aircraft mechanics, while I concentrated on flight-testing pilots and supervising their written examinations. As was inevitable, the operators on the field found out about Scotty not being a pilot, but by this time they had come to like him so much that it didn't much matter. Scotty, a little, skinny guy about five feet four, would entertain us by the hour imitating various characters in his Scotch brogue.

One day, a barnstorming pilot flew in to Richards Field in an old beat-up Laird Swallow. I have forgotten the pilot's name, but he very much wanted me to fly his airplane, of which he was extremely proud. I had learned from other pilots that this airplane had been staked down in some farmer's field for several winters in all kinds of weather and was not in very good condition. I kept stalling the pilot with one excuse after another, for I had no desire to fly his airplane. However, one day he caught me off guard when I had run out of excuses, so I reluctantly agreed to fly the old Laird. As luck would have it, there was a strong wind blowing, as it often does over the flatlands of the Midwest, and I knew it was going to be a rough flight.

I took off and had reached an altitude of 200 feet with the airplane bouncing around like a cork. I started to make a turn to the right, but when I tried to move the control stick, it simply wouldn't move. I used all the strength I had, but I still couldn't budge that stick. It had jammed somehow. This meant I had no lateral control whatever. And, in this bumpy air, I needed all the control I could get. My paramount concern now was getting back on the ground all in one piece. I managed to skid the airplane around with the rudder, heading downwind toward the end of the field from which I had taken off. There, again using the rudder, I managed to get the airplane headed into the wind for the approach for landing. As I glided towards the field, the gusty wind would toss me around like a feather, but I was able to keep the plane headed straight with the rudder. I finally hit the ground on one wing and a wheel. There was no damage except a broken wing skid, a sort of half-loop of wood attached to the underside of the wing, which protected the wing in the event of a ground loop.

I taxied the airplane into a hangar and proceeded to inspect the aileron-control system. I found that the cable running from the control stick to the aileron had frayed where it runs through a pulley on the wing spar and the few strands of wire left had jammed between the pulley and the flange. I had indeed been lucky, but I had also learned a lesson: from now on, I would first inspect the airplanes and *then* fly them.

One day, I received a wire from Clarence Young ordering me to report back to Washington for another assignment. A replacement would be sent to Kansas City to take over my duties. I had organized the territory and made friends for the government, and, now that things were going smoothly, my successor would have no trouble taking over. I felt the lasting satisfaction of accomplishment.

Chapter 7   Detroit

When I arrived at Ford Airport, Dearborn, Michigan, in the late summer of 1927, the Ford trimotor, later to be known as the Tin Goose, had only been in production for a short time. The plane was designed by Bill Stout, an aeronautical engineer who had also designed the first all-metal plane for Ford. This was a single-engined airplane, powered with a 400 H.P. Liberty engine, which, like its successor, the trimotor, was built of corrugated aluminum. At the time of my arrival (again, I had the dubious honor of being the *first* inspector in the territory), these aircraft were being flown on a scheduled airline, operated by Ford, to Grand Rapids and Chicago.

The first trimotor airplane to be operated commercially in this country was the Fokker F-7, built in Holland and designed by Tony Fokker. This airplane, unlike the Ford trimotor, was built of wood and fabric. The wing structure was of plywood and the fuselage fabric-covered. Stout's plane was, of course, all metal (corrugated aluminum), but, nevertheless, Bill was accused by many of merely copying Tony Fokker's design.

By this time, the word had gone around that the department inspectors were a fairly capable group of pilots who were qualified to judge the capabilities of other pilots flying commercially. So, unlike the situtation at our first cold reception at Kansas City, we were greeted warmly by the Ford pilots, who were most cooperative. There was Eddie Hamilton, Larry Fritz, Perry Hutton, John Collings, and Shorty Schroeder. These pilots flew the run to Chicago and Grand Rapids and also acted as test pilots for the aircraft coming off the production line at the Ford factory.

I immediately decided to waive the flight-test part of examining these pilots, for it was obvious that these men, veteran airline pilots, needed no such flying examination by me. For the record, though, I would have them complete the written examination, which only concerned air regulations.

The airplane factory was located at the east end of the airport while the administration building, which was also the engineering building, was located at the west end of the field. I had been instructed to report to a Mr. Walker, whose office was located in the administration building. When his secretary admitted me, Walker, a thin man of medium height with dark-brown hair, arose from his desk and greeted me affably. However, his cold, piercing brown eyes told me that here was a no-nonsense man who, if need be, could prove himself a tough character to tangle with.

Walker seemed to have no particular title, but I soon learned that as far as the operations of the Ford Motor Company at Dearborn were concerned, all matters of any importance had to be channeled through his office. After a few minutes of general conversation, mostly about the operation of the airplane factory, Walker called in his secretary and said, "Ask Mr. Dahlinger if he will please come to my office as soon as convenient." In a very few minutes, there appeared a short, stocky man whom I guessed to be about thirty-five years old. His light-brown hair, thinning on top, was brushed straight back, and his deep-blue eyes seemed to look right through me. He too gave the impression of being a rather tough character.

After Dahlinger had entered the office and closed the door, Walker said, "Ray, I want you to meet Frank Jerdone from Washington, who represents the Department of Commerce and who will be in charge of licensing our pilots and airplanes." Dahlinger shook hands and said he was glad to meet me. He seemed a bundle of nerves, unable to sit still a minute. I was to learn very soon that indeed this man's energy was boundless and he gave the illusion of being at several different places at the same time.

Walker explained that Mr. Dahlinger was manager of Ford Farms at Dearborn and this included the airport. But I was also to learn that Ray Dahlinger was much more than a farm manager. He was Henry Ford's man Friday, his personal bodyguard, the chief of security for all operations at Dearborn, and Ford's personal representative in all matters pertaining to the operation of the Dearborn plant of the Ford Motor Company.

After a few minutes, Ray took his departure, saying, "Anything I can do for you at the airport, just let me know." Walker, too, offered to assist me in any way possible. Although these men were officials of one of the most powerful organizations in the world, they seemed to have tremendous respect for United States government regulations and were anxious to comply with these regulations.

The atmosphere surrounding the Ford Airport contrasted greatly with that of all other airports which with I was familiar. In the first place, there were strict regulations that were rigidly enforced. I remember my first day on the flight line, I pulled out a cigarette and lighted it, but I had hardly taken a puff before a guard appeared and, in no uncertain terms, ordered me to put it out. And it would be too bad if anyone was caught drinking or had in his possession any liquor in the vicinity of the airport or, for that matter, anywhere else on Ford property. I had the feeling that I was being watched constantly, and constant surveillance proved to be true, especially for the employees of the Ford Motor Company, including the pilots.

There were several speakeasies up the Detroit River, as well as in the city itself, that served not only alcoholic beverages but excellent food. Some of the pilots and I would often have dinner at one of these establishments. The day after one of these evenings out, Eddie Hamilton came up to me and said that he had been called to Dahlinger's office and told by Ray that he had been seen at a certain speakeasy and that it would be wise for him to stop patronizing such places. All during my assignment at Dearborn, I could sense that "cloak and dagger" atmosphere that so pervaded the premises of the Ford Motor Company.

One late afternoon, I was standing in one of the hangars talking with a couple of pilots when there landed a small low-wing monoplane. The pilot taxied up to the hangar, crawled out of the cockpit, and introduced himself as Phil Downs. This airplane was of much interest to me, for I had never seen this design before—a low-wing monoplane, externally braced by compression struts extending from the top of the fuselage at about a forty–five degree angle connecting with the front and rear wing spars. This was a rather innovative design, contrasting greatly with that of the standard biplane of that day.

I introduced myself to Downs as a Department of Commerce inspector and asked him a few technical questions. After a brief conversation, he asked, "Would you like to fly this airplane?"

"I sure would," I replied.

"It's too late now, but meet me here tomorrow morning. I think you'll like the way she flies."

"Okay, I'll be here at 9 o'clock ready to go."

When I arrived at the hangar the next morning, Downs was sitting in the cockpit with the engine running. He motioned me alongside and said, "I'm just going to take her up for a short flight, and then you can have her." I walked up to the operations office and got my helmet and goggles from my locker. As I was walking back towards the hangar, I saw Downs take off, climb to about 400 feet to the north, turn, and come back over the south end of the field. At this point, he put the airplane into a shallow power dive to within about fifty feet off the ground and then pulled the plane up sharply into a steep climb. At 200 feet, there was a loud noise, as if someone had shot off a high-powered rifle. At that instant, I was horrified to see the right wing fold over the cockpit and the plane go into a vertical dive, crashing to the earth with a loud, crumbling sound.

I ran toward the scene, arriving at the same time as a woman whom I later learned was a nurse from the Ford Hospital. Downs was dead, killed instantly by the impact.

Now this airplane was classed as "experimental." There had been no "airworthiness certificate" issued. Therefore, there was really was no knowledge as to its structural strength available. In fact, we were just beginning to inspect aircraft factories for airworthiness certificates for various types of aircraft. This procedure was quite involved; not only must the materials used in the construction process meet certain standards, but the engineers were required to run stress analyses on the various components to determine their structural strength.

Phil Downs had been flying this airplane for over two months and had experienced no trouble whatever. Why had this structural failure occurred at this particular time, causing this tragic accident? It could just as well have occurred on a previous flight, or it could very well have happened on the next flight, when I would have been flying the airplane. In fact, I would have put the airplane through much more violent maneuvers than had Downs. Fate seemed to be playing strange games with me—first the jammed aileron control at Kansas City, now this fatal crash. What next? I do not like playing Russian roulette.

I was awakened early one morning in my hotel room by the persistent ringing of the telephone. It was Bob Gast calling from the lobby.

"Bob, I'm sure glad to hear your voice. What brings you to Detroit?"

"Come down and have breakfast with me, and I'll tell you all about it."

I dressed hurriedly and joined Bob in the dining room.

"There's an air meet starting tomorrow at Ypsilanti. You and I are to go up there and license the pilots and airplanes."

"Why both of us?"

"Clarence Young's orders. He thinks it will take the two of us to handle it." Bob continued. "A sort of 'flying entrepreneur' by the name of Pete Goff is conducting the meet. Pete called on Bill MacCracken and told him that if he would send a couple of inspectors to Ypsilanti, he would make it a requirement that all pilots and their airplanes be licensed before they could enter the various events."

"It looks as if we'll have our hands full."

"Yeah. It might be a lot of fun, too," replied Bob.

Bob himself was a lot of fun. A stocky man of medium height, with pale-blue eyes and a bald head, he was far from handsome, but what a personality! A brilliant conversationalist, full of wit and dry humor, he, in spite of stomach ulcers that seemed to give him constant pain, was almost always cheerful. A great drinking companion, he would, when the occasion arose, match drink for drink with the best of them, completely ignoring his ulcers.

When we arrived at the air field at Ypsilanti, there was a confusion of pilots, aircraft, mechanics, and spectators. We found a little shack with a sign on the door that said : "Operations Office." Pete Goff was sitting at a desk that occupied most of the room. He got up and shook hands with us, saying, "Welcome to Ypsilanti." He seemed genuinely glad that we were there and informed us that he had arranged with the high-school principal for the use of the classrooms in which to give the pilots their written examinations.

There were about a dozen pilots awaiting flight tests, so Bob and I started right to work. By the end of the day, we had finished with the flight tests, and after dinner we arrived at the schoolhouse to conduct the written exams.

Bud Wyman, a reporter for the *Detroit News,* had followed us to Ypsilanti. His assignment: to cover the air meet and to interview Bob and me on the subject of air regulations and their impact on the industry. Bud had approached me late that afternoon, but it was obvious that he had had a few too many, so I told him I was too busy and to see me tomorrow.

When Bob and I arrived at the schoolhouse, there was Bud waiting for us. Bud was a tall, good-looking chap and very likable, but he was still not very sober. He decided he wanted to help us with the exams, but in trying to pass out papers, he only stumbled into people and fell over desks, creating a nuisance.

The meet lasted three days and was quite a success. Bob and I returned to Detroit and checked into the Fort Shelby Hotel. As I was dressing for dinner that evening, there was a knock on the door and when I opened it there stood Bud Wyman and he was far from sober. I had told Bud repeatedly that when he sobered up I would grant him an interview. However, this evening he was very insistent, so, to get rid of him, I said, "Okay, Bud, what do you want to know?" He asked a few pertinent questions, took a few notes, thanked me, and said goodnight. The entire so-called interview had lasted only twenty minutes.

The next evening, I picked up a copy of the *Detroit News,* and to

48

my amazement, there on the front page was a three-column heading with Bud's byline. It was a two-thousand–word story, one of the most coherent and intelligently written articles I had ever read. It was undoubtedly the finest piece of interviewing I had ever experienced.

During the time I was stationed at Dearborn, Ford's engineers developed a small low-wing airplane dubbed the Ford Flivver. It was supposed to be the "Model T of the Air" that would make it possible to put a plane in every garage. However, this never came to pass for many reasons, one of which was that it was a single-seater, therefore it would be impossible to teach anyone to fly it.

Harry Brooks, a favorite of Henry Ford, was the test pilot on this project. Brooks set some time and distance records for a single-engine aircraft before he was killed off the Florida coast. He had landed at an airport, where he refueled and remained overnight. It was rumored that he stuck a toothpick in the gas-cap breather vent to keep the sand, which was blowing over the airplane, from entering the gas tank. Shortly after taking off the following day, the engine quit and Brooks landed in the ocean. He was last seen standing on the wing just before the plane sank. His body was never recovered.

It was said that after Harry Brooks's death, Henry Ford lost all interest in airplanes. Eventually the Ford factory was closed down. This was unfortunate, for the Ford trimotor was a good airplane. Several hundred had been built, and, for a considerable time, it was flown by practically all domestic airlines as well as those of many other countries. There are still a few trimotors flying today.

49

Chapter 8   Los Angeles

The Santa Fe *Chief* with the aid of two huge steam locomotives (this was before the advent of diesels) threaded its way through the mountains of New Mexico and Arizona. The *Chief* was an extra-fare, deluxe train running between Chicago and Los Angeles. It was (within the limitations of train travel) the ultimate in comfort and service.

The stars, directors, producers, and assorted executives of the motion-picture industry were patrons of the *Chief*. For these denizens of the "world of make-believe" to travel by ordinary train would be unthinkable. The perquisites of these God's favored people demanded the very best.

We were now coasting lazily down toward the Colorado River, which we would soon cross into California at Needles.

As we started our long trek across the Mohave Desert, the sun burst forth over the horizon with a roar of color and a promise of intolerable heat that would blanket the desert during the emerging day.

Sitting across from me in the lounge car was a very beautiful blond whom I recognized as one of Hollywood's better-known stars. Sitting opposite her was a heavyset man of apparently medium height engaged in deep conversation with the actress. I guessed correctly that he was her director. There were other couples scattered throughout the car whom I judged to be professional people and their wives. I was somewhat puzzled that I had not seen any of these people all the way from Chicago. In fact, I had hardly seen anyone, even at mealtimes. It was as if by instinct they could smell the California air and as we approached that golden land they all emerged from wherever they had been hibernating.

Having paused briefly at Barstow, we were now approaching San Bernadino, where we would stop for breakfast at the Harvey House. These Harvey House restaurants had been established along the route of the Santa Fe to accommodate the passengers and relieve the heavy workload of the train's dining car service. The food served at the Harvey

House was of excellent quality, and the passengers welcomed this break in the long train journey.

The waitresses, all attractive young ladies who had come west seeking adventure and very probably husbands, too, were known as the Harvey Girls. A very fine motion picture by the same title, depicting the lives of these women, proved to be a great box-office success.

The two-hour run down to Los Angeles was a welcome relief after the searing, dry heat of the Mohave Desert. We were now passing through well-cultivated orange groves, and from the observation platform one could smell the distinctive odor of orange blossoms that seemed to pervade most all of Southern California.

Wesley Parks (not his real name) met me at the Union Station and offered to drive me around to look for an apartment. As it was early in the morning, we would have the whole day in which to find a place to live. Wesley had been the first inspector to arrive in California. As Los Angeles was his hometown, he naturally knew his way around. We found an attractive bachelor apartment on Cahuenga Drive, and by early afternoon I had moved in bag and baggage and settled down to contemplate this, to me, strange land of Southern California.

Parks had been assigned an airplane for his official use, a Ryan Brougham, a commercial version of Lindbergh's *Spirit of St. Louis*. The plane was hangared at the national-guard field in Griffith Park. As I enjoyed equal status with Parks, I had, of course, equal use of the airplane. I soon learned that Parks was not one of the better pilots around the Los Angeles area and, probably for this reason, made little use of the airplane. This suited me fine, for I liked to fly and used the plane on every possible occasion.

One day an amusing incident occurred. After landing at Clover Field, Santa Monica, I came in over the fence, made a short landing, and taxied up to the flight line. I had hardly switched off the engine when some chap climbed up on the wheel and peered into my open window at me. "I knew this wasn't Parks," he said. "Too good a landing."

I soon learned, too, that Parks had a few delusions of grandeur. He seemed to think that in addition to being an aircraft inspector for the Aeronautics Branch of the Department of Commerce, he was also a traffic cop. He always carried a whistle tied to a string around his neck, and when driving along the street if he happened to see a motorist speeding or otherwise breaking a traffic regulation, he would drive alongside the offender and whistle him over to the curb. He would then proceed to bawl the driver out and emphatically advise him of his wrongdoing.

This sort of procedure would inevitably get Parks in trouble, for he had no authority to proceed in this manner and no badge or other identification to back him up. One day I was following Parks up Wilshire Boulevard when I suddenly saw him pull a car over to the curb. By the time I pulled up behind them and parked, the driver whom Parks had apprehended was out of his car and telling Parks off in no uncertain terms. The guy was about six-feet-two and weighed at least 200 pounds, and I could see he was mad enough to beat the hell out of Parks and was just about to do it. I stepped in between them, hoping I wouldn't get myself hit, and tried to reason with this giant. Of course, I didn't have much of an argument, but somehow I managed to get him calmed down and told Parks to get into his car and get going.

Later, I said to him, "Wes, what in hell is the matter with you? You know damn well you have no authority to act in this manner.

"And," I added, "the Los Angeles Police Department would take a dim view of your trying to do their job. Furthermore, you are very likely to get the hell beat out of you one of these days. You would have this morning if I hadn't been along to break it up."

Parks made no reply. He just looked at me and grinned. I decided then and there that this guy was a little nuts and would prove to be an embarrassment to me as long as I was associated with him in Southern California.

Aviation, in that year of 1927, was experiencing a terrific boom. This was especially so in the Los Angeles area, where dozens of flying fields had sprung up in the outlying districts. There was more activity here than any place I had been stationed previously. This was due to a combination of circumstances: the California weather, where one could fly the year around, and Lindbergh's recent nonstop transatlantic flight. (His Ryan monoplane had been manufactured in San Diego.) Also, the motion-picture industry greatly influenced the growth of aviation. They were just beginning to make full-length pictures with aviation as the theme. This created a demand for pilots, mechanics, and almost all types of aircraft, as well as for engineers, technicians, and various types of executives with an aviation background.

I was much impressed with Southern California—its salubrious climate, its rugged mountains, and its vast agricultural areas and acres and acres of beautiful orange groves. However, Los Angeles, it seemed to me, had attracted almost all of the world's screwballs. There were more screwy political organizations advocating all sorts of ridiculous schemes, as well as some peculiar religious cults, including that of Aimee Semple McPherson. Even the pilots with whom I came in daily contact (for, after all, I was granting them their license to fly) were of a different breed from those I had known in the East. At every field there were students, instructors, and hangers-on, and for the most part they wore boots and riding breeches, helmets, and goggles. They wore this attire not only when they were flying, but at all times. It was as if they were ready to go on the set and face the cameras for a take. Indeed, I suppose they were playing a part.

After a few days of getting acquainted with Los Angeles and its environs, I decided to call J. B. Alexander. I found his name in the book and dialed the number. J. B. answered the ring immediately.

"Hi, J. B.," I said. "I'm the guy who flew you across the Alleghenys to Pittsburgh the hard way."

"It's good to hear your voice," he replied. "Welcome to California."

"It's good to be here, J. B. How about meeting me for a drink? I take it you know a good speakeasy."

"I sure do. How about 6 o'clock?" He gave me an address on Santa Monica Boulevard.

J. B. was waiting when I arrived promptly at six. He had found a booth where we could talk with some measure of privacy. We ordered a drink.

"I'm glad they sent you out here to help with the licensing," J. B. said. "We not only need additional help, but that screwball Parks is sometimes impossible to deal with. I think he's a little bit nuts.

"And," he added, "he's a lousy pilot."

"I've already found that out," I replied.

"By the way," J. B. asked, "did you ever catch up with the French minister?"

"Yeah, finally. I had to fly all the way to Quebec, though, to get him. Got him and his secretary back to Roosevelt all in one piece. Luck was with me on that flight.

"Are you still working for Howard Hughes?" I asked.

"Yes, but my regular job is as general manager of American Aircraft out on Angeles Mesa Drive. We have a Fairchild and Waco agencies and do some instructing and charter work in addition to selling airplanes. As a matter of fact, I'm teaching Howard to fly and he's about ready to solo. As soon as he gets in his time, I want you to give him his private pilot's license."

"Sure thing, but you seem to have your hands full. I've heard that Hughes is very demanding."

"He is that," J. B. said. "He calls me at all hours of the night and sometimes wants me to meet him at the most unlikely places or else yack for an hour over the phone. Sometimes I get very little sleep.

"By the way, I've got to call Howard now, so I'll probably be tied up for the rest of the evening. Sorry I have to run, but how about meeting me at the field tomorrow morning?"

"I'll be out about nine-thirty. If you have any candidates for licensing, I'll run them through the tests."

"Fine. See you in the morning."

There were three flying fields on Angeles Mesa Drive. As one approached from the east, the first field was operated by Pacific Air Transport, a scheduled airmail carrier between Los Angeles, San Francisco, and Seattle. The next adjoining field was operated by American Aircraft, J. B.'s outfit. The third was operated by Maddux Airlines, a passenger line between Los Angeles and San Diego.

All three fields were merely turf strips, and the usual approach was over power and telephone lines, and even with the slow-landing aircraft of that day, the fields were none too long.

When I arrived at J. B.'s office the following morning, I was introduced to a Mr. Hull, a Texan who was the principal owner of American Aircraft. I also met Charlie LaJotte, an instructor who was later to become Wallace Beery's personal pilot. J. B. handed me a list of a half-dozen students who he said were ready for their flight test for a private pilot's license. There were several Waco 10s on the line, and J. B. said to take any one for checking the students. I spent the rest of the day in the front seat of the Waco, correcting the mistakes of the student behind me. Some were very good and some were very bad.

The days dragged on into weeks, and the routine became monotonous—conducting written examinations, passing out mimeographed questions and correcting answers, and flight-testing inexperienced pilots, some of whom were dangerous to ride with. Sometimes on a rare occasion a student would become panicky and "freeze" the controls and I would have to fight him off—a contest of pure physical strength. This was a nerve-wracking job, to be sure.

The one thing that made my job interesting was meeting new people—quite a few celebrities and some who would later become world-famous. One day at the Lockheed plant in Burbank, I ran into Carl Ben Eilson, with whom I had been associated at Langley Field and later with the department in Washington. Ben had been assigned to me on several inspection trips in the field, and we had become good friends. Because of Ben's pioneer flying in Alaska, he had been engaged by Sir Hubert Wilkins as his personal pilot, and together with Sir Hubert navigating, they were to fly from Point Barrow, Alaska, over the North Pole.

Lockheed had designed a new type of aircraft that only recently had been put into production. This airplane was known as the Lockheed Vega. The wing was the cantilever type mounted on a monococque

54

fuselage. It was constructed entirely of plywood, which with its light weight and ultra streamlining gave it a high crusing speed: 150 MPH, which at that time was higher than that of any other commercial aircraft. Sir Hubert had purchased the second production model to come off the production line.

Ben and I greeted each other warmly. "Well, Ben," I said, "Langley, Washington, Cleveland and Detroit, and now Los Angeles. It's good to see you again."

"It's good to see you again, Frank. We've had some good old times together."

We were sitting in Lockheed's reception room when Sir Hubert Wilkins walked in. Ben stood up, looked at Sir Hubert, and said, "I want you to meet Frank Jerdone, an old friend from the army and Department of Commerce days." (This was before Sir Hubert made his historical flight over the North Pole, and at that time he had not been knighted. I still can't remember ever having heard Ben address him by any name, either Hubert, Mr. Wilkins, Wilkins or whatever.)

This man who now greeted me so cordially was a very distinguished-looking gentleman. He was above medium height, with broad shoulders and not an ounce of surplus fat. He wore a well-trimmed goatee, and his distinguished appearance would dominate any group of people anywhere. He was a native of Australia, but when he spoke I could detect no trace of the usual Australian accent.

I knew that Ben and Sir Hubert would have business at several of the airfields in the Los Angeles area and that transportation would be a problem for them. So I said to Ben, "Look, I have a Ryan out at Griffith Park, which I have use of most of the time, and I would be glad to ferry you and Sir Hubert around the area at any time you have need of some transportation."

For the next few weeks I spent a great deal of time flying Ben and Sir Hubert around the Los Angeles area. Los Angeles was such a vast area (it was thirty miles from Santa Monica on the Pacific Ocean to Burbank) that an airplane became very useful indeed. Also, I too, in the course of my work, had to visit these various flying fields, so I managed to accomplish quite a bit on these short hops as well as accommodate Ben and Sir Hubert.

One late afternoon at Maddux Field on Angeles Mesa Drive, a Lockheed Vega landed and taxied up to the administration building. The pilot was Lockheed's sales manager, whose name I have forgotten. However, he approached me, introduced himself, and asked me to fly the airplane. Now at that time most airplane manufacturers and owners, too, would often request that I fly their airplanes. Their idea was that if a government official flew their airplanes and stated that they were favorably impressed with the performance, it would be of considerable help in their sales promotion.

This airplane was either the first or one of the first production models, and frankly, I was a little reluctant to fly it. In the first place, the airplane was so streamlined that it had a reputation for landing at a high rate of speed. Then, too, this plane was so radically different from anything I had ever flown that I didn't want to be rushed into flying it. This pilot salesman was so insistent that in the end I had really no alternative but to accept his offer. As I climbed into the pilot's seat (this was a single-control airplane and you were really on your own), I glanced back into the cabin and saw some guy and a girl sitting in the rear seat. As I had never seen either of them before, I thought briefly of asking them to get out, but then I decided if they were crazy enough to be flying with me, then let's go.

I took off and flew around for about ten minutes, making some steep turns and some stalls with power off, to get the feel of the ship. Now I noticed with some misgiving that twilight had set in and darkness was fast approaching. This was a time of day that made landing difficult. It was not dark enough to use landing lights, yet the twilight made it difficult to judge distance. I came in on my approach over the power lines (which seemed always to surround most flying fields) and leveled off a little high, and as I hit the ground, I felt the left landing-gear strut shear off where it was attached to the fuselage. I skidded along on the left wing for several hundred feet and then came to an abrupt stop. I climbed out of the cockpit into the cabin and saw that the young man and his girl friend were unhurt, although a little pale.

As I stepped out of the airplane, a crowd of people rushed up, the first of whom was Sir Hubert Wilkins. His first words were, "Gee, I'm glad you did this. I'm going to have Lockheed beef up this landing gear fitting." And he added, "You didn't drop her hard enough for this gear to have collapsed."

Frankly, I didn't think so either, but I was extremely embarrassed—a government inspector's cracking up a company airplane on his first flight was certainly not very reassuring to any one concerned. The sales manager was most gracious, however, and insisted that I fly the airplane again after repairs had been made. I did just that later on, with no disastrous results.

In the meantime, I had seen a great deal of J. B. Alexander. We were becoming very good friends, for there was mutual respect. I admired his business and sales ability, and he respected my flying ability, and I had been successful in making friends in the industry. He had

56

on many occasions invited me to his home for dinner, and he and his pretty blond wife, Ruth, always made me feel right at home.

One morning as I walked into J. B.'s office at the airport, I noticed a tall, thin man (he was probably six feet, three inches) standing in front of a wall map. J. B. got up from his desk and said, "Howard, I want you to meet Frank Jerdone, who will check you out for your private license this morning." So this was the fabulous Howard Hughes. We shook hands and admitted that we were glad to meet each other. I had been told that Hughes was somewhat deaf, and I found that I did have to raise my voice to make him hear me.

I climbed into the front seat of a Waco with Howard in back and told him to take off and make some steep turns, a power-off stall, and three turns of a spin from 3,000 feet. From the moment we became airborne, I could tell that this guy was a natural-born flyer and with a lot of experience would make a superb pilot. He went through the morning's maneuvers without a hitch. His handling of the ship was smooth and precise, and his three landings were all excellent, not a bounce on any of them.

"Congratulations, Howard," I said as I signed his license form. "You did just fine."

"I had a good instructor." Howard grinned, looking at J. B. I was to learn very soon that Howard Hughes was not much on the small talk. He was, for the most part, a very serious young man.

At the time of which I speak, Hughes had already started producing his movie *Hell's Angels*, an epic World War I picture starring Ben Lyon, James Hall, and Greta Nissen. Howard was buying up old warplanes by the dozen and hiring scores of pilots, and for the most part J. B. Alexander, in addition to his many other duties, was commissioned to acquire these planes and hire the pilots.

Somehow, Reginald Denny, the actor, had acquired two World War I Sopwith Snipes. These were single-seater "pursuit" planes with rotary engines. That is, the entire engine revolved around the crankshaft. This rotary action of the engine produced a tremendous amount of torque, and when the pilot opened the throttle for takeoff, it was necessary to hold full right rudder to correct for this. The Snipe was a tricky airplane to fly, and it took a skillful pilot to fly it with safety. Howard had purchased these planes from Denny for use in *Hell's Angels.*

Howard Hughes had built up considerable flying time in the months after I granted him his pilot's license, but for the most part he had been flying only Wacos and Fairchild 51s. They were shooting on location at Mines Field (now Los Angeles International Airport), and the script called for a side slip into the camera angle from an altitude of a few hundred feet. The stunt pilot involved refused to do it under a thousand feet. "Below this altitude the maneuver is too dangerous," the pilot told Hughes.

"Ridiculous," replied Hughes. "I'll do it myself." He climbed into the Sopwith, took off and circled into camera range at 300 feet, put the plane into a left-hand slip, and crashed in a cloud of dust. He was rushed by ambulance to the hospital, where surgery was performed on his badly crushed face. The surgeons did the best they could, but it was impossible to repair the cheekbone. It was too badly crushed. There was an indentation in Howard's cheek which remained with him the rest of his life.

Howard at another time had purchased a Boeing P-4 "pursuit" plane designed for the military. The plane had been at the Douglas Santa Monica plant undergoing various modifications for almost a year. During this time, Howard had done very little flying and, of course, none on the P-4. The plane was now hangared at the Burbank Airport, and one day Howard, J. B., and I were walking toward the Lockheed hangar, where at orders from Howard the plane was being rolled out onto the apron and refueled for flight. It was a bright, sunny afternoon with only scattered cumulus clouds dotting a blue sky. Howard had announced his intention of flying the P-4, but I felt that this was not a wise decision, with his having been off flying for such an extended period.

As we walked along, I said, "Howard, don't you think you should fly a smaller, less complicated airplane," raising my voice to overcome his deafness, "before trying out the Boeing?"

"Naw," he drawled. "I can handle her all right." Howard was not known for lack of confidence.

He climbed into the Boeing, started the engine, and taxied out onto the field. He opened the throttle wide and started down the runway, but just before becoming airborne, he cut the throttle and jammed on the brakes. He repeated this performance a half-dozen times, while J. B. and I anxiously looked on. Finally, Howard taxied to the end of the runway, headed into the wind, and this time took off. He flew around for about fifteen minutes and then started his approach for a landing. The touchdown was smooth and on three points. He taxied up to where we were standing, cut the engine, looked at us, and grinned, as if to say, "See? I told you I could do it."

A few years later, I was living in East Orange, New Jersey, and flying Eastern out of Newark when I received a message from Noah Dietrich's office in Hollywood requesting me to go into New York and talk with the manager of the theater where *Hell's Angels* was to open

58

soon. I have forgotten just what I was supposed to do for the Hughes organization in this regard, but anyway I did what was asked of me and forgot about the incident.

Some time after the New York theater incident, I was in Hollywood, and together with J. B. Alexander, I visited the offices of the Caddo Company at 7000 Romaine Street. The Caddo Company was the operating company for Hughes's motion-picture enterprises. I was seated in the reception room reading a magazine when Noah Dietrich came to the door and asked me to come into his office. I had met Dietrich when I was stationed in California as an aircraft inspector for the Department of Commerce. I had been much impressed with Noah Dietrich and consider him one of the finest gentlemen I have ever met. It is my personal opinion that if it were not for Noah Dietrich's shrewd and able management of Hughes's vast financial empire, Howard would never have become the fabulous billionaire that the world came to know so well.

After we seated ourselves, Noah said, "Frank, what do we owe you for that work you did for us in New York?" I was somewhat startled at the question.

"You owe me nothing, Noah; I was just doing you and Howard a friendly favor. Besides, it was no trouble anyway."

In spite of my protests, before I left the office he handed me a most generous check.

I had been in Southern California now for over six months, and while I found the Hollywood atmosphere most interesting and the people I met fascinating, I was becoming increasingly annoyed with Wes Parks. While I felt that those in the aviation industry—pilots, mechanics, and executives—all liked and respected me, the antics of Parks were detrimental to the prestige of the department and humiliating to me. So I finally decided to take some action. I wired Clarence Young in Washington the following: "Refuse to be associated with Parks any longer. Request assignment to another territory."

A few days later I received a reply: "Your request granted. Return to Washington for reassignment."

So my tour of duty in Southern Cal rnia came to an end. It was with some reluctance that I boarded the ain for the long journey back to Washington. After all, I had had a fabulous experience in that incredible place called Hollywood.

Chapter 9   **Seattle and Portland**

When I arrived back in Washington, I immediately learned that Clarence had departed for Honolulu the previous day. His secretary informed me that he had tried to get in touch with me by phone at our Los Angeles office. It so happened that my last week in Southern California was devoted to inspecting the Ryan factory at San Diego for an Approved Type Certificate (ATC). This involved inspecting the factory for materials, workmanship, quality control, and various other functions necessary to the production of an airplane. For this specific job, I used the Ryan to commute from Los Angeles to San Diego. For some reason, Clarence had assumed that I had moved down to San Diego for this particular job. He had been trying to contact me in every place except where I actually was every night—my apartment in Los Angeles.

In previous correspondence I had requested of Clarence that I be given the Saint Louis territory and he had indicated his approval of this transfer. However, his secretary now informed me that he had left orders for me to proceed to Portland, Oregon, and to establish an office there that would be my headquarters for the territory comprising Oregon, Washington, and Montana.

I had set my heart on the Saint Louis territory, and I had no desire whatever to go to the Pacific Northwest. Apparently Clarence had become miffed at failing to communicate with me in Los Angeles and had switched territories on me, I suppose as a disciplinary action. I asked his secretary if there was any way I could reach Clarence by phone somewhere along the way. She said that he had planned on laying over a day or two in Chicago and would be registered at the Sherman Hotel. That evening I placed a person-to-person call for him at the Sherman. Fortunately, he was in his room and answered immediately.

"Hello, Clarence. Sorry you were unable to reach me in Los Angeles."

"Where were you anyway?"

"Clarence, I commuted each day to the Ryan plant. I saw no reason to move down there when Ryan was available."

"Well, it's important that I be able to reach you inspectors at all times." I was getting a cool reception over the phone.

"Your secrectary informs me that I am to take over the northwest territory."

There was a long pause. . . .

"We need an experienced man to organize that territory. It's just as important as Saint Louis."

"But, Clarence, you as much as promised me that Saint Louis area. That is where I really want to go."

"Yeah, but I've changed my mind." Clarence was adamant. "You can have a couple of days off and then leave for Portland. And," he added, "don't stop over in Chicago." I had on a previous occasion run into Bob Gast and Ben Eilson in Chicago and the three of us had thrown a party that lasted for days. This time, too, Clarence was unable to find us, and, of course, he was furious. So I knew what he was thinking with the warning "Don't stop in Chicago."

I knew that Ben and Bob were still in Chicago, and sure enough, as I was checking into the Hayes Hotel I saw them sitting there in a corner of the lobby grinning at me. After an enthusiastic greeting, the three of us repaired to a speakeasy down the street away from the hotel. Ignoring Clarence's edict, I spent three days in Chicago. Ben and Bob had a couple of airplanes out at Ashburn Field—a new Laird and an old airmail D.H. Each day we would go to the field and fly the Laird, even in the rain, for this was a superb airplane, and it was a delight to fly it. Matty Laird, in designing this plane, had done a magnificent job.

I decided that the time had come for me to leave for Portland. If I stayed around Chicago much longer, Clarence would surely find out and would again be mad at me. So it was with some reluctance that I boarded the Great Northern's *Empire Builder* for Seattle and Portland.

The scenery along this northern route was most spectacular. I remember crossing the Continental Divide with the early-morning sun glistening on the snow-covered mountains and the tall trees shrouded in white. We dropped down off of the divide heading for Spokane, where we stopped briefly before winding through the Cascades into Seattle and thence to Portland, our destination.

I reported to a Mr. Peeples, the district manager for the Department of Commerce, who maintained offices in the post-office building. Peeples greeted me warmly and proved to be most cooperative all during my tenure in the Pacific Northwest. He had prepared an office for me down the hall from his own and offered me the services of his secretary. I checked into the New Heathman Hotel, which at that time was new and the accommodations excellent. As I would be traveling a great deal between Portland, Seattle, and Spokane, I decided to make the hotel my headquarters. The rates were reasonable and I didn't want to be bothered with an apartment.

That evening as I was preparing to go down to dinner, the phone rang, and a rather meek voice said, "I'm Jack Truebridge of the *Portland Oregonian*. I learned of your arrival in town and would like to talk with you."

"I'm just getting ready to go down to dinner. Could you make it sometime tomorrow?"

"Sure, but I haven't had dinner either. Would you mind if I joined you?"

"No, of course not. Be glad to have you," I replied. After all, I was alone in a strange city and the company of a newspaper reporter might prove interesting.

As I stepped off the elevator, I was greeted by a young man of medium height, somewhat on the thin side, with blond hair and pale-blue eyes. For a reporter, I thought Jack was indeed a quiet, unobtrusive person who seemed even a little embarrassed to ask a question—not at all like most of the newspeople I had previously met, who were for the most part an aggressive, bold lot. The dinner progressed pleasantly enough, in a low-key, conversational manner. Jack asked me about my work in licensing pilots, mechanics, and aircraft and seemed interested in the implementation of the new air regulations. I didn't suspect it then, but Jack was to become almost a constant companion during my stay in Portland.

At breakfast the next morning, I received a telephone call from Tex Rankin, a prominent pilot who operated a Ryan agency and flying school out at the Portland Airport. Tex had heard of my arrival, too, and offered to come by the hotel and take me out to the airport. Tex arrived about twenty minutes later. I was a little surprised to see a big, heavyset man with dark hair and piercing brown eyes.

"I'm Tex Rankin," he said. "Welcome to Portland."

"Glad to meet you, Tex. I've heard a lot about you."

"And I've heard a lot about you, Frank."

"Well, I hope that what we've heard about each other has been mutually good," I replied, laughing.

In later years, Tex was to become famous as an acrobatic pilot. We arrived at the field and drove up to a hangar with a huge sign on it proclaiming that this was the "Rankin Flying Service." A four-place

Ryan Brougham was parked on the apron in front of the hangar. While Tex and I were talking, a car drove up and out jumped Jack Truebridge. Jack and Tex greeted each other as old friends.

Tex said, "Frank, we'll take the Ryan and fly around the area, and you'll see some of Oregon's beautiful scenery."

We took off with Jack in the rear seat. As a newspaperman, he wasn't going to miss any possible story. We climbed 8,000 feet and headed toward Mount Hood. It was a beautiful, clear day—just a few cumulus clouds dotting the blue sky. Visibility was unlimited and off in the distance we could see Mount Saint Helens and Mount Baker over in the state of Washington. We circled Mount Hood, the highest mountain in Oregon (11,245 feet), its snowcapped peak glistening in the morning sunlight—a magnificent sight, unlike anything I had ever seen. After about an hour of observing the scenic wonders of Oregon from on high, we landed and Tex took me around the field, introducing me to various pilots, mechanics, and operators, all of whom made me feel most welcome.

Again that evening Jack showed up just before I was ready to go down to dinner. But this time he was a little the worse for wear. I was to learn soon that while Jack was inherently a very nice fellow and an intelligent reporter, he was unfortunately addicted to bootleg gin. He suggested that we go to a place called the Oyster Loaf, a seafood restaurant just down the street. We enjoyed a delightful dinner (the crab cocktail supreme was the best I had ever tasted), and as usual the conversation was all about flying, with me doing most of the talking. In spite of Jack's overload of booze, he seemed quite lucid and listened attentively to my stories of "derring-do" in the Wild Blue Yonder. I must admit that most of my tales were a gross exaggeration of the truth.

At breakfast the next morning I was thumbing my way through the *Oregonian* when on the second page a bold-type headline captured my attention. The caption, prominently displayed, proclaimed that "Tex Rankin takes Jerdone for a Flight around Mt. Hood." Truebridge had developed a rather interesting story from a simple pleasure flight around Mount Hood. There were to be many articles about my activities in the Portland area throughout my tenure of duty, all appearing in the *Portland Oregonian* with Jack Truebridge's byline. Jack had a subtle way of obtaining material for a story. We often had dinner and drinks together, and I always assumed, naively, that we were just enjoying each other's company—a social event to pass away a pleasant evening. However, almost invariably there would appear the next morning an article by Truebridge developed from our conversation of the previous evening.

One morning while I was still in bed, my room phone rang, and after sleepily answering it, I heard a voice with a deep southern accent come floating over the wire. "This is Penn Taliaferro [pronounced *Tolliver*]. I'm from the Airways Branch of the Department of Commerce. I saw your name in the paper and would like to meet you."

"Fine. I would like to meet you, too. As soon as I get dressed I'll be down and we can have breakfast together." I knew instinctively that this guy was a fellow Virginian. The accent was unmistakable, and, besides, there was a family of Taliafferos who were neighbors of ours on our farm in Virginia.

As I stepped off the elevator, a tall, very handsome young man with dark hair and deep-brown eyes greeted me with a sly grin that I was to become so familiar with in days to come. We introduced ourselves and proceeded into the dining room for breakfast. I learned almost immediately that his full name was A. Pendelton Taliaferro, Jr., that he was a graduate of Cornell University, and that he had served in Italy as a naval aviator during World War I. Also during breakfast, I learned that Penn was indeed a relative of Charlie and Barcley Taliaferro, my neighbors on the farm in Virginia.

Penn's job was to survey routes throughout the Pacific Northwest for installation of rotating beacons that would serve as aids to navigation for pilots of that day flying night air-mail. The Airways Division of the Department of Commerce, headed by Dr. Hingsburg, was responsible for this pioneering work. (I might add that since the development of very sophisticated electronic systems these lighted beacons are no longer in use. In fact, they have been obsolete for many years.)

Penn had informed me that he had to go to Seattle in a few days and suggested that we meet at the Olympic Hotel, as that seemed to be headquarters for all who were in any way connected with aviation. When I checked in to the Olympic, I was assigned a room on the third floor. I soon learned that because of our reputation as a hell-raising bunch whose habit of throwing wild parties seemed to be too well known to most all hotel proprietors, the third floor was reserved for us only—the reason, of course, being that by isolating us on the one floor we would be in no danger of disturbing the other guests of the hotel.

Flying activity in the Seattle area was confined to three fields, Boeing, the largest, was open to general aviation, including airline, charter, and student instruction. There was a small field north of town used almost exclusively for student instruction, and the Sand Point Naval Air Station, headquarters for both the naval reserve and the army reserve. This field was situated on Lake Washington and consisted of a rather narrow turf runway. Due to the prevailing wind, the approach was usually over the water. Being a reserve officer, I was permitted to fly the army training planes assigned to their reserve squadron.

Commander Campman (a fellow resident of the third floor) was commanding officer of Sand Point Naval Air Station. The commander and I soon became good friends. We often dined together at some of Seattle's better restaurants.

There was a marine-corps–reserve officer named Kluky who, as a member of Campman's squadron, flew out of Sand Point. He had made application for a transport pilot's license. (This designation was later changed to commercial rating.) He made an appointment for a flight test, and I, being an army reserve, took him up in a PT1 training plane. We took off with me in the front seat and flew around for a while at 2,000 feet. His air work was sloppy but passable, so I told him to go in and land. Our approach, as usual, was over Lake Washington. As we neared the edge of the field at about fifty feet altitude and still over the water, this guy seemed to have no intention of breaking his glide or even applying more power in order to reach the runway. In spite of my frantic motions and yelling at him, he did nothing to recover. Grabbing the control stick, I pulled back hard in an effort to get him off the controls, and at the same time I jammed throttle wide open, hoping to get the airplane on to the turf runway. (I was not a bit interested in landing in Lake Washington.) It turned out to be a close call; in spite of my efforts to wrestle the controls from this marine, we hit wheels first and bounced about ten feet in the air. Fortunately the landing gear withstood the shock and we finally came to a stop. I was so damn mad that I just walked away with Kluky running after me, pleading for another chance.

That evening, Commander Campman dropped by my room and pleaded with me to give his marine another chance. His argument was that the reserve officer was totally unfamiliar with the army PT and that if I would ride with him in a navy Vought Corsair with which he was thoroughly familiar, Campman was sure that he would pass with flying colors (pardon the pun). After all, Campman pleaded, the marine had proven to be a good pilot while flying under his command. Because of my fondness for Commander Campman, whom I admired as an officer and a gentleman, I reluctantly agreed to give this guy another chance, this time in the navy Vought.

The following morning, I appeared at the air station to find my candidate sitting in the Vought warming up the engine. I climbed into the front seat. (This time it was I who was unfamiliar with the airplane.) We took off and climbed to 2,000 feet. I motioned to Kluky to do some steep turns, a power-off stall, and three turns of a spin. This time his air work was somewhat improved from the previous day's performance. With some apprehension, I finally told him to try a landing. He brought the Vought in for a normal approach and, to my relief, made a good landing. I had completely relaxed, thinking that this time Kluky had done all right, when suddenly near the end of our roll, the airplane started into a left turn of a ground loop. There was a deep ditch running along the edge of the field, and before I could take any corrective measures, we hit. Fortunately, we were going slowly enough that damage to the plane was light, but this time I was really angry. By the time I unbuckled my belt and crawled out of the cockpit (Kluky had already jumped out), Campman had come running and I could see that he too was angry as a wet hen. He barked an order for Kluky to meet him in his office, and away they went. Needless to say, that was the end of Kluky's effort to obtain a pilot's license.

I was relaxing in my room late one afternoon when the phone rang. I picked up the receiver, and a voice that I immediately recognized floated over the wire. "Hi, Frank. This is Les Tower. Heard you were in town and am anxious to see you."

"Les, I apologize for not calling you, but I got involved with too much work too soon.

"And," I added, "this wild gang on the third floor is hard to break away from."

"Frank, how about having dinner with me tonight?"

"Fine. Where and what time?"

"Meet me at the Rainier Club. It's right across the street—say around six?"

"My, have you come up in the world. I'm glad to know someone who is a member of such a prestigious club."

"Well, Boeing has been good to me. See you later."

It was good to see Les again, and we enjoyed reminiscing over a good dinner. We arranged to meet the following morning at the Boeing plant. When I arrived at the gate, a security guard greeted me and asked if I were Mr. Jerdone. After my admitting that that was indeed my name, the guard escorted me across a wide expanse of concrete and into the administration building. We walked down a long corridor flanked on each side with offices until we came to a door marked "Chief Pilot." I thanked the guard and entered to find Les sitting behind a huge desk, talking on the phone. He motioned me to be seated. My eyes took in this plush office with its deep-pile carpet and mahogany furniture, and I thought back to the Langley Field days when I first laid eyes on this gawky-looking cowboy from a Montana ranch. Now looking at him, I found his sitting behind this desk making like an executive seemed to me a bit incongruous. Les had come a long way.

Les finished his conversation, arose from his chair and said, "Let's go meet my boss. Claire Edgvedt is vice-president of the company."

Edgvedt greeted me cordially. He was of medium height with hair on the blond side and piercing blue eyes. We passed a pleasant few minutes, during which time I was reminded that Boeing's production was at least 95 percent military. Therefore, I would have very little business with the company, as I was concerned only with commercial aircraft. However, it was good to establish friendly relations with Boeing, as they would no doubt in the future get into commercial production, as indeed they did. Today Boeing's huge backlog for commercial airliners far overshadows their military business.

Commander Campman, Les Tower, Penn Taliaferro, and I would often dine toegether, and needless to say, we did a lot of "hangar flying." Penn and Campman were both fine raconteurs, which made the evenings always interesting. Penn announced at dinner one evening that he'd had to go to Spokane and suggested we could make it a joint venture. This I agreed to, for I did have plenty of work to do in Spokane.

After a train ride through the Cascades, we arrived in Spokane and checked into the Davenport Hotel. I had just stepped into my room when the phone started ringing. It was Nick Mamer, a prominent local pilot, suggesting that he arrange a party for us at the hotel that evening. (News of our arrival certainly had spread quickly.) Nick showed up around six with several other pilots and a bevy of girls. (Nick Mamer was later to become one of the founders of Northwest Airlines and one of their first captains.)

The party was a huge success, lasting until the early hours of the morning. The trouble was that this bit was repeated, to the detriment of our sleep and rest, for the next three nights of our stay. Spokane and the Davenport, in particular, were lively spots in those days.

During the day, I was busy licensing pilots and mechanics. Penn would drift off on some vague Airways business. There was a reserve squadron at the airfield consisting of five PT1 trainers and one DeHaviland 4B. Almost all of the pilots were reserve officers, so I used the squadron's planes for flight testing. Nick was the first pilot I licensed, and that broke the ice for all the others, who seemed eager to get their commercial licenses.

We finished our work in Spokane, so the time had come to return to Seattle. Nick, several of the pilots, and some of the young ladies came down and escorted us to the train. What a hospitable bunch! But I am sure the Davenport Hotel was never the same after our short visit.

For some time, I had been toying with the idea of leaving the department. I had, in the course of my travels, been offered several lucrative positions. But all of them were of an executive nature, and I was not interested in being tied to a desk. I had long since decided that as far as a career was concerned, the government was not for me. The Aeronautics Branch was expanding rapidly, and already politics and bureaucracy were showing their ugly heads. So upon my return to Portland I made up my mind to make the break and wired Clarence Young my resignation.

It was with some reluctance that I said goodbye to all my newfound friends in the Pacific Northwest and boarded a train to Washington.

Upon my arrival back at the office, I learned that several other inspectors had resigned to accept jobs in the industry. Clarence seemed a bit disturbed at losing some of his key men, but accepted it all graciously. One of the first persons I ran into was Bob Gast, one of my best friends in the department. He said that he too had just resigned and suggested that we have sort of a farewell dinner together that evening.

We were having oysters on the half-shell at the Occidental when Bob said, "I've decided to go back to Louisville and start a flying service at Bowman Field. Lee Miles (we call him Uncle Lee) the Hertz taxicab man in Louisville, has agreed to finance me. We will take on an agency for a couple of airplanes, probably Fairchild and Waco, do some instruction and charter work—all that sort of thing."

"That's fine, Bob. You're a big man in Louisville, and you should do well."

"What are your plans, Frank?"

"Well, Bill Brock has offered me a job as a pilot-salesman. He and Ed Schlee have formed a corporation, Schlee-Brock Aircraft Company, with headquarters in Detroit. They have acquired the distributorship for Lockheed comprising all territory east of the Mississippi.

Bill Brock and Ed Schlee had attempted to fly around the world in a Stinson monoplane recently and had gotten as far as Tokyo. However, upon their arrival in Tokyo, our State Department refused them permission to continue across the Pacific, claiming it was too hazardous an undertaking. However, Bill and Ed had made a record-breaking flight that far, and, of course, received a great deal of publicity.

"Sounds like an interesting project, Frank. Big territory and a fine airplane, way ahead of its time. Lots of luck to you!"

"Thanks, Bob, and success to you in Louisville."

We said adios that night, each going his separate way. We didn't know it then, but our paths were to cross again—in fact, many times—in the not-too-distant future.

Chapter 10   All Points East and West

Les Tower and I were having dinner at the Racquet Club in Washington. Les had been sent east by Boeing to conduct flight tests on one of their fighter planes at the Anacostia Naval Air Station. As we were leaving the dining room, Les paused by a table where two young men were engaged in earnest conversation. Les introduced one of the men to me as Ralph O'Neill, who had represented Boeing in Argentina.

It seems that one day flying a Boeing "pursuit" plane from Buenos Aires to Montevideo, O'Neill ran into a fog-enshrouded mountain on the outskirts of the city. It was a bad crash, and O'Neill spent considerable time in the hospital recuperating from his injuries.

Les and I proceeded to the lounge and were joined shortly by O'Neill, a rather short, balding man of stocky build whom I judged to be in his late thirties. As the three of us sat there in the lounge, O'Neill told of his futile efforts to obtain financing for an airline from New York to Buenos Aires. He said that while recuperating in the hospital, he had conceived the idea of an airline from the United States to Buenos Aires via the east coast of South America. At that time, Pan American, together with W. R. Grace and Co., had formed a joint venture, Panagra, and were operating from Miami down the west coast of South America to Santiago, Chile, and thence across the Andes to Buenos Aires.

O'Neill pointed out the need for an air route along the *east* coast of South America, mentioning the large cities to be served and the vast amount of raw products—coffee, cocoa, and various minerals—that we import mostly from Brazil. He said that before leaving Buenos Aires, he had obtained an Argentine concession to carry airmail from that city to New York. This concession, he said, had been signed by Irigoyn, who at that time was president of Argentina. This was the instrument by which O'Neill hoped to obtain financing. Of course, this "concession" on the face of it wasn't worth much. For an airline from New York to Buenos Aires via the east coast of South America to be economically feasible, it would be necessary to obtain an airmail contract from the United States Post Office Department. O'Neill realized this, but his thought was that by starting this line he would qualify for a United States mail contract without any trouble.

O'Neill was a good salesman. He even got me all hopped up about his scheme. While he was talking, I happened to think of Nate Brown, whom I had known in Detroit when he was a Ford pilot. I knew that he was now flying a Ford trimotor for James Rand, Jr., of the Remington-Rand Corporation. I mentioned this to O'Neill with the suggestion that possibly Mr. Rand would be interested in helping him to finance his project. O'Neill became excited immediately and asked if I could get in touch with Brown. I happened to have Nate's telephone number, so I called him and asked him to come over to the club.

Brown, too, was impressed with what O'Neill had to say and agreed to introduce O'Neill to Mr. Rand and let him tell his story. It so happened that the three of us boarded a train for New York that very night. Of course, I had no further part to play in this drama. I had introduced O'Neill to Brown, and he in turn was to introduce him to James Rand, Jr. I only tagged along that night because I had some personal business in New York the following day.

Some months later, I had a letter from O'Neill stating that while Rand had evidenced some interest in the project, there had been a change of government in Argentina and the "concession" he had so relied upon as a basis for promoting initial capital had been canceled. He further suggested that he was in financial straits and wondered if I knew of any jobs in the industry. I replied that this being a depression year, jobs were indeed scarce and I felt lucky to be on somebody's payroll myself.

Bill Brock and Ed Schlee had opened an office in the Fisher building in Detroit under the firm name of Schlee-Brock Aircraft Company. They had also built a large hangar on the new Detroit Municipal Airport on Gratiot Avenue. I remember that there was a huge water tank at the intersection of the two runways, and I wondered at the time just how long it would be before some guy flew into this tank.

When I arrived on the scene in February of 1929, the company had on hand one Lockheed Vega demonstrator, the only airplane in that huge hangar, the construction of which had just recently been completed. For the next six weeks I demonstrated the airplane to prospective customers in the Detroit area as well as in other Michigan cities, such as Grand Rapids, Benton Harbor, and Ypsilanti. The weather, typical for this area, was cold, with much snow and ice. On some of the fields we flew out of the snow was so deep that it was difficult to get the plane off the ground.

Bill Brock, a native of Tennessee, was a man of medium height, very heavyset—in fact, much overweight—and extremely nervous. He seemed never able to relax and constantly paced up and down, whether in his office or at the hangar or wherever he happened to be, and he smoked one cigarette after another. But he was an excellent pilot, as his record attests. Bill called me into his office one day and said, "Frank, we're leaving for Los Angeles the latter part of March."

"That's fine, Bill, but why are we going to Los Angeles?"

"We've ordered nine Lockheed Vegas and one Air Express model, and they will be ready for delivery around April 1. So we're going out and fly them back here as a group, a sort of convoy."

"Where are we getting the pilots? There are only two of us."

"Well, Vance Breese [a well-known engineering test pilot] will fly the Air Express. There are a couple of Lockheed pilots available, and we'll hire the others."

"Okay, Bill, let me know the exact date we will arrive in Los Angeles."

In recent months, I had been thinking seriously of marriage. I was now twenty-six years old and felt that it was time I settled down. This bachelor life had been a lot of fun, but I needed some stability to my life. While in Seattle, I had met a very pretty woman, Thelma Davis, a blond with sparkling blue eyes and a lovely complexion, typical of so many girls of the northwest. We had seen a great deal of each other during the short time I was in Seattle, but nothing serious had developed between us. Since my return east, I had thought of Thelma often and we had established a fairly regular correspondence. Now that my thoughts had turned to matrimony, Thelma's image seemed to be constantly on my mind. So, being the impetuous guy that I am, I wired Thelma that I was arriving in Los Angeles the last of March and would she consider meeting me there with the idea of getting married? Somewhat to my surprise and pleasantly so, I received a wire agreeing to meet me at the time I requested.

Bill and I arrived in Los Angeles on March 28. I had arranged to meet Thelma, who with her older sister, Leta, would arrive by train from Seattle on March 29. I was at the station at least an hour early and, I have to admit, plenty nervous. When the train finally arrived, we greeted each other affectionately and Leta seemed affable enough, so in that atmosphere, I calmed down considerably. We took a cab to the Ambassador Hotel, where I had reserved rooms for Thelma and her sister. After an excellent lunch in the hotel dining room, Thelma and I took a cab to the municipal building to get our marriage license. We obtained our license all right, but the clerk also reminded us of the California three-day waiting period. It seemed that because of so many of what were known in that day as gin marriages, California had passed a law requiring a waiting period of three days from the time the license was granted until the marriage ceremony was performed.

I had not known of this law, or if I had, I had forgotten about it. However, it posed a real problem for me and Thelma. We were scheduled to take off from Van Nuys Airport early on the morning of April 1st. We only had two days left, so what to do about that three-day law? I explained my problem to Bill, and he in turn spoke to Whitney Collins, secretary-treasurer of Lockheed. Whit told Bill that he knew Buron Fitts, at that time attorney general for Los Angeles County, and that he would explain the situation to him. He admitted that he didn't know Fitts very well and could promise nothing. However, that evening he phoned and said that Fitts had agreed to waive the three-day provision under these extenuating circumstances.

Somebody arranged with a Presbyterian minister to marry us at 7 o'clock on the morning of April 1. After this brief ceremony, we dashed to the airport, from which I took off promptly at 9 o'clock for Detroit.

I was flying one of the Vegas powered with a Pratt and Whitney 450 H.P. Wasp engine. This was one of the faster airplanes in the fleet. My passengers included Whitney Collins, who had obtained my three-day waiver and Margaret Bartlet, the daughter of Reno's famous divorce judge. Our itinerary called for a first stop at Phoenix and thence to El Paso. On the takeoff at Phoenix, one of the other aircraft broke a tail wheel and was forced to remain over a day for repairs. For some reason I've forgotten, I was elected to remain overnight and accompany the other pilot to El Paso the following day. When we were unloading the airplane preparing to leave for the hotel, we discovered that mine and Thelma's baggage had been placed aboard another airplane. So there we were in Phoenix and our baggage in El Paso. One of the girls loaned Thelma a nightgown, and Whit Collins loaned me a pair of pajamas. Incidentally, when I tried to return the pajamas, Whit said no, to keep them as a wedding present. Anyway, I wore those pajamas for several years.

Our flight from Phoenix to El Paso the following day was uneventful. By late afternoon, all ten of the airplanes had arrived safely. Just before dinner that evening, my room phone rang and the guy on the other end said, "This is Henry Unverzagt. I saw in the paper that you had arrived and would like to see you." Henry and I had sort of grown up together and had attended grammar school together in Falls Church, Virginia.

"Well," I said, "this is a pleasant surprise, Henry. How about having dinner with me?" Henry informed me that he was in the Foreign Service and was now assistant vice-consul at Juarez, Mexico. He also mentioned that he had never been up in an airplane. "Okay, Henry, if you will get out to the airport early tomorrow morning, I'll take you up for a short hop."

"That'll be fine; I'll be there waiting."

Sure enough, Henry was waiting at the airport when I arrived the next morning. I took off, flew around for a few minutes, and decided to give Henry a thrill or two. I did a couple of wingovers and some steep banks, but upon looking back, I saw that Henry was not a little bit frightened. So I cut out the funny stuff and went in and landed. Henry was little pale, but thanked me for the ride. It was good to see an old childhood chum after so many years.

We continued on that day, with the "convoy" intact, via Dallas, Oklahoma City, and Indianapolis and landing finally at the Ford Airport in Dearborn. The flight had been very successful and, for my part, enjoyable, and the attendant publicity didn't do Schlee-Brock Aircraft or Lockheed any harm. The highlight of the trip for me, of course, was getting married and taking off immediately on a 2500-mile flight to Detroit. I was a little surprised that the passengers were willing to ride with me. A bridegroom is supposed to be a bit nervous; at least, that is what I had always been told.

Shortly after Thelma and I settled into an apartment on Grand Boulevard, I approached Bill with what I thought would be a good scheme to sell some airplanes.

"Bill, you know that Akron, Ohio, being the center for the tire industry, there is probably a lot of money floating around among the sons and grandsons of the tire magnates. And some of them no doubt are very much interested in aviation."

"So?" Bill asked.

"I would like to fly a demonstrator down there and spend some time with those guys. I think I can help them organize a flying company or an intrastate airline and at the same time sell them a flock of airplanes."

Bill lit another cigarette, thought a minute, and said, "Sounds like you might have something there, Frank. What've we got to lose? Get the hell down to Akron, and good luck!"

When I landed at the Akron Airport, "Shorty" Fulton, the manager, greeted me, and I explained to him the object of my visit. I knew that Shorty would cooperate with any scheme to stimulate the airplane business in Akron. The next morning, I took Shorty for a short flight and then let him fly the Vega. I knew that he would be enthused with the flying qualities of the airplane and therefore be enthusiastic in helping me sell some airplanes.

Shorty was on speaking terms with some of the officials of Goodyear, Firestone, and Goodrich and proceeded to introduce me around. There began a series of meetings, parties at country clubs, and daily flights with the younger executives of the rubber companies. I flew back to Detroit and brought Thelma back with me. She seemed to enjoy the social whirl revolving around this wealthy country-club set.

I spent a month in Akron, at the end of which time we had formed a corporation chartered to operate a flying service and airlines to various cities within the state. Shorty Fulton was jubilant and I was walking on cloud nine. I flew back to Detroit with firm orders and deposits for eighteen Lockheed Vegas, which at that time sold for $18,500 each. This was not only a nice piece of business for the company, but also meant a fat commission for me. Bill Brock was ecstatic and congratulated me heartily on a job well done. Not only that, but the night after my arrival he threw a big party for all concerned at their suite of offices in the Fisher building.

A few days after the party, Bill called me in and said, "How would you like to move to New York?" I was somewhat startled by the question and hesitated for a moment.

"Well, fine, I guess. Why?"

"You deserve a promotion for pulling off that Akron deal, so I'm giving you the New York territory."

"That's great, Bill, and I certainly appreciate your confidence."

"Homer Berry has been representing Lockheed in New York, but he hasn't done much with the territory. That's a fertile area, which also includes eastern Canada, so it should prove very lucrative for all of us."

"Okay Bill, when do I get started?"

"You and your wife can start driving east anytime. You'll need your car to get to and from the airport. Get an apartment convenient to Newark Airport, and after you get settled come back here and pick up your demonstrator."

We soon found an efficiency apartment in East Orange, New Jersey, about twenty minutes' drive from the airport. I then took a train back to Detroit, picked up my demonstrator, and flew it back to Newark. Now this airplane Bill had assigned me was no ordinary Lockheed. In fact, when I first saw this airplane standing outside the hangar at the Detroit Airport, I was amazed. The plane was painted a cream color, and the interior was fitted with bedford cord upholstery and mahogany trim. The metal fittings were chrome-plated. This was indeed one deluxe airplane.

Bill had instructed me to take over Homer Berry's office in the Graybar building in downtown Manhattan. When I arrived at the office, Homer was packing up his personal belongings preparatory to leaving for Chicago, his hometown. I introduced myself, trying to be as pleasant as possible. Homer was affable enough, but seemed a little sad. He had the reputation of being an excellent pilot, but apparently he wasn't a very good salesman.

It wasn't long after settling in my new job in New York that I decided to fly to Montreal and demonstrate the Lockheed Vega to Canadian Airways. Soon after my arrival in New York, I had met a chap named Johnny Poulin who was vacationing in New York from his job as a geologist with an oil company in Venezuela. We had become friends quickly, so I invited Johnny to accompany me to Montreal, as he was a bachelor and kind of at loose ends. Anyway, he was most appreciative of my invitation.

So, with Thelma and Johnny aboard, I flew to Albany, the airport of entry for Canada, cleared customs for Montreal, and a couple of hours later landed at Saint Hubert, Montreal's official airport. While I was clearing Canadian customs, the airport manager approached me and introduced himself. I noted at the time that his greeting was not too friendly. Thinking that was just his manner, I gave it no further thought.

We checked into the Mount Royal Hotel, where I had reserved rooms, and after freshening up, the three of us went up to the roof garden for some drinks before dinner. This was indeed a treat, being able to order alcoholic beverages free of the restraining influence of Prohibition. As we were being seated, I noticed two men at an adjoining table who observed our approach with what appeared to be considerable interest. Presently, the taller of the two, a clean-cut, handsome man with a short, well-trimmed mustache, got up and walked over to our table and introduced himself as Captain Spooner of the Royal Flying Corps. He seemed to know somehow that we had just landed at the airport from the States. In those early days of aviation, pilots seemed to recognize one another instinctively. Spooner was most gracious and asked if we would care to join him and his friend at their table. We accepted gratefully, for after all, we were strangers in a strange land and were pleasantly surprised with this show of hospitality.

Captain Spooner introduced us to his companion, a Captain Hill who was in Montreal organizing a "Light Aeroplane Club" that was equipped with small DeHaviland Moth airplanes. It developed later in the evening that Captain Spooner was the brother of Winifred Spooner, who had the previous year won the King's Cup race from London to Sydney, Australia, the first and only woman of that era to be so honored.

It didn't take long before we were all old pals (of course, the drinks helped) speaking the same language. I impulsively invited Spooner and Hill to meet me at the airport the next morning and I would let them fly a *real* airplane. After an excellent dinner and a few more drinks, there was dancing to a very fine orchestra. Both Spooner and Hill kept Thelma busy on the dance floor. It was getting late, and I had a 9 o'clock appointment the next morning with Colonel Mulock, the managing director of Canadian Airways. So I reluctantly bid our newfound friends goodnight, thanking them for a delightful evening and promising to meet them later the next day at the airport.

Colonel Mulock was a short, stockily built man in his early forties. I had arrived at his office promptly at nine, and he immediately ushered me into his office. My first impression was that this was a no-nonsense, hard-boiled executive. After questioning me regarding various technical aspects of the Lockheed, he called in his assistant, a younger man, who was also a pilot on Canadian's route to Nova Scotia. The colonel introduced me to Dave, whose last name I've forgotten. He said, "Dave, I want you to go fly this Lockheed aircraft with Mr. Jerdone and tell me what you think of it."

"I've heard some good reports about the Vega and will be happy to fly it."

"Fine," I said. "If it's convenient for you, we can go out to the field and do some flying this morning."

Colonel Mulock nodded his approval, stood up, and shook hands with me, saying, "I will be in touch with you later."

Dave drove us to the airport in a company car. As we walked into the terminal building, the airport manager, who had the previous day introduced himself with a somewhat hostile attitude, greeted us suspiciously.

Dave said, "Hello, Harold." The man's name proved to be Harold Cromly, which I hadn't heard when he had mumbled his name to me before.

We cranked up the Lockheed and warmed the engine. I gave Dave a brief cockpit check, explained the characteristics of the airplane to him, and said, "Take her off, fly around, and do whatever you feel like. It's a good airplane and it won't fall apart." Dave made a smooth takeoff, I could tell immediately that he was a good pilot. He did some steep turns, stalls, and a couple of wingovers, then came in for a perfect landing. I could tell by the grin on his face that he was very pleased with the airplane's performance. When he left to return to his office, he said, "I'll give the colonel a good report on this machine."

"Very good," I replied. "When can I expect to hear from you or the colonel?"

"Either Colonel Mulock or I will call you sometime tomorrow."

As Dave drove away, Spooner and Hill came dashing up to the terminal building in a little Austin.

"How are you guys feeling this morning?" I asked.

"Very good, considering last night," replied Spooner. "We carried on till quite late, you know."

"All right, you two. Let's fly this airplane for a while. Which one of you wants to be first?"

Spooner elected to be the first, so I went through a routine check and told him to take off. After about fifteen minutes, Spooner landed and then Hill took over. They were both good pilots and were most appreciative of the opportunity of flying the Vega.

We had another session on the Mount Royal roof that night. These two British flyers were a lot of fun to be with, and I felt very lucky to have met up with them.

Promptly at 10 o'clock the following morning, I received a call from Colonel Mulock. He said that Dave had given him a good report on the Vega, but before he made a final decision on purchasing the airplane, he would like me to fly to Ottawa and demonstrate the airplane to the Air Ministry. I told him I would be glad to do so and would leave for Ottawa that morning. I said to Thelma, "Pack up; we're leaving for Ottawa. And call Johnny and tell him to get ready; we will leave for the aiport in fifteen minutes."

Upon arriving at the airport, I had started to clear customs for Ottawa when Cromly, the ubiquitous airport manager, sidled up to me and said, "Sorry, but you can't clear for Ottawa."

"Why not?" I asked.

"Because you are here on a visitor's permit. You have no commercial entry permit, so you are not permitted to do business in Canada." (I had been told by Spooner that Cromly, in addition to his duties as field manager, was also the Travel Air distributor for eastern Canada.)

I now realized what this was all about. I was in direct competition with Cromly. He wanted to sell the Travel Air to Canadian Airways.

"Okay Cromly, I'll call Colonel Mulock and see what he has to say about this." I was confident that the colonel would straighten things out. However, when I finally got him on the phone, I was astounded to hear him say that he couldn't do anything about it. If the officials refused to clear me for Ottawa, that was that. By this time, I was really mad. I was the victim of cheap politics. While it was true I did not have a commercial entry permit, it was usually not required. Canada had always in the past welcomed American aircraft, and, in fact, most of their commercial aircraft were of U.S. manufacture.

I turned to Thelma and Johnny. "I'm through with this mess. We'll clear for Albany and be on our way in half an hour; they can't keep us from going back home."

Under a bright blue sky dotted with scattered cumulus clouds, we flew down the Saint Lawrence River, over Burlington, Vermont, and on to a landing at Albany. In another two hours, we would be on the ground at Newark Airport. My dream of selling a flock of airplanes was ended. *But,* I thought, *we did have a lot of fun.*

Chapter 11   **To South America**

As I approached the entrance to the Graybar building one hot July morning, I came face to face with Ralph O'Neill, who was just leaving the building. This was indeed a surprise. Ralph's name had not crossed my mind for some time, and I had forgotten all about this airline to Argentina project. He greeted me effusively and explained that he had obtained a new concession from the Argentinean government and through James Rand, Jr., had obtained sufficient financing to start operating the airline.

"We're taking delivery of our first airplane, a Sikorsky S-38 amphibian next week," O'Neill said. "The plane is now at Bridgeport, Connecticut and will be christened the *Washington*." O'Neill paused. "I'll be leaving immediately after for Buenos Aires with the *Washington*, and I want you as pilot."

"Well, Ralph," I replied, "things are coming at me a little too fast; I need a moment to catch my breath. In the first place, I couldn't possibly leave with you next week for Buenos Aires. If I did decide to throw in with you, I would have to give Schlee-Brock sufficient notice, at least two weeks!"

"Okay. I understand that," O'Neill continued, "but anyway I would like you to join the company as division superintendent between Rio and Buenos Aires." He mentioned a salary with an unlimited expense account that really startled me.

"That sounds very enticing, Ralph. By the way, what's the name of your new airline?"

"New York, Rio and Buenos Aires Airline, Inc.—for short, the NYRBA Line."

Ralph explained that if I decided to accept his offer, I should call on a Mr. Wilson, his assistant, whose office was on the same floor as mine. Ralph said that he would be out of town for several days, but I should more or less write my own contract and Wilson would be authorized to sign it.

"By the way, Frank, as you will not be able to fly down with me, you had better book passage on a steamship leaving as soon as possible. Also, I want you to hire another pilot and take him with you. Our first project will probably be a shuttle run between Buenos Aires and Montevideo across the Rio de La Plata. Wilson will arrange for booking your passage and letter of credit." He talked as if I were already an executive of NYRBA. All this conversation had taken place with us standing on the sidewalk in front of the Graybar building, both sweltering under a hot July sun.

For the next twenty-four hours, I gave almost continuous thought to O'Neill's offer. My association with Bill Brock had been pleasant and interesting. I was happy with my work and, until O'Neill came along, had no thought of making a change. However, this offer of O'Neill's was indeed challenging and very much appealed to my sense of adventure—faraway places, strange, exotic lands, and all that sort of thing. However, one thing did disturb me a little. For over a year I had heard nothing from O'Neill, and then suddenly by accident I had run into him on a New York street and I was immediately offered this very good and lucrative position in South America. What was the catch? Why had not O'Neill advised me of all that had taken place in forming the NYRBA line? These disturbing questions I finally brushed aside. My desire for adventure in faraway places overcame any skepticism I may have had. I had made up my mind I would see Wilson the next day.

Wilson proved to be a rather large man in his late thirties with a pleasing personality. He had obviously been briefed by O'Neill regarding my situation. We discussed the salient points to be incorporated in my contract, and for the most part our talk concerned what Wilson knew of future plans for the NYRBA Line. Our conversation ended. I stood up, shook hands with Wilson, and said, "I'll have my attorney draw up the contract and bring it back to you in a few days for your signature."

My aunt Ida's husband, Walter Wiechmann, an attorney, was a senior partner of the prestigious Wall Street law firm of Sullivan and Cromwell. That evening, I visited Ida and Walter at their apartment on East 72nd Street. I had made notes of certain provisions I wanted to be made part of the contract, and I went over these with Walter, who added other points that I, not being a lawyer, would never have thought of. Upon leaving their apartment, I said, "Listen, Walter, make this thing ironclad. I'm going a long way from New York, and I want ample protection under the law."

A couple of days later, Walter called and said the contract was ready. I went by his office, picked up the contract, and continued on to Wilson's office, where we both signed together with the signatures of two witnesses.

Back in my office, I called Bill Brock in Detroit and explained my plans. I told him that I was mailing my official resignation to him that day and would fly my demonstrator back to Detroit the following day. Bill sounded disappointed, but was gracious about my decision to leave his employ. He understood very well my desire to seek "new worlds to conquer." He had shown a like spirit by trying to fly around the world.

Upon my return to New York, my first piece of business was finding a pilot who would accompany me to South America. The first person I thought of was Ed Conerton, who at the time was flying amphibians and flying boats for the Curtiss Flying Service at North Beach, Long Island. Ed was an old friend of mine with whom I had served as a cadet in the old army air service, back in the early twenties. Also, we as reserve officers had done some flying out at Mitchell Field. Ed was an excellent pilot on both land planes and flying boats. He was also at that time flying Sikorsky S-38s for the Curtiss Company.

I called Ed at North Beach, explained briefly what I wanted, and asked him to meet me at the NYRBA office and we would discsuss my offer in detail.

After I told Ed what little I knew of the planned airline operation to South America, Ed said, "Okay. It sounds interesting to me; I'll give Curtiss a couple of weeks' notice." Ed too could hear the call of faraway lands.

I introduced Ed to Wilson and asked him to put Ed on the payroll as of that date. I also asked Wilson to book passage for us both and our wives on the first steamship sailing for Buenos Aires after the first week in August and to prepare a letter of credit for me drawn on the National City Bank of New York.

The week prior to our departure for South America proved to be one continuous party with old flying friends who coincidentally happened to be in New York at that particular time. There were Ben Eilson, Shorty Cramer, Bob Gast, and myself, who were all preparing to leave for various parts of the world. Ben, the pioneer Alaskan pilot, was returning to Alaska as head of a corporation that had consolidated most of the bush pilots' operations and was to be known as Alaska Airways. Shorty was preparing to fly to Germany via the Arctic. Bob Gast was leaving for China to fly for China National Airways, partly owned by Pan American Airways. And of course I was leaving for the far south to Buenos Aires.

The four of us had taken adjoining rooms at the old Astor Hotel on Times Square, and each night we patronized a different speakeasy.

This was a memorable week for many reasons, not the least of which was that we were all, with the exception of Bob Gast, destined never to meet again. Ben was killed flying to a stranded fur ship in Siberia. Shorty was lost somewhere in the North Sea. Neither his body nor the wreckage of his aircraft was ever found. Bob Gast was later killed when his Sikorsky amphibian flew into Hangchow Bay, China. What was left of his body was only found some months later.

So it was that I was the only one of the four of us to return home from some adventurous flying in Argentina and Brazil. I often wonder by what means Fate selects some of us, while still in our early youth, to journey across the river Styx, while others live to a ripe old age and often die in bed. For no conceivable reason, I am still around and at eighty-two enjoying reasonably good health. I know that I am living on a lot of "borrowed time."

On August 3, 1929, Thelma and I, accompanied by Ed and Edith Conerton, sailed on the SS *Van Dyck*, of the Lamport and Holt Line, for Barbados, Rio, Montevideo, and Buenos Aires. We arrived in Buenos Aires on August 25, twenty-two days out of New York. The voyage down had been uneventful—long monotonous days at sea on an old tub of a ship that had seen better days. The *Van Dyck* was a sister ship of the *Vestris*, which had, a couple of years previous, gone down off Cape Hatteras in shark-infested waters with a tremendous loss of life.

Our ship lay over in Rio for several days, discharging and taking on cargo. One morning as Ed and I were entering the National City Bank, who should we meet coming out but Ralph O'Neill? I was quite surprised to see him, for I had thought by this time he would be back in New York.

Ralph proceeded to brief us on the situation in Buenos Aires. The Sikorsky *Washington*, which he and pilot Kluky had flown down from New York, was anchored in the harbor of Buenos Aires adjacent to the Yacht Club Argentina. It seems that at Port-au-Prince, Haiti, they were unable to get off the water with the heavy fuel load plus spare parts, so they had decided to remove the landing gear and leave it at Port-au-Prince. Ralph informed us that he had hired a mechanic from Aeropostale (now Air France) who would have to work on the plane at its mooring, there being no way of getting the aircraft onshore for routine maintenance. This was an unsatisfactory procedure, for inevitably the mechanic would drop tools and parts overboard.

O'Neill said that I should report to a Senor Alejandro Bunge, whom he had appointed as our Argentinean representative. O'Neill explained that Bunge was a prominent Buenos Aires economist and would be very helpful in helping me get started in setting up an airline operation.

Our first project was to inaugurate a twice-daily schedule across the Rio de La Plata to Montevideo, a distance of 125 miles. O'Neill's ship sailed for New York a day ahead of our departure for Buenos Aires with a day's stopover at Montevideo.

The Rio de La Plata is probably one of the widest and shallowest rivers in the world. The channel is provided with a system of buoys from the mouth of the river near Montevideo all the way to the harbor of Buenos Aires. Even so, sometimes ships drag bottom while still in the middle of the channel. It is not unusual for winds emanating from the Pacific cyclone, blowing down off the Andes and sweeping across 600 miles of pampas to attain a velocity of over 70 MPH before hitting Buenos Aires. When this occurs, the wind actually blows a lot of water out of the river and ocean-going vessels lying in the harbor keel over on their sides.

We were greeted upon our arrival at Buenos Aires by a young man with a blond mustache who introduced himself as Roberto Bunge, the eldest son of Alejandro Bunge. Roberto took us in tow, got us through customs, and then drove us to the Jousten Hotel, where he had reserved rooms.

Chapter 12   Buenos Aires

The offices of Bunge and Co., S.A., were situated in downtown Buenos Aires. The building, with its spacious rooms and high ceilings, indicated a nineteenth-century style of architecture. Entering an outer office, I was greeted by a rather stout dark-haired woman whom I judged to be in her early fifties. In almost perfect English, she informed me that she was Senor Bunge's private secretary and without further ado escorted me into Bunge's office.

Behind a huge desk some thirty feet from the entrance, sat a middle-aged man with blond hair and rimless spectacles. He arose from his chair, shook my hands, and asked me to be seated. Almost immediately there appeared a servant bearing a tray with a carafe of coffee and demitasse cups. I was to learn that the coffee ritual was strictly adhered to in all business offices in Argentina. While greeting me affably but unsmilingly, I knew immediately that this was a no-nonsense man, totally lacking in humor.

Bunge proceeded to advise me of the political situation in Argentina, particularly as it pertained to NYRBA; various problems confronting the development of the airline; a project to build a seaplane hangar in the harbor adjacent to the Planta Electricid; organizing an office staff; and many other details. Bunge said that his son, Roberto, would be at my service and devote all of his time to helping me get things started. He said that he had obtained office space in the Avenida Roque Saenz Pena and had already moved in the furniture.

We found Luis, the Argentinean mechanic, recently of Aeropostale, working on the *Washington,* anchored in the harbor near the Yacht Club Argentina. Ed and I climbed aboard from the dinghy and introduced ourselves. Luis, a smiling, affable young man, spoke not a word of English. He was a resourceful mechanic and proved himself more and more so as time went on. He had persuaded a friend who was fluent in English to translate the Pratt and Whitney engine manual into Spanish, no mean accomplishment considering the difficulty of a technical translation.

NYRBA Ford over Santiago, Chile

As I had never flown a Sikorsky S-38, it was up to Ed to check me out on this particular aircraft. So we motioned to Luis to start the engines and prepared to take off. After about an hour of practice landings and takeoffs on the Plata River, Ed pronounced me qualified, so from there on out I was on my own. As this was an amphibian, we were supposed to be competent on both land and water. Therefore we were required to obtain a license from both the Argentinean army and navy. Ed and I made three landings each on the water with an army pilot aboard observing our actions. (With no landing gear, we of course had to dispense with the land phase of the tests.) Then we made three more landings with a navy pilot aboard. Both pilots seemed satisfied with our performance and told us that after passing our physical exams, we would in due course receive our licenses.

Kluky, the pilot who had brought the *Washington* down from New

Hangar and ramp under construction at Buenos Aires (1929). A Commodore flying boat is sitting on the ramp.

York, was still in Buenos Aires when we arrived. Just before his departure for the north, he insisted on flying us over to Montevideo, "to show us the route." On the morning of our takeoff, the wind, what there was of it, was blowing offshore, so Kluky taxied far out into the river and started his takeoff toward the city. It was a most peculiar takeoff. Kluky, instead of easing back on the control column, shoved it forward into the instrument panel and held it there. The throttles were of course wide open. As a consequence of this unorthodox maneuver, the plane started pounding on the step until I thought our back teeth would fall out. Finally, however, the plane bounced into the air, and fortunately we remained airborne. Ed and I just looked at each other in amazement. We understood now why he had left the landing gear in Haiti.

We had decided on two round trips daily between Buenos Aires and Montevideo, leaving Buenos Aires at 9:00 A.M., arriving at Montevideo about 10:15, and returning to Buenos Aires at 12:00 noon. Again we would depart Buenos Aires at 2:00 P.M., returning to Buenos

Aires at 4:30 P.M. This shuttle run proved to be a bonanza from the start. Our only competition was the Mahanovich Line, an overnight steamship run between the two cities.

At both ends of the line the passengers were ferried out to where the aircraft was moored to a buoy and boarded the plane from the motor launch, and when we landed we would taxi up to the mooring buoy and make fast and the launch would come alongside and take the passengers off. It was not a very satisfactory operation, but the only one possible. Bunge had hired a young man of eighteen or nineteen, Tito Villegeas, who acted as a dispatcher and operator of the motor launch and also acted as my chauffeur. Tito's parents were very wealthy Belgians who had emigrated to Argentina in the late nineteenth century. His father had given Tito a red Auburn convertible for his birthday, and he was very proud indeed of this sporty-looking car. Tito would pick me up at my hotel each morning and take me to the office or, if I were flying that day, to the yacht club. Like most Argentineans, he drove like a maniac, and by the time he got me to wherever I was going, I would be a nervous wreck. To make matters worse, Tito's car was standard American make, designed for driving on the right-hand side of the road. In Argentina, however, all traffic moved on the left side of the road, so this, coupled with Tito's inherent reckless driving, resulted in some nerve-wracking experiences for me.

All funds for the operation of the airline were deposited by NYRBA in the Buenos Aires branch of the National City Bank of New York. Through doing business with the bank, I met Boyce Hart, executive vice-president of National City for all of Latin America. Boyce was a man in his late thirties, rather tall, very personable, and a raconteur of no mean ability. We soon became good friends and I was invited aboard his cabin cruiser, which he kept at the Tigre Yacht Club some distance up the Tigre River. It soon became a weekly ritual that almost every Sunday afternoon Boyce and I, together with Nelson Riley, the Associated Press manager in Buenos Aires, and a few others would cruise up and down the Tigre. Both Boyce and Nelson were two-fisted drinkers, and the scotch flowed freely. The boat, very appropriately, was named the *Say When!*

Buenos Aires in the year 1929 was often referred to as the Paris of South America. Its beautiful parks and wide boulevards were outstanding features of this magnificent city. The Avenida Mayo, probably the widest boulevard of any city in the world, led to the Plaza de Mayo and the Casa Rosado (the Pink House), the presidential residence. The Calle Florida in downtown Buenos Aires was a street of elegant shops where the very wealthy women spent much of their time shopping.

There were many tearooms that after 4 o'clock were filled with patrons having their afternoon tea. This location was convenient to our office in the Avenida Roque Saenz Pena, so every afternoon at 4 o'clock we would close the office and proceed to a tearoom in the Florida. But instead of tea we usually drank beer.

There was also La Boca, at that time a tough section of town located adjacent to the municipal docks, where rusty freighters from all parts of the world were tied up. There were numerous saloons, nightclubs, and brothels frequented largely by gauchos in from the pampas for a little diversion from the heat and dust and rain of herding cattle. They were a tough lot, reminding one of our own hard-drinking, carousing cowboys of the West during the latter part of the nineteenth century.

In contrast to La Boca there was a posh nightclub, La Taboris, patronized by the wealthy young men and women of Buenos Aires, of which there were indeed many in that prosperous city of that era. As one entered La Taboris, directly ahead was a huge dance floor flanked on each side by tables for dining. On the podium at the far end of the dance floor were two orchestras, one playing tango music and the other American dance music. On the second landing, a balcony on both sides of the room overlooking the dance floor, there were also tables for dining.

There were hostesses of all nationalities, very beautiful in their evening gowns. Any young blood with sufficient cash, patience, and staying power could, after plying one of the young ladies with champagne and waiting until 3 o'clock (closing time), accompany the young lady to her apartment and there remain the rest of the night.

At the time of which I write, Buenos Aires was the world's greatest market for the white-slave trade. Shortly after my return to the States, I read a book titled *The Road to Buenos Aires*, by a writer named Londres. The book told of the operation of a white-slave ring that procured its girls from various sources in Paris and the girls' voyage to Montevideo, where the laws of Uruguay pertaining to prostitution were very lax. Some of these girls were only thirteen, and some had been kidnapped and others tempted by promises of high-paying jobs as entertainers in Buenos Aires. On the last segment of their journey they were smuggled across the Rio de La Plata on the Mahanovich Line.

The best of the girls were established in elaborately furnished houses in downtown Buenos Aires, the next best went to nightclubs such as La Taboris, and the rest were shipped off to the provinces—Rosario, Cordoba, and Mendoza.

The Hotel Jousten, situated on the corner of Avenida Corrientes and the Viente Cinco de Maya, soon became the headquarters of all pilots and other aviation personnel flying into or stationed in Buenos Aires. There was "Red" Williams of Panagra, who flew a Ford trimotor from Santiago, Chile, over the Andes to Buenos Aires; Eddie Hamilton, a former Ford Airline pilot, also flying a Ford for our (NYRBA) land-plane division to Santiago and return. Ed and Edith Conerton and Thelma and I were at that time living at the Jousten. Every evening at six, we would all meet in the bar for drinks. The waiter always served us caviar with grated onion on toast, a very tasty hors d'œuvre to have with a drink. Around 9 o'clock we would move into the dining room and order a full-course dinner, usually with filet mignon as the entrée.

The shuttle operation to Montevideo was going very well, with Ed and I flying the run on alternate days. Luis was doing a magnificent job of maintaining our one airplane in flying condition, considering the fact that all work had to be done while the aircraft was tied to its mooring. Inevitably, some tools and a few spark plugs were dropped overboard. The contract for the seaplane hangar had been let, and construction was underway. On my days off from flying, I had to super-vise the work on the hangar in addition to my other duties of a routine nature.

After months of operating the shuttle with our one lone Sikorsky, new aircraft began arriving from New York. The pilots were, with one exception, all junior officers of United States Naval Aviation formerly assigned to the Pacific fleet. Like so many of the military pilots of those boom days of aviation, these officers had resigned their commis-sions to accept more lucrative positions as commercial-airline pilots.

The first Sikorsky to arrive was piloted by Robin McGlohn, a former navy enlisted pilot. His co-pilot was Johnny Shannon, a former lieutenant junior grade, United States Navy, and a graduate of An-napolis. Johnny told me shortly after his arrival that he resented hav-ing been assigned as co-pilot to a former navy enlisted pilot. He thought that being a former commissioned officer, he, instead of McGlohn, should have been airplane commander. I told Johnny to forget his rank and first-pilot business and from now on all NYRBA pilots would have equal status. Nevertheless, I liked Johnny and recognized his potential ability both as a pilot and an executive. I devoted considerable time instructing Johnny in the tricks of commercial flying, such as landing and taking off in crowded harbors, taxying on the step, and other methods in saving time and, consequently, money for the company. These pilots of the Pacific fleet were used to having all sorts of facilities available to them that commercial aviation could not afford. This was an entirely new ball game.

There followed after McGlohn and Shannon in rapid succession five or six airplanes, all with ex-navy crews. Ed and I found ourselves the only army-trained commercial pilots completely surrounded by the United States Navy. The harbor being too crowded for all these planes, I had the pilots fly their ships over to Moron, the military airfield, lower their landing gear and land, taxi over to the edge of the field, and park their airplanes. From one lone Sikorsky, which we had been flying over five hours a day and barely keeping in the air, we now had gone to a great surplus of airplanes, for which I really had no immediate use.

Now with this abundance of equipment, the time had come to prepare to start the Rio–Buenos Aires segment of the line. Initially we would fly one round trip a week between these two points. I selected one of the new Sikorskys, test hopped it for about an hour, and, satisfied with its performance, ordered the mechanics to prepare it for flight to Rio.

To my surprise, there appeared in my office, a couple of days before my scheduled departure, John Montgomery, a NYRBA vice-president whom I had met in the New York office just prior to my departure for Argentina. John had somehow acquired a large twin-engine Sikorsky land plane that had been built especially for Rene Fonck for a transatlantic flight that never materialized. Johnny flew the airplane down the west coast of South America to Santiago, Chile, and then attempted a flight over the Andes to Buenos Aires. Unfortunately, due to some mechanical trouble, he cracked up somewhere near Mendoza in the high Andes. Considering the rugged terrain, he was lucky to have been able to walk away from the wreck. With the help of a native, he made his way to Mendoza, and from there he bummed a ride on Panagra to Buenos Aires.

I explained to Johnny that I was leaving the following day on a survey flight to Rio, and he immediately suggested that he go along. As he was, when I left New York, a vice-president of the company and, as far as I knew, still was, I was in no position to refuse him. My passenger list besides my crew chief now consisted of my wife, Thelma, Fritz Hoffman, a former employee of an oil company in Tulare, Peru, whom I had hired as sort of an assistant manager, and, much to everyone's disgust, a scrubby-looking German Shepherd that Johnny had picked up in some Andean village through which he had passed. Fritz was a huge man, about six-feet-four and weighing well over 200 pounds. Fritz was fluent in both Spanish and Portugese, which was a great help to me, as I could, at that time, speak neither language.

The weather on the morning of our departure was almost perfect, visibility and ceiling unlimited. Our first stop would be Pelotas in southern Brazil. I had arranged with Standard Oil of Brazil to have gasoline available at the dock upon my arrival. However, when we came in over Pelotas, there was a 20 MPH wind blowing directly across the river. With such a wind, a safe landing on the water was impossible. So I lowered the landing gear, flew over to the Aeorpostale Field, and landed. I spotted a huge cache of five-gallon tins of gasoline. I taxied up close and switched off the engines. There was no one around; the field was completely deserted. We had no time to wait for someone to show up, so we proceeded to fill our tanks from the five-gallon tins. When we had finished refueling, I left a note stating the amount of gasoline we had taken and explained that they could replace this with the gas I had ordered at the dock in Pelotas. As I taxied out for the takeoff, there came roaring down toward us a little Peugot, filled with Frenchmen yelling and shaking their fists at us. I simply opened the throttles and took off. I wasn't about to stick around and argue with a bunch of Frenchmen.

Our next stop was Florinapolis, where we landed on a large lake close to the city. Almost immediately, a motor launch came out to take us into town. Strangely, no customs or immigration people appeared, nor did we see any government officials during our overnight stay. The hotel we were escorted to was a third-rate fleabag with uncomfortable beds and lousy food. After a restless night, we were all very happy to once again board the Sikorsky for the flight to Rio.

This morning, the weather deteriorated and we flew in and out of rain showers all the way to Rio. From Florinapolis, the coastline curves to Santos. I elected to fly a direct course to Rio, which took us about a hundred miles out to sea. About midway on our flight, I spotted a large passenger ship southbound to Buenos Aires. The ceiling was only 500 feet in light rain, so I dropped down low as I approached the vessel, which proved to be the *Caparcona* of the Italian Line, one of the largest ships in the South American trade. The decks were lined with passengers as I flew low over the bridge, turned and came down the starboard side, turned sharp again, and flew down the port side. The passengers were waving frantically and probably shouting, too, for after all this was 1929 and having an airplane buzz your ship in what seemed like the middle of the Atlantic Ocean was, to say the least, a bit unusual.

In the early afternoon, still under low clouds and rain, we flew into the harbor of Rio, passing close by Sugar Loaf Mountain, and turning left into Botofoga Bay, we landed and taxied up to a Standard Oil barge. The barge attendant, an American, took our lines and tied us up in a secure manner. He refused to let us off the airplane until

Customs and Immigration came aboard. After a short wait, two little men in black suits and black straw hats appeared and we helped them aboard. After the formalities were over and I, as captain of the ship, had signed various papers, one of the little men asked if there were any stowaways. Fritz, the only one who could talk to them in their language, shook his head. Then the little guy pointed to the dog and grinned. We all laughed with him, but everyone aboard was damn glad to be rid of that dog, which had been seasick all during the flight.

Chapter 13   Rio de Janeiro

We checked into the Gloria Hotel, situated off the Avenida Rio Branca, overlooking Botofoga Bay. There was much work to be done preparatory to establishing the Rio—Buenos Aires segment of our route from Miami to Buenos Aires.

I first called on Jack Thomas, local manager of the National City Bank. Jack had been in Rio for many years and knew almost everyone of importance. He proved to be of immense help to me in my efforts to get the airline started.

Jack was a man I judged to be in his early thirties, of medium build, who wore horn-rimmed glasses. He was outgoing, affable, and friendly. We immediately hit it off well together. Soon after our first meeting, he invited me to his home in Ipenama Beach, where he and his charming wife, Jean, a native of New York who had fallen in love with Brazil, made me feel very much at home.

Later that day I called at the offices of Standard Oil of Brazil and met with Mr. Humpstone, the president. Together we went over plans for refueling facilities at Santos, Florianopolis, Porte Alegre, and Pelotas. Mr. Humpstone was most courteous and promised me his full cooperation.

After a busy week in Rio, I decided to fly over to São Paulo on a sort of survey flight, for we were to establish a branch line from Rio to take care of the heavy traffic between the two cities. Also, it would feed passengers and mail into our international route.

São Paulo, the industrial center of Brazil about 220 miles from Rio, was at that time the second largest city in the republic. It was situated about sixty miles inland from the port of Santos. Therefore, it would be necessary for us to use the existing airfield at São Paulo.

I decided we could do with a little publicity on the first flight, so I invited the Associated Press manager, Jack Thomas, a Standard Oil official, and their wives to accompany me on this first flight.

The weather the morning of our departure was good—ceiling and visibility unlimited. About an hour and a half out of Rio, I could see smoke from the city of São Paulo. In another thirty minutes I was over the airfield and started my approach for landing. This field proved to be very small indeed. While I had no difficulty landing, I was really concerned about the takeoff with full load.

We took a taxi into town and had lunch at the Esplanade Hotel. I noticed my passengers were having quite a few drinks before lunch, but at the time I was not concerned.

After lunch, they all wanted to do some sightseeing and shopping, so I told them to meet back at the hotel not later than 3 o'clock. I wanted to be sure to arrive back in Rio before dark, and I also was worried about my takeoff from this very small field.

Three o'clock came and no passengers. Finally at 3:30 they came wandering in—not really drunk, but I could tell they had had quite a few more drinks. By the time I could herd them into taxis and get out to the field, it was becoming very late, and I didn't look forward to a night landing in Botofoga Bay.

The takeoff, as I expected, was a close one. We barely missed the treetops at the end of the field. Thirty minutes out of Rio, it began to get dark. In these latitudes there is virtually no twilight.

Far ahead, the lights of the city shone brilliantly against a black sky. As I approached the landing area in the bay, I could see the bright lights illuminating the boulevard along the shore. This gave me a reference point by which to land. Fortunately, the shore lights proved adequate; I made a good landing and taxied up to the mooring buoy. Now the problem was how to get ashore.

The only lights on the aircraft were the navigation lights on the wingtips and tail. These hardly would attract any attention from the shore. The motor-launch operator who ferried us from the yacht-club landing to the aircraft long since would have given us up and gone home. If I could attract some attention onshore, somebody might realize our predicament and alert the coast guard.

I got out our emergency kit, which contained a Very pistol, shoved a shell into the chamber, and shot off a flare. Nothing happened, so I fired another flare. This time I could see motorists along the boulevard stop to watch the pyrotechnical display.

After about an hour during which I futilely tried to attract some attention, there appeared out of the darkness a huge white yacht, bearing down on our little craft at what seemed to me full speed ahead. I felt sure he was going to ram us, and I started yelling and trying to wave him off. At the last moment he slowed, put his engines in reverse, and then hove to.

94

The crew put over a little dinghy, and a sailor rowed over to us and proceeded to take off our passengers one by one and deposit them on board the yacht. I, of course, was the last to be taken off. As I climbed up the gangplank, on the deck stood a rather handsome Brazilian with a very pretty girl. He said he had been cruising around the bay and spotted our navigation lights. He also had seen our flares and decided we needed help. He introduced himself as Dharky Mattos and proceeded to take us to the yacht-club dock.

A sequel to this episode occurred two years later while I was aboard an airplane en route from Lakehurst, New Jersey, to Roosevelt Field on Long Island.

I had been visiting my friend Ed Conerton at his home in Hempstead, Long Island, when he received a cable from Bill Leeds, the heir to a tinplate fortune who had financed Ed in a flying venture, stating he was flying up from Pernambuco, Brazil, on the *Graf Zeppelin*. He asked that Ed charter the largest airplane he could find and meet the *Graf Zeppelin* at Lakehurst. Ed arranged for a big twin-engine Sikorsky based at Roosevelt Field and invited me to go along.

The huge dirigible landed on schedule at Lakehurst, and Bill, with six or eight Brazilians with whom he had made friends on the flight, boarded our chartered Sikorsky.

On the flight back to Roosevelt, I found myself sitting opposite a young Brazilian whom I engaged in conversation. The man looked vaguely familiar to me, and in the course of our conversation he mentioned cruising his yacht around Botofoga Bay. Suddenly I remembered him.

"You," I said, "are Dharky Mattos. You took me aboard your yacht one night about two years ago when I was stranded on the bay with my Sikorsky amphibian."

He remembered, all right, and became very excited over this coincidence.

Dharky, a very wealthy man, was at that time the "cocoa king" of Brazil. We became very friendly and enjoyed several parties with our host, Bill Leeds, at his Oyster Bay home and also at his apartment in Lower Manhattan.

Shortly after our São Paulo adventure, I received a cable from Pernambuco (now Recife) signed by O'Neill requesting me to fly to Pernambuco and bring him and his associates back to Rio. The message stated further that he had crashed off Fortaleza and had been picked up by a coastal steamer and taken to Pernambuco.

I knew that Kluky had gone north to take delivery of our first Consolidated Flying Boat, a large twin-engine craft with a passenger capacity of about thirty persons. Having flown over to Montevideo with Kluky and experienced that peculiarly rough takeoff, I could guess what had happened off Fortaleza.

I learned later from O'Neill the details of the crash. Sure enough, I had guessed right. It seems that on the takeoff, he had started pounding on the step so hard that the starboard engine broke loose and dropped down low enough for the propellor to cut the hull nearly in half. Fortunately, no one was hurt and the rescue boat appeared soon after the crash.

Johnny Montgomery (still with me in Rio) suggested that he accompany me on the flight to Pernambuco. I was glad to have Johnny aboard. As a pilot, he could relieve me of some of the flying; besides, I liked the guy. I also asked Fritz Hoffman to come with us.

Pernambuco (or Recife) was some 1,400 miles north of Rio, so it would be necessary to stop overnight at Bahia—now called Salvadore, how these names have changed! We refueled from a Standard Oil barge stationed in the harbor and then checked into a hotel. This city is situated on two levels; you either walk up a long flight of stairs or take an elevator to the upper level, where our hotel was located.

The next morning, under clear skies we proceeded to Pernambuco, where in the early afternoon we landed in a crowded harbor. I had cabled O'Neill our estimated time of arrival and fully expected him to meet us. However, after waiting around the dock for more than half an hour, we took a taxi to the hotel where we knew O'Neill was staying. We entered the lobby and signed the register, but still no O'Neill.

I asked the desk clerk for O'Neill's room number and proceeded to knock on his door. O'Neill opened the door and greeted me with a scowl. He obviously was in a very bad humor. He said, "I see you've got Montgomery with you."

"Yes," I replied. "He came up from Buenos Aires with me."

"Well, he's our enemy," O'Neill continued. "He and Bavier and others have been trying to get control of the company from me."

So that was it. A political feud, of which I had no knowledge, had developed in New York. I said, "Listen, Ralph. When I left New York, Montgomery was vice-president of the company, and when he appeared in my office in Buenos Aires, as far as I knew he was still vice-president. I was not about to refuse a vice-president a ride in a company aircraft. As to the political feud you say has developed in the home office, I, of course, had no knowledge of it. So Montgomery's request to accompany me on this flight was, to me, an order from a higher company official."

O'Neill's reply was merely a grunt of acknowledgment. It was obvious to me that O'Neill was convinced I had entered into some conspiracy with Montgomery in opposition to him. "Okay, Ralph," I said, "we'll take off tomorrow morning at 8 o'clock for Bahia, an overnight stop, and we should arrive in Rio early in the afternoon of the next day."

The atmosphere at dinner that evening was, to say the least, restrained. O'Neill introduced us to Dick Ingalls, a man of medium height, dark hair, and considerable excess weight. Dick, formerly of National Air Transport, was to be our chief engineer. O'Neill merely nodded to Montgomery, and neither spoke to the other during the entire meal.

Promptly at eight the next morning I took off with Johnny in the copilot's seat and O'Neill, Ingalls, and Fritz Hoffman as passengers. After a smooth five-hour flight, we landed at Bahia.

The following morning, under scattered clouds we took off for Vitoria, where I had scheduled a stop for refueling. Two hours out of Bahia, the weather started to deteriorate, with lowered ceiling and a threat of rain. We landed in the harbor of Vitoria during a heavy squall. After refueling from a Standard Oil barge, we took off on a course to Rio that took us some distance from the coast over rugged mountain ranges.

About an hour out of Vitoria, still in heavy rain with a lowering ceiling, I could see ahead that the clouds had dropped down to the base of the mountains. I now found myself in a bad situation. I couldn't continue on my course, and, looking back, I could see the clouds now were obscuring the mountaintops. So returning to Vitoria was out of the question.

I continued on for another ten minutes, hoping for a break in the weather ahead. Now, ahead and below, I spotted what appeared to be the outline of a very small lake. I immediately throttled back to go down and have a look at this little body of water that seemed to offer the only possible chance of a safe landing.

As I continued to lose altitude, I saw there was habitation on the shore of the lake—an Indian village and half-naked Indians running around pointing upward to this big bird flying over their heads. Now, as we were circling at 100 feet over the jungle, the "lake" seemed little more than a millpond.

However, there was a strong wind—I estimated at about twenty knots—blowing from the direction toward which I wanted to land. I could see the lake was very shallow, but with this wind I knew I could make a safe landing, even on this miniscule body of water. And, what was more important, if the wind continued at this velocity, I could also takeoff.

Circling into the wind, I started a long power-on approach, and when the hull of my plane cleared the trees surrounding the shoreline,

I cut the throttles and made a stall-landing with plenty of room to spare. When the airplane slowed down and the hull sank to the water-line, I could feel her dragging bottom.

I taxied over in front of the Indian village and placed my right-wing pontoon as near shore as possible. I cut the engines and looked at Johnny. We both grinned, and I turned and glanced back at my passengers. They were a little pale, but also smiling with relief. My only remark was, "Let's hope this wind holds out."

Now the Indians were wading out into the water and milling around the aircraft. The thought had crossed my mind when I first spotted this village that this could be a hostile tribe. There were many tribes in Brazil that were particularly hostile to the white man. However, these Indians so far seemed friendly—fortunately for us.

My immediate concern was for a safe takeoff, when the time came. I had spotted some *cayukas*, dugout canoes, pulled up on shore in front of one of the native huts. What I had in mind was trying to get one of the Indians to paddle me around the lake to see if there were any submerged objects just below the surface.

Fritz had tried his Portuguese on some of the Indians, but to no avail. They apparently spoke some dialect, so we had to resort to pantomime. I was standing on the wing trying in sign language to make them understand I wanted to be taken ashore (I didn't want to get my feet wet) and paddled around the lake in one of their canoes. Pointing to the canoes and then to myself and waving my arms around produced only wide grins and a lot of chatter.

While I was standing on the wing, a tall, very handsome Indian waded up in front of me. He wore some distinctive design on his loincloth and another device in his hair, something made of bone. This obviously was the chief of the tribe.

As he approached, I again started my pantomime, the silent litany of the *cayuka*. Wasted effort. The chief just grinned at me. He turned slowly, and now his back was in front of me.

Suddenly I jumped on his shoulders, with my arms around his neck. What prompted me to pull a damn fool stunt like that I will never know. I suppose his broad back offered too tempting an invitation for transportation ashore.

Anyway, there I was aboard the chief's back, and to my vast relief, all the Indians started jumping up and down, screaming and yelling as if this was the funniest thing they ever had seen. And I suppose it was.

The chief seemed amused, too. He turned his head and gave me a wide grin and proceeded to walk ashore.

Once on dry land, I jumped down and, leading the chief over to the *cayukas*, managed this time to make him understand what I wanted to do. He obligingly paddled me around the little harbor, and I satisfied myself there were no submerged obstacles in my takeoff path.

When I was back aboard the aircraft (the chief graciously ferried me through the water), the others aboard made some snide remarks about my trying to get them killed by a bunch of Brazilian Indians.

O'Neill pulled out a flask and offered everyone a drink. So there we sat in the remote Brazilian jungle, flanked by a bunch of primitive Indians, and drank a toast to our, for the time being, good fortune.

After about two hours, the weather improved gradually. I could see a break in the clouds far ahead, and the top of a lone mountain peak emerged into view.

"Come on," I said. "Let's get out of here while we've got this wind."

I started up the engines and, waving good-bye to my Indian friends, taxied to the far end of the "millpond." I stuck the tail of the airplane into the bushes and opened the throttles. With assistance of the twenty-knot wind, the amphibian seemed to leap onto the step. In a minute we started picking up speed and in another few seconds were airborne.

Once again we arrived at Botofoga Bay after dark. But this time I knew my wife would be having dinner on the balcony of the Gloria Hotel. So I flew down low over the hotel and dropped my left wing with its red navigation light almost on top of the heads of the diners. This, of course, alerted my wife to arrange for the launch to pick us up at the mooring.

In those days, there were no air regulations. If I pulled such a stunt today I would, on top of losing my license, no doubt spend some time in the local slammer.

O'Neill's irascibility was becoming more pronounced each day. There were times when in conference with Humpstone, Jack Thomas, and various government officials he became rather insulting. This was embarrassing to me, for I had established very good relations with these officials. This was not the O'Neill I had known in Washington and New York. His attitude toward me had become so belligerent that it was impossible to talk to him.

Leigh Wade, one of the army air-corps pilots first to fly around the world, was in Rio representing Consolidated Aircraft. Leigh was staying at the Gloria Hotel, and we soon became good friends, meeting each day with Fritz Hoffman and others for cocktails and dinner. Leigh had observed the actions of O'Neill, and I could sense on his part a certain sympathy for my position.

This state of affairs continued into Christmas week. I decided the time had come for me to return to New York. O'Neill was unapproachable. Therefore, my usefulness to the company had come to an end.

I knew that Bill MacCracken, my former boss in the Department of Commerce, had become chairman of the board at NYRBA. As I had enjoyed a good relationship with MacCracken during the days of Inspection Service; I felt he would at least give me a sympathetic ear.

Fritz Hoffman asked to accompany me to New York. I, of course, said yes, that I would be glad to have his company. O'Neill had taken him off the payroll anyway, so there was no point in his hanging around. So I booked passage on the *American Legion*, sailing January 1 for New York.

Jack and Jean Thomas had invited Fritz, Leigh Wade, Dick Ingalls, and me to a party at their Ipenama home one day during Christmas week. After a delightful lunch, we decided to go for a swim.

When we arrived at the beach, we found a heavy surf rolling in, no good for swimming. However, Dick and Fritz waded out to some depth while the rest of us went just far enough to get wet. We could see that there was a strong undertow washing the sand out to sea.

Presently we were startled to see the current taking Dick out to sea. We watched his attempt to swim ashore and realized he just could not make it. None of us was strong enough a swimmer even to get to him against the incoming surf.

Fritz, six feet, two inches, and a tower of strength, started swimming toward Dick, who by this time seemed completely exhausted. Fritz reached Dick and with an arm under his shoulders started swimming back to shore. When they finally reached the beach, Fritz was exhausted and Dick had swallowed a lot of water. We gave him some artificial respiration. After an hour's rest, he once again was back to normal. If Fritz Hoffman had not been there to drag Dick to safety, he would indeed have drowned. None of us had the brute strength to swim against the current as did Fritz.

After a late New Year's Eve party, Jack and Jean, Leigh Wade, and Thelma all came down to the dock to see Fritz and me off for New York. Thelma was to return to Buenos Aires and close our apartment and then follow on the next available ship out of Buenos Aires for New York.

All the party came aboard, carrying much champagne. They stayed until the signal "All ashore that's going ashore" sounded. Promptly at 9:00 A.M. January 1, 1930, the *American Legion* cast off her lines and set sail for New York. It was a festive occasion.

We were off the coast of Brazil where the landmass forms a hump protruding out into the Atlantic. It was midnight, and Fritz and I were sitting on deck looking out at a sea bathed in moonlight. "See that ship," said Fritz, pointing to the north.

There appeared the lights of a large ship approaching us on our starboard bow. "Probably the *Southern Cross* southbound for Rio and Buenos Aires," I said.

Just then our engines slowed and died and we hove to. The other ship also hove to several hundred yards off our starboard quarter. Now, to our astonishment, a lifeboat was lowered with our Captain Sadler accompanied by several sailors aboard. The boat hit the water with a splash, and the sailors started rowing toward the Southern Cross.

Presently we could see a lifeboat from the *Southern Cross* being rowed toward our ship. As the boat came alongside, the captain of the other vessel clambered up a rope ladder to the deck of our ship.

Now this was indeed an unusual drama at sea: two large passenger liners exchanging captains at midnight off the north coast of Brazil. It was not until the next morning that we learned the reason for this peculiar drama.

The captain of the southbound *Southern Cross* had received a radio message that his wife was probably dying in a New York hospital. He immediately sent a message to the *American Legion* requesting an exchange of captains so that he could return to New York, possibly in time to see his wife while she was still alive. Of course, Captain Sadler, our skipper, gladly agreed to this exchange. Anyway, Fritz and I had witnessed a drama that would happen only once in a hundred years.

On January 15, under gray skies and with a temperature of forty degrees, our ship docked in Brooklyn. After clearing customs, Fritz and I took a taxi to downtown Manhattan and headed for the first haberdashery we could find. After all, we were shivering in summer whites, having left Rio in ninety-degree heat.

The next morning promptly at 9 o'clock we appeared in MacCracken's office in the Graybar Building. He greeted us pleasantly enough, and I explained the situation that had developed in Rio as briefly as possible. MacCracken listened attentively, but I could see he was both surprised and puzzled by my summation of the events that led to our being in his office in the first place.

"What do you propose to do now?" he asked. His tone was not altogether friendly.

"That's up to you, Mr. MacCracken," I replied rather coolly. "Remember," I said, "that I have a contract that has more than a year to run." I was becoming annoyed at MacCracken's rather chilly attitude.

After a long pause he said, "Due to ice in the river at Buffalo, we are having the Consolidated boats shipped to Langley Field for assembly at their seaplane hangar on Back River. I could send you down there to run the flight tests. We expect this to take about a month."

"That's okay with me," I replied. The idea of revisiting my old air-corps station was rather appealing.

MacCracken stood up, shook hands with Fritz and me, and said, "Come by the office tomorrow morning, and I will have your travel orders ready. You then can leave on the first available train for Langley."

That evening, Fritz and I had our last dinner together. Fritz was leaving that night for Chicago, his hometown. "You know," he said, "I'm going to marry my old high-school sweetheart. I don't know how we are going to live, because, as you know, I have no job and not much money saved up. But I'm going to take the plunge."

I said good-bye to Fritz, wishing him all the happiness possible. I was going to miss the big lummox, for in spite of our troubles with O'Neill, we had had some good times together. Sure enough, about a month later I received an announcement of Fritz's wedding. I hope he had a long and happy marriage.

It was good to be back at Langley. There had been little change in the four years that had elapsed since my tour of duty ended in May of 1926. Some of the same officer friends were still there, and they made me feel very much at home. I was assigned quarters in the same Bachelor Officers Quarters (BOQ) that I had occupied previously as a young bachelor officer.

I occupied my time watching the assembly of the first of five Consolidated flying boats that, after more than a week, was not yet ready for flight test.

One morning as I walked into the hangar, I was surprised to see "Rabbi" Hawkins talking with the foreman of final assembly. "Rabbi" (obviously he had obtained this nickname from his classmates at Annapolis because of his religion) had flown one of the Sikorskys down to Buenos Aires just before I left for Rio. Having known the man for only about a week, I naturally knew little about him.

"Well, Hawkins," I said (purposely omitting the "Rabbi"), "what brings you to Langley?"

"O'Neill sent me up here to do the flight testing on the Commodores."

I replied, "That makes two of us to do the same job. MacCracken sent me down here from New York for the same purpose."

Of course, I was mad as a wet hen, realizing that I was the victim of conflicting orders from higher up. But there was no reason to be sore at Hawkins. He was just carrying out *his* orders.

Later that day, I got through to MacCracken. "Hawkins is here with orders from O'Neill to do the flight testing. You don't need two pilots for this assignment, so what do you want me to do?" I asked.

"I can't very well go against O'Neill's orders," MacCracken mumbled.

"Okay, Bill. I'm leaving on the next train for New York. See you in your office tomorrow morning."

The atmosphere in MacCracken's office was distinctly cool. "Mr. MacCracken [being formal again], there obviously is nothing more I can do for you or NYRBA, so you might as well pay me what's due on my contract and I shall bid you good-bye."

Looking somewhat pained, MacCracken said, "According to the terms of your contract, we would have to pay you your full salary for the remaining time the contract has to run. We couldn't possibly settle for the full amount, so how much would you be willing to settle for?"

I answered, "Bill, from what you have just said, I know you have read the contract, and you, being a lawyer, realize that this document was also written by a lawyer and a very competent one at that. So, therefore, I expect you to abide by the terms of the contract. If you don't see fit to do so, you may call my attorney at Sullivan and Cromwell."

"Okay, Frank, come by the office in the morning and we will settle this business to, I am sure, your satisfaction."

So the next morning I said adios to NYRBA and MacCracken and walked out of his office.

On the street outside the Graybar Building, I breathed a sigh of relief. It was good to be free again, free from all the petty politics and the squabbling among company officials.

No, I didn't get *all* the money that my contract called for, but I got *most* of it, and that was all right with me.

Chapter 14   Atlanta

The spring of 1930 was hardly a propitious time to be out of work. The stock-market crash with its resultant mass unemployment was, as far as I was concerned, good cause for alarm. I admit to quite some concern for my future.

Thelma had finally arrived from Buenos Aires, and we had rented a small apartment in Garden City, Long Island. I immediately started calling my old pilot and executive friends in the aviation world to learn of any new developments and, of course, any possible openings for anyone of my qualifications.

At the time of which I write, there was no airline passenger service operating in the continental United States. There was, however, a network of airmail routes operating under authority of A.M. Route certificates issued to the various operators by the U.S. Post Office Department.

One of the first things I learned upon my return to New York was that the postmaster general had ordered all airmail contractors to inaugurate passenger service as soon as feasible, which really meant immediately. Now this was most unwelcome news to the airmail contractors. They had a good thing going. They were being paid by the mile, usually anywhere from a dollar or more, depending on the route, to carry a bunch of mail sacks from city to city along their route. They could use small, single-engined airplanes with mail compartments, seldom with a capacity of over 500 pounds. One pilot sitting on a parachute would fly a 500-mile segment of the route day or night as the schedule called for. As an aid to navigation at night, the Department of Commerce had installed rotating beacons along the route. In good weather, the pilot could usually see three of four beacons ahead, making it virtually impossible to get lost. When the weather closed in and visibility was practically zero, the pilots later learned to fly by instruments.

Frank Jerdone and John "Army" Armstrong. Armstrong was the author's first copilot.

Now this type of operation suited the contractors just fine. It was a lucrative business with a minimum of headaches, and it was understandable that they resented having to engage in public transportation. Juggling a bunch of mail sacks was one thing. Dealing with a bunch of passengers, some of whom would prove cantankerous, was another. Anyway, the postmaster general had decreed: Start carrying passengers or lose your airmail contract.

I learned from friends (who were presently employed) that Eastern Air Transport (now Eastern Airlines) was about to start their passenger service and that Harold Elliott, a former navy flier, had been appointed vice-president in charge of operations. I had known Harold slightly over the years and in fact had talked with him shortly after my return. Now I knew that Harold would need to hire some pilots, and I lost no time in calling him on the phone.

"Harold," I said, "I understand you are about to hire some pilots for your passenger division, I would like to apply for a job."

"Sure, Frank. I would have called you before, but I didn't know you wanted just a pilot's job."

"Listen, Harold, times being what they are, the depression and all, a pilot's job suits me just fine."

"Okay, Frank, you're it. I've hired only one pilot, Pete Parker, a guy whom I flew with in the navy, so you're number two."

"Thanks, Harold. When do I go to work?"

"Tomorrow, if you wish. I have an office out at North Beach, so come around 10 o'clock and I'll fill you in on all the details."

So I had a job, so soon, and number two on the pilots' list. How lucky could I get?

North Beach was a combination airport and seaplane base situated on the edge of Flushing Bay, the approximate present site of La Guardia Airport. For land planes, there were two runways running north-south and east-west, both rather short even for the slow-landing aircraft of that era.

I entered Harold Elliott's office promptly at 10 o'clock. Sitting beside his desk was a ruddy-faced, dark-haired man whom I judged to be in his early thirties.

Harold looked up at me and said, "Good morning, Frank. Meet Pete Parker, with whom you will be flying very soon."

Pete stood up, shook my hand, and said, "Glad to know you." He was well dressed in a business suit, white shirt, and blue tie, and his six feet, three inches towered above me. I learned that Pete was from Maine—a rugged guy from a rugged country.

106

Harold explained to us the equipment we would be flying when we opened the New York–Richmond division a week hence. There were two Ford trimotors, one equipped with the 225 H.P. Wright J-5 engines, the other with the Wright J-6 300 H.P. engines. There were two Curtiss Condors, powered with two 600 H.P. Curtiss Conqueror engines, liquid-cooled. These aircraft carried fifteen passengers plus crew, the largest commercial aircraft in operation at that time. In addition, Harold informed us they would lease two Fokker F-10 trimotors equipped with three Pratt and Whitney 450 H.P. Wasp engines. This was a conglomeration of all the aircraft suitable for passenger service at that time. This lack of standardization was going to cause a lot of maintenance problems later on.

Pete and I, in one of the Fords, flew the inaugural flight on the New York–Richmond segment, with stops at Philadelphia and Washington and with Baltimore as a flag stop. After a few round trips to familiarize us with the run, we started a regular schedule with Pete flying one day and me the next, each, of course, completing a round trip every other day. Harold had hired two copilots, Johnny Armstrong and Del Hendrickson. Johnny, my first copilot, usually flew with me, Del with Pete. Johnny was an excellent copilot and went on to become a senior captain of Eastern Airlines. He is retired now, having reached the mandatory age of sixty a few years ago.

One day Harold called me into his office and said, "Frank, I want you to go over to Teterboro and take delivery of one of the Fokker F-10s and bring it back here to North Beach. One of the Fokker pilots will check you out, so you shouldn't have any trouble."

I arrived at the Teterboro airport early the following afternoon and reported to the Fokker Company's office. There was a good-looking blond chap sitting at a desk who upon my entrance rose, shook my hand, and said, "I'm Bernt Balchen." This of course was the Bernt Balchen of Arctic fame, who would during World War II add further luster to his fame as a colonel in the U.S. Army Air Corps.

Bernt led me out to an F-10 parked on the apron. We climbed into the cockpit, and Bernt proceeded to show me the location of all the instruments and how to start the engines and explained the various peculiarities of the airplane.

Having rehearsed all the cockpit procedure over and over, I finally said, "Okay, Bernt, how about checking me out in the air? Just give me two or three landings, and I think I can handle it from there."

To my amazement, he said, "Oh, no, Frank, I'm not supposed to fly with you, not in my contract. You go ahead; you'll be all right."

Now I must explain that this to me was a huge airplane much larger than the little Ford I had been flying. The idea of my taking this plane off and landing it at North Beach without even a copilot aboard was, to say the least, frightening. Bernt just sat there grinning at me. Now what should I do? Harold had told me to bring the airplane back to North Beach. I just sat there for a few minutes, visualizing overshooting the runway at North Beach and landing in Flushing Bay. I knew that with the prevailing wind direction that day, I would have to use the short runway that extended to the edge of Flushing Bay. My approach would have to be over Jackson Heights, then dropping down over a high precipice onto the runway. This was a difficult approach even for a smaller plane with which I was throroughly familiar. I wasn't particularly worried about the taking off and flying the plane in the air. But landing it at North Beach was a different matter.

I finally turned to Bernt. "All right. I'll try it, so get out and let me go commit suicide."

He patted me on the shoulder. "You'll do all right." He added, "Good luck."

I started the engines, warmed them up, and taxied out to the end of the runway. I took off, climbed to 3,000 feet, and headed for North Beach. Arriving over the field, I noted that the wind was just right for the short runway. Fortunately, it was blowing at about ten knots. That would help slow me down before going into the drink. I came in low over Jackson Heights, almost scraping the rooftops. I was making a power-on approach, and as I cleared the cliff at the edge of the runway, I cut the throttles and dropped down on the runway. I hit hard, but all things considered, it was not too bad a landing. Now the waters of Flushing Bay were coming up to meet me, fast. I jammed on the brakes and hoped for the best. The airplane came to a stop just thirty feet from the water's edge. I turned and taxied up to the hangar. As I climbed out of the cockpit, I noticed that my hands were shaking and cold sweat was pouring from my forehead.

Harold came out to look the airplane over. "How'd it go?" he asked.

"Fine," I lied. I saw no point in telling him I had soloed the airplane without a check ride.

"Okay," he said. "Take her on the run tomorrow morning. You have a full passenger load."

It was March 28, 1969. I was a guest at the Explorer's Club sixty-fifth annual dinner at the Waldorf-Astoria. There, at the table sat Bernt Balchen, still ruggedly handsome in his dinner jacket. Thirty-nine years had elapsed since that time at Teterboro when he gave me a cockpit check in the Fokker F-10. After the last speaker had finished his address, I walked over to Bernt's table.

"Well, Bernt," I said as we shook hands, "it's been a long time since we last met at the Teterboro Airport." I doubted very much if he would remember me, for I hadn't seen him in all those years. But he remembered all right.

"Sure, Frank," he said, "I checked you out on the F-10." (He even remembered my name.)

"Yeah, but only on the ground, you refused to ride with me in the air."

He just grinned at that. "You did all right, though; I knew you didn't need me."

We reminisced a while and the party broke up. That's the last and only time I saw Bernt Balchen since I first met him at Teterboro. Several years later I learned of his death.

Pete and I continued to fly the New York–Richmond division for the next few months, each flying the route every other day. For our Philadelphia stops, we used the field at Camden, New Jersey, across the river from downtown Philadelphia. At Washington we landed at Hoover Field, the only commercial airport serving the capital city. The field was situated across the Potomac in Virginia, about where the Pentagon is today. The field itself was just a narrow turf strip and not too long for our larger two- and three-engined airplanes. To make matters worse, the prevailing wind was such that we had to come in low over high-tension wires, using every available foot of landing area before coming to a stop just short of a highway that bisected the lower end of the field.

After many complaints on our part, the authorities concerned decided to install a gate across the road, and whenever an airplane approached for a landing, they would lower the gate, stopping all traffic until the airplane had landed and was taxiing back to the terminal. Of course with traffic stopped we had ample room to continue our landing roll across the road.

In the meantime, we had moved our base of operations from North Beach to Newark. This necessitated Thelma and me moving from Garden City to East Orange, New Jersey, which was convenient to the Newark Airport. We found a small (I use the word euphemistically) apartment hardly bigger than a broom closet. The bed pulled out of the wall, and the entire kitchen pulled out of the wall. However, it was modern and clean and would suffice temporarily.

It was my day off and I was sleeping late when the phone rang insistently. I reached for the receiver and grumbled, "Hello." It was Harold.

He said, "Meet me at the airport as soon as possible. I want you to fly me to Atlanta.

"And," he added "pack a bag; you'll be in Atlanta for quite a while."

"Okay, Harold. I'll be there within the hour."

I dressed hurriedly, packed a bag, and gulped down some coffee and toast. With Thelma driving, we made a dash for the airport. Harold was waiting for me, standing by a peculiar-looking airplane that I had never seen before. He informed me that this was a Curtiss Kingbird. It was a high-wing monoplane powered by two Wright 300 H.P. J-6 engines, and there were seats for eight passengers.

"All right, Frank, you do the flying; we'll land first at the Pitcairn plant at Willow Grove, Pennsylvania."

"*Me* do the flying? Look, Harold, I've never even seen this thing before." I thought, *Here we go again; everybody seems to think I can fly anything. No need for any instructions, no check ride, just get in and away we'll go.* Unlike the Fokker F-10, this was, fortunately, a simple airplane—only two engines and the instrument panel was not cluttered with a lot of strange, sophisticated instruments.

As I throttled back for the approach to Willow Grove, I realized that this airplane's gliding angle was like that of a brick. It literally fell out of the sky. In order to maintain flying speed, I seemed to be diving for the airfield. I managed to pull out of the dive just a hair's breadth before the plane hit the ground, luckily on all three points.

We had lunch, courtesy of Mr. Harold Pitcarin, and proceeded on to Washington. Harold had some business with the Post Office Department, so I was left to my own devices. I called an old friend of air-corps days, and we had a good dinner reminiscing about the carefree days of army life.

When I arrived at old Hoover Field the following morning, there was a solid overcast with intermittent rain. The reports south indicated that the weather was deteriorating but Richmond was still open. Harold said that he wanted to get at least as far as Raleigh, North Carolina. I said "Okay, Harold, we'll land at Richmond and see how the weather is south." At Richmond we learned that the weather south was not at all encouraging. Raleigh was still open, but the weather was deteriorating fast. I frankly did not want to continue. In my judgment, the weather reports did not justify continuing the flight. However, Harold was insistent that we continue. So, he being the boss and I not having the guts to argue with him, we took off for Raleigh. Almost immediately, I regretted this decision. We were flying in heavy rain under a 500-foot ceiling, and visibility was practically zero. After about an hour of flying in and out of low-flying scud, we found ourselves over a small town that proved to be Franklinton, North Carolina. Now the ceiling all around us suddenly dropped into the treetops. There was no going ahead nor turning back. I looked out to my left and saw a narrow field running uphill at an angle of about twenty degrees. I was circling the town not over a hundred feet above the rooftops. I yelled to Harold, "Fasten your seat belt; we're going in to land." It was now raining hard. I could just barely see the outline of the hay field ahead. I literally flew the airplane onto the field. With all that rain, the ground was soft, so I kept pumping the throttles, holding the tail down, trying to keep from going on my back. It was a very short landing, and when we came to a stop the wheels very quickly sunk to the axles. Anyway, we were down safely, no damage done.

By this time the rain was coming down in sheets, so we just sat in the airplane, waiting. There was a road running parallel to the field, and very soon there approached a farm wagon pulled by two horses. Harold jumped out of the plane and hailed the farmer. He agreed to take us into Raleigh about eight miles away, for a price. After about an hour and a half and with Harold and me soaking wet, the farmer pulled up in front of a hotel and deposited us at the door.

The rain stopped during the night, and the morning brought clear weather with abundant sunshine. I hired a taxi and drove back to the farmer's field, leaving Harold at the hotel. With such a wet, soggy field I was doubtful if I could get up sufficient speed to take off. The wheels were still sunk up to the axles. I climbed aboard, started the engines and with throttles wide open managed to get the airplane moving. I continued on up the hill at a speed of at least 10 MPH. Finally reaching the top of the hill and still moving, I headed downhill, and slowly picking up speed, I was able at the very bottom of the hill and the end of the field to force the airplane into the air. It was a close squeeze, but I was now airborne, and in ten minutes I was landing at the Raleigh Municipal Airport.

Harold was waiting for me, so after refueling we took off for Atlanta. The flight to Atlanta was uneventful. Harold's business was to arrange with the proper authorities for the opening of the New York–Atlanta division of our passenger service.

On December 7, 1930, Harold called me into his office and announced his intention of starting the New York–Atlanta segment, leaving Newark on the morning of December 9. "There will be six aircraft participating in the flight to Atlanta—two Fords, two Fokkers, and two Curtiss Condors.

"Pete," he added, "will be the pilot of one of the Condors, and you will fly the other one."

"Sounds very impressive," I replied. "We'd better not fly over Atlanta in formation; they'll think it is the second coming of Sherman."

Harold grinned. "Okay. We'll leave Newark at noon on the ninth, fly down to Washington, where we will remain overnight, and continue to Atlanta early the following day." Harold explained that the Washington stop would enable him to attend a banquet given by the postmaster general, whose guests would be other high government officials, members of Congress, and executives of the various airlines.

As I was about to board my airplane the following morning, I spotted Doug Davis, who along with the other passengers was also getting ready to go aboard. When Doug entered the cabin, I greeted him and asked him if he would care to occupy the copilot's seat on our flight to Atlanta. He seemed pleased at my invitation and said he would he happy to be up front with me.

Now, I didn't know Doug very well, having met him only a few times before. He had acquired some fame as a racing pilot, but as far as I knew had had no commercial experience. I also knew that he had no knowledge whatever of the Curtiss Condor, probably having never been inside the cabin before. His reputation as a pilot, I felt, would be of more value to me with him acting as my copilot than would be that of Del Hendrickson, who had acted as copilot on the flight down from New York the day before.

Del had very little experience on any type of aircraft. In those days, those of us who had acquired a fair amount of flying time, either in the military or barnstorming, were hired as captains. None of us had ever served as copilots. Now, of course, due to the seniority system, a young man hired as a copilot could remain a copilot for as long as fifteen years—a long apprenticeship indeed.

As for copilots, anyone who had soloed an airplane was eligible for the job—the idea being that sitting in the right-hand seat, flying with a senior pilot day in and day out, you would soon learn enough to be of some help. Most captains would give their copilots occasional landings and takeoffs so that eventually they would, in case of an emergency be able to land the airplane safely.

I had been instructed, before leaving Washington, to land at Spartanburg and pick up a newspaperman for the final run to Atlanta. We landed on schedule and our passenger was waiting as we taxied up to the terminal.

Shortly after taking off and reaching cruise altitude on the course to Atlanta, one of the passengers came forward and touched me on the shoulder. He said, "I want you to look out the right window." I motioned to Doug to take over and stepped down into the cabin. The passenger, a newspaperman (there were several aboard this flight), pointed to the forward window. I looked out and what I saw I didn't want to believe. The landing-gear strut had sheared off at the ball-and-socket joint, allowing the wheel to drop down and dangle under the belly of the airplane. My mind was slow in grasping the import of this spectacle. I seemed to be thinking in slow motion.

I recalled my previous landings and takeoffs. Both at Washington and Spartanburg, they had been fairly smooth. Nothing could possibly have fractured a piece of metal an inch and a half in diameter. Yet there it was the strut with wheel attached had completely severed its connection with the other parts of the landing gear and was now hanging uselessly beneath the airplane. Not only was it useless, but a menace to the airplane, the passengers, and the crew.

I looked at my friend, the newsman, the bearer of an unwelcome message. He was an observant young man, and it was fortunate that he had been sitting in that particular seat, had looked out that particular window, and had realized that what he saw was not all that it should be. It was fortunate, too, that he saw fit to inform the crew of this unusual spectacle. From my seat on the left side of the cockpit, I couldn't possibly have seen the right landing gear, and the chances are Doug would not have noticed it.

As it was, the incident posed a potential disaster. If I had attempted a normal landing at Atlanta without knowledge of the broken gear, it surely would have resulted in a bad crash and possible fire, with a resultant loss of life.

The newsman was staring at me, his face a question mark. He was waiting, I am sure, for some remark from me, some judgment of an encouraging nature, for he was an intelligent young man and knew full well that we were in a dangerous situation. But at the moment I could think of nothing to say. My mind was still not functioning at its normal pace. So, muttering a, "Thanks for telling me about this," I returned to the cockpit.

The Curtiss Condor that I was flying, was, at that time the largest passenger aircraft in service. But compared to the modern jet liner of today, the speed, configuration, and payload of our airplane was that of an ox cart. Although I was the captain of this airplane, it actually was quite unfamiliar to me. I had only a few days before been "checked out" on the airplane by a Captain Courteney, a British pilot employed by the Curtiss Company. Although Captain Courteney had pointed out the location of the various instruments and allowed me to land the airplane a few times, I was by no means "experienced" on this aircraft. It was also of no help that I had never been over this route before and had never landed at Candler Field, Atlanta. However, Doug Davis, who was a native of Atlanta and thoroughly familiar with this part of the country, was of considerable help.

We were now about an hour and forty minutes from Atlanta, with plenty of time to plan our landing procedure. I knew, of course, that there had been numerous one-wheel landings with small single-engine airplanes. The pilot simply switched off the engine and hoped for the best. Even so, the result was almost always considerable damage to the airplane and sometimes injury to the pilot and his passengers.

We were now faced with an entirely different situation. We were flying a big twin-engined airplane with eighteen passengers aboard, many of whom were distinguished citizens: the postmaster general and his wife, several senators and congressmen and their wives, and the president of Sperry Rand Corporation, a rather impressive VIP list.

I thought of all possible procedures I could use in this fast-approaching one-wheel landing at Candler Field. Finally, I decided on a plan that I thought offered the best chance of getting down with maximum safety. This plan, which I carefully outlined to Doug, was: I would make my approach to the field at as slow a speed as possible and still retain lateral control. I would attempt to land the airplane on the one good wheel, coming in with the right wing high. I told Doug that I would have my right hand on the throttles and my left hand on the brake lever and that when the airplane started its inevitable "ground loop," I would brake it with the left brake and at the same time shove the right throttle wide open, thus stopping the gound loop almost before it began. I further instructed Doug that at the moment we hit the ground, no matter in what fashion, he was to hold the control wheel all the way back, thereby keeping the tail down. I also told him that in the event we started going on our back, he was to cut the master ignition switch, the location of which was nearer his position than mine.

Now Candler Field lay directly ahead and we were passing Stone Mountain close by our starboard wing. I flew low over the field to get a good look at the terrain and to decide on the exact spot where I would touch down. (Doug had warned me that the turf field was rough in spots.) I had noticed a crowd of people at the far end of the field, the city fathers out to welcome us and celebrate our arrival on this inaugural flight. As we passed low over their heads, I hoped they would see that wheel hanging down below the aircraft and understand our predicament.

In the early days of pioneering passenger routes, our equipment was primitive indeed, our aids to navigation practically nonexistent. At the time of this inaugural flight, our airplanes were not even equipped with two-way radios. There was no such thing as air-traffic control. Without two-way communication, we couldn't call the Atlanta tower and inform them of our predicament. There was of course no ambulance or firefighting equipment on hand in the very likely event that we might indeed need such help.

I circled the field and lined up for a long approach. I glanced at Doug. "Okay," I said, "here we go." He just grinned. He seemed not the least bit disturbed, as cool as if he were sitting in his living room reading the funny papers.

We came in over the fence, right wing high, and touched the ground lightly—so lightly that we seemed to just skate on to the turf. This was the best landing that I probably ever made, before or since, but of course it was just damn good luck. We rolled a long way, and finally the tail got light and I thought, *Here we go on our back*, but the tail dropped back down and then the plane started its inevitable "ground loop." I braked hard and opened the right throttle full out. We did a quarter-turn of a ground loop and came to an abrupt stop. The passengers started filing out; most of them didn't even know what had happened. Doug and I, for a long moment, just sat there looking at each other. Neither of us said a word. Finally with a sigh of relief we stepped out of the airplane.

This unusual accident caused considerable excitement among those awaiting our arrival at Candler Field. Aboard our flight was a quiet, unobtrusive young man by the name of Ernie Pyle who at that time was a correspondent for the Washington *Daily News*. Pyle was later to become one of the nation's finest war correspondents and columnists, known to millions the world over. Perhaps the events of the day can best be summarized by the following excerpts, which appeared in the *Daily News* under Ernie Pyle's byline:

> The opening of Eastern Air Transport's passenger air service between New York and Atlanta saw what fliers term one of the finest pieces of piloting ever done in aviation.
>
> Frank Jerdone, one of Eastern Air's pilots who will fly the Atlanta-Miami run, was the hero of the occasion. Jerdone, by a skillful one-wheel landing at Candler Field, averted a serious accident and brought 17 people to the ground without even shaking them up.
>
> [Pyle elaborated]: There have been scores of such one-wheel landings but never before has a pilot been faced with the task of preserving the lives of 17 passengers in such an emergency. [The future famed correspondent did not overlook the passengers whose lives were saved.] If those people [said Pyle] ever forget the name of Frank Jerdone, they are ungrateful wretches.

The damage to the aircraft was slight. The right wing was not even damaged. Only the trailing edge of the aileron was damaged. The bad wheel had been forced up into the engine nacelle and damaged the various controls. A new landing-gear strut was flown down from New York on the night mail plane. Mechanics worked throughout the night repairing the damage, and with all but a few of the same passengers aboard, I flew the plane back to New York the next day.

Chapter 15   Miami

It was the day after Christmas, a bitter-cold day at Newark. Industrial haze mixed with low, scudding clouds in the fast-approaching darkness blotted out all horizontal visibility as I landed my flight from Richmond.

When I entered Operations, Harold came out of his private office and said, "After you've checked in, Frank, I want to see you." When I entered Harold's office, I saw Pete Parker sitting at one side of his desk. Harold, offering me the other vacant chair, said, "Sit down, Frank. What I have to say concerns both you and Pete.

"On January 1, we will start the Atlanta-Miami division. This final segment will complete Eastern's route from New York to Miami. Now Pete, as chief pilot of the Northern Division, will be responsible for operations from here to Atlanta. I am promoting you, Frank, to chief pilot of the Southern Division, and you will be responsible for the operation between Atlanta and Miami. You will be based in Atlanta."

Now this came as a most-pleasant surprise. I was hardly expecting a promotion of this kind so soon. I suspected that my one-wheel landing at Atlanta may have gained me the promotion.

"You might as well leave tomorrow with the Kingbird," Harold continued. "This will give you a few days to look for a place to live in Atlanta. By the way, I've hired Doug Davis, so you and he will start the run, each flying the round trip every other day. This will entail a lot of flying, but I will get another pilot as soon as possible."

"That's great, Harold. I like Doug and he will add much to the prestige of the company."

I drove home, told Thelma, emphasizing my promotion, and explained that I was leaving in the morning so that I would have a few days in Atlanta to look for a place to live. She agreed to close up the apartment, drive to Washington, and stay with Aunt Kitty until I got things under control in Atlanta.

I arrived in Atlanta in late evening and checked into the Ansley

Hotel. The following day, I found a furnished house in College Park, convenient to Candler Field. The house was situated right across the street from the residence of Slim Thomas, an Eastern mail pilot, and at least Thelma and I would have congenial neighbors.

I decided to fly the Kingbird down to Miami and bask in the sun while waiting to take the inaugural flight to Atlanta on January 1. I phoned Thelma, told her of renting a house, and asked her to come down any time during the week of January 1.

On the morning of December 29, I took off for Miami in the Kingbird. This would be the type of plane we would use in this division, and Harold had promised early delivery of additional aircraft from the Saint Louis factory.

Arriving in Miami, I checked into the Everglades Hotel, where Eastern had arranged for a company room to be used by Doug and me, as we would alternate one-night stays in Miami.

I hadn't been in my room ten minutes when the phone rang. It was Harry Rogers, for whom I had a couple of years before flown a few charters in flying boats. Harry at that time was manager of the Curtiss Flying Service at North Beach. He had somehow learned of my arrival in Miami and called to ask me to go deep-sea fishing with him. "Frank" he said, "a couple of friends of mine and I have chartered a sport-fishing boat for a couple of days. It's completely provisioned with captain and mate and there's plenty more room, so we would like you to come along."

"Thanks, Harry, I'd be delighted." (I had nothing to do anyway for several days, so this would be a pleasant way to occupy my time.)

"Fine, Frank. I'll meet you in the lobby in half an hour. I have a rented car, so we'll drive down to the dock together."

When we arrived at the slip, there standing alongside a sleek forty-eight-foot Sport Fisherman were Bob Gast and Duke Schiller, Harry's "two friends." Bob was a former pilot for Colonel McCormick, owner of the *Chicago Tribune*. The colonel had decided to get rid of his Sikorsky amphibian, thereby throwing Bob out of a job. (I have to explain that this was, of course, before Bob went to China and was killed in a crash of his plane in Hang Chow Bay.)

Duke Schiller, whom I had known for many years, was now the personal pilot for Gar Wood. We all greeted each other effusively and then climbed aboard the Sport Fisherman. Two days in the Gulf Stream produced few fish. But there was plenty of beer, good food, and sun, and we just relaxed and enjoyed the lazy days.

I awoke early on the morning of January 1, 1931, to clear skies, bright sunshine, and a strong northwest wind. My schedule departure time was 11 o'clock, so I arrived at the airport at 9:00 and preflighted my plane and taxied it up to the terminal building. There a large crowd of people milled around, so I just stood by the plane waiting for the passengers to get aboard. The mayor of Miami came up and shook hands with me and introduced some of the passengers, all of whom seemed quite pleased to have been invited on this inaugural flight. One of them was Ed Valerie, the postmaster of Miami, but more about him later.

My weather report indicated clear skies and unlimited visibility all the way to Atlanta, but strong northwest winds of twenty knots gusting to twenty-five and more. This wind would cause considerable turbulence and delay my arrival in Atlanta. I was scheduled to land at Vero Beach, West Palm Beach, and Daytona Beach. At each stop were city officials, newsmen, and photographers, all trying to make the most of the occasion. Each of these towns was apparently the home of one or more of my passengers, so by the time I was over Jacksonville, Ed Valerie was the only one left.

It was now getting dark, and of course I had never been over this route before at night. In fact, my ferry flight down from Atlanta was my first over this territory. However, I could see the beacon lights ahead and I had no trouble following them into Atlanta.

In January 1957, Eastern celebrated its fifty millionth passenger. Twenty-six years had elapsed since I flew Eastern's first schedule from Miami to Atlanta. Having flown the first passenger from Miami north, I was invited to attend the ceremonies at Miami International Airport. Bernard Gimbel, the department-store tycoon, was flown down from New York as the fifty millionth passenger. There was, of course, Eddie Rickenbacker, then board chairman of Eastern Airlines; and Capt. John A. Armstrong, a senior captain of the line who had been my first copilot on the New York–Richmond division. There were also Elmer Sperry of Sperry Gyroscope fame and various other department heads who kept Eastern's Miami maintenance base operating efficiently. And there was Ed Valerie, still postmaster of Miami, my lone passenger who had accompanied me all the way to Atlanta. When Bill Wooten, Eastern's vice-president for Public Relations, phoned to ask me to participate in welcoming Bernard Gimbel, he wanted to know if I remembered any of the passengers' names. I told him I hadn't the faintest idea who they were and in fact had forgotten the details of the flight. Now here was Valerie, who recognized me instantly and seemed anxious to talk. He recalled every detail of the flight, and one incident (which I found very amusing) had made a deep impression on him. He said, "Frank, when we were over Jacksonville and it was getting dark, you

Left to right: Elmer Sperry, inventor of the Sperry gyroscope; Frank Jerdone; Ed Valerie, postmaster of Miami; Eddie Rickenbacker; and Bernard Gim-

called me up front and asked, 'Do you know where we are?' and I said 'Hell, no, I've never been in one of these things before.' " Well, I had forgotten this little tête-à-tête, but Ed recalled it to mind. I was either trying to be funny or to make conversation, but I can imagine that my question was, to say the least, a little disconcerting to a passenger aboard an airplane, especially one who had never flown before.

The ceremonies went off well, and I enjoyed the reunion with some of my old friends, especially Johnny Armstrong. The event was covered by newsmen and photographers. Bill Wooten had done a good job.

Doug and I started flying the route immediately. Our schedule called for leaving Atlanta about 11 o'clock in the morning and arriving at Miami at four that afternoon, with stops at Macon, Jacksonville, and Daytona Beach (where we had a connecting shuttle to Tampa). Our departure time from Miami was 11 o'clock the following morning, with plenty of time for some social activity. Bob and Dorothy Gast had rented a house in Coral Gables that, due to their unbounded hospitality, became the headquarters for all those of us in the Miami aviation fraternity seeking refreshment and companionship. It became almost routine that upon my arrival in Miami and after freshening up at my hotel room, I would get in the company car and drive out to Coral Gables. Bob and Dorothy would greet me effusively. There would always be plenty of food and drink, and soon the house would be filled with fellow aviators and their wives and girl friends. It was always a stimulating evening, and I would usually be the first to leave in order to fly back to Atlanta the following morning.

Quite a few Eastern pilots were based in Atlanta at this time. Among the pilots who flew the night mail were: Dick Merrill, Leland Jameison, Larry Pabst, Slim Thomas, Fritz Schaummle (who later became a Delta Airlines executive), Doug Johnston, Frank Andre, and Gene Brown.

Bob Hewitt, Doug Davis, Frank Kern, Bill Seivers, and myself flew the passenger routes. Of course we also carried the mail, but unlike the regular mail pilots, we were not required to maintain the rigid schedule expected of them. These pilots had become very proficient on instruments and flying alone, sitting on a parachute; they could and did take chances that we who were responsible for the safety of the flying public could not afford to take.

While the mail planes were equipped fully with instruments and reliable radios, our aircraft were not so elaborately equipped. Radio transceivers had recently been installed in our Kingbirds, but were far from reliable. For instance, I would be within twenty miles of

Jacksonville, wanting to give a position report, and I simply couldn't raise Jacksonville, but presently Newark, a thousand miles away, would come in loud and clear. And I would have to relay my message to Jacksonville, twenty miles away, through Newark, a thousand miles distant. This phenomenon was known as "skip-distance" and occurred quite frequently in those early days of airborne radio.

One afternoon after landing my flight from Miami on schedule, I got in my car and drove to my home in College Park. Most of the pilots lived in either College Park, Hapeville, or East Point, all within minutes of the airport. I had changed from uniform to civilian clothes and was about to get in my car to drive downtown to Atlanta when I looked toward the airport and saw a huge cloud of black smoke billowing high into the sky. It looked as if all the buildings at Candler Field were on fire. I drove madly over to the field (less than five minutes away) and was startled to see my airplane burning on the ramp.

It seems that the maintenance crew had checked the airplane and corrected whatever faults I had reported, then refueled the plane and rolled it into the hangar. This was routine procedure. Now I learned that the airplane with no one anywhere near it had suddenly burst into flames. A couple of alert mechanics had spotted the fire almost immediately and succeeded in pushing the plane out of the hangar onto the concrete ramp, thus saving the other aircraft in the hangar from destruction.

The routine investigation that followed showed the fire had been caused by faulty wiring to the navigation lights. A short-circuit had occurred, and presto! Up she went in flames.

Now this incident disturbed me greatly, to say the least. It so happened that on this flight I had a full passenger load. I realized only too well that this fire might have occurred while in flight. By the grace of God and extreme good luck, the airplane had been considerate enough to wait until it was safely deposited in the hangar before deciding on self-immolation.

Officials in charge decreed that all Kingbirds (some six or eight in the fleet) would have all wiring replaced—a wise decision. But in the meantime we were to continue flying these planes—not a comforting thought for any of us. It would take quite some time to run the entire fleet through the electrical shop, and who was to say that one of these planes that had not yet received its new wiring might self-destruct over the states of Florida or Georgia?

I, for one, decided that until I was assigned an airplane that had been rewired, I would not attain an altitude of over 800 feet. Thus in case fire did occur, I could quickly slip the airplane onto the ground and possibly save myself and my charges from being cremated. Fortunately, no further incidents of fire among the Kingbirds occurred, and in due course, all of the planes had been rewired and we pilots resumed our normal routine without the specter of possible disaster hanging over our heads.

It is the desire of all good airline pilots to maintain as perfect a schedule as possible. In addition to possible mechanical trouble, very rare in these days, the weather was our most formidable adversary. Today the captain of an airliner has an awesome responsibility. He is the commander of an aircraft possibly worth $30 million or more. He may be carrying 300 or more passengers for whose lives he alone is responsible. He has served long years of apprenticeship as a copilot and, of course, has developed impeccable judgment about weather conditions. Therefore he knows just what weather he can safely negotiate and that which his experience and judgment tells him not to attempt. The modern airliner is equipped with sophisticated instruments that permit the pilot to fly safely through almost any weather and land under minimum visibility. His electronic navigation system enables him to fly thousands of miles without viewing the ground.

Thus it was that both Doug and I made every effort to maintain as perfect an on-time schedule as possible, commensurate, of course, with safety. In this regard there developed between us a friendly rivalry as to which one of us could maintain the best on-time schedule. There were only two causes for any delay or cancellation of a scheduled flight: weather or mechanical trouble, neither of which could be blamed on the pilot. Usually the worst weather encountered on our route occurred between Atlanta and Daytona Beach. North of Daytona, if the weather ahead looked dubious, I would get on the teletype and request Jacksonville for a detailed report. If it looked at all possible, I would take off and make a try at it, but I would often have to turn back at Daytona. At the time of my arrival at Daytona, Doug Davis would be leaving Jacksonville, and if all went well, we would pass each other somewhere around Saint Augustine. Now if I were forced to return to Daytona I would immediately get on the teletype and ask if Davis had left Jacksonville, the rivalry showing up strong. If the message stated that Davis had cancelled, then I would sigh with relief, sit back, and wait for the weather to improve. I am sure Doug was following the same procedure from the Jacksonville end and with the same apprehension.

By this time, the Department of Commerce had established auxiliary fields along the air routes of the continental United States. These fields were usually boundary-lighted and equipped with a rotating beacon. Such fields along our route were located at McRae and

Hazelhurst in Georgia and Melbourne and Vero Beach in Florida.

On one northbound flight, I was forced to land at Hazelhurst due to local thunderstorms. After I had spent about two hours on the ground, the storm passed over, followed by clearing weather. I took off, landed at Macon, a scheduled stop, refueled, and took off for Atlanta, only about seventy miles away. About twenty minutes out of Macon at an altitude of 800 feet (I was bucking a strong northwest wind), the oil pressure line on the starboard engine broke and oil started spurting all over the engine nacelle. I realized that I had only a minute or two before I would have to shut down that engine, as I would be out of oil. I immediately started climbing and managed to get to 2,000 feet before having to shut off the engine. I had a full passenger load and several hundred pounds of mail, so I knew this airplane would not fly very far on one engine.

I continued on the course to Candler Field, losing altitude all the time. Now I had the field in sight but I was down to a thousand feet. Could I stretch the "power glide" far enough to land at the airport? Below, the terrain consisted of terraced cotton patches. A landing on this rough ground would be certain disaster. Finally I was within gliding distance of the field. I had 200 feet left out of the 2,000. (I'm glad the field wasn't a couple of miles farther ahead.) Disregarding wind and traffic, I made a straight-in approach landing within the boundaries of the airport.

I struggled up to the ramp (taxiing was difficult on one engine) and shut off the remaining engine. Following the last passenger out of the plane, the dispatcher greeted me with "Congratulations, Frank, you have a daughter."

"Thanks, Jim, for the good news, I had a hard-enough time getting home to hear it."

I hurried home, called the hospital, and asked for Thelma's doctor. Some other doctor came on the line. "Congratulations, Frank, you have a son."

"Now wait a minute," I said. "They told me at the airport I had a daughter. Now which is it?"

Just then our doctor came on the line. "It's a fine daughter, Frank; she and your wife are doing fine." I dashed down to the hospital and greeted my first offspring, a beautiful baby girl.

Harold, true to his word, soon hired another pilot, Bill Sevier, a former marine-corps flyer. With three pilots now flying our route, the workload eased considerably. Even so, we were still flying over a hundred hours per month, which was a lot of flying with no copilot to relieve us.

For some time now, I had been giving a lot of thought about my future. I was not at all sure that my career should be that of an airline pilot. True, the pay was good and there was ample time off during which I could indulge in sports or even establish a small business of my own. However, for the most part, I found airline flying rather boring. You took off from Atlanta and flew to Miami, and the next day you took off from Miami and flew back to Atlanta. Except for occasional bad weather, especially at night, this was a somewhat dull routine. A saying among some of the present-day pilots describes airline flying as 98 percent utter boredom and 2 percent stark terror. Be that as it may, 98 percent boredom was too much for me.

Not long after this, the decision of whether to fly or not to fly was forced upon me. While I was happy enough flying for Eastern and continued to enjoy excellent relations with Harold Elliott, my relations with Carl Dolan, the operations manager at Atlanta, were, to say the least, restrained. As I recall, it was probably a personality clash, but I was not very happy having Dolan for my immediate superior.

For some time, I had recommended transferring Sevier to the night mail. It was my opinion that he was not the type of man to deal with the public, and I had received several complaints about his abrasive manner. As far as I knew, no action had been taken on my recommendation. However, one night in Miami, Sevier appeared in my hotel room and accused me of getting him fired. The evening had begun pleasantly enough, but after a few drinks Sevier began to get belligerent. I tried to explain to him that I had nothing to do with his being fired, that I had only recommended that he be transferred to the night mail. Anyway, the evening ended on a lot of unpleasantness, and I considered the matter closed. However, upon my return to Atlanta, Dolan called me into this office. Somehow he had learned of my altercation with Sevier, and I suppose he considered that a good excuse to get rid of me. Well, I also considered that Dolan's attitude regarding the Miami incident was good reason to leave the company.

I have always had what some people call an itchy foot. I like to travel and meet different people in different parts of the world. I am fortunate in that almost everything in life interests me. I have known so many pilots for whom flying is their sole life. They have no other interests, and if they are airline pilots and reach the mandatory retirement age of sixty, they are indeed lost souls. These pilots have my deep sympathy. I could probably have remained an airline pilot and, as aviation progressed, flown better, faster, and more sophisticated airplanes and made a salary far beyond my dreams, but I have never regretted my decision. While the going has not always been easy, I have had a most interesting life. For the most part, I have continued to fly airplanes, pioneering airlines over the jungles of Central America, developing gold mines by air, and having many adventures on the ground, all of which will be related in coming chapters. There was nothing routine about all this and never "utter boredom."

I drove home, greeted Thelma with the [good? bad?] news and said, "As soon as we can pack up and get out of here, we're driving to California." I don't know why, but for some time I had been dreaming of going back to California. I still had a few friends out there, and I very much wanted to go west again.

Chapter 16   Hollywood

It was a Sunday afternoon in Hollywood. I was a guest at a cocktail party hosted by some movie star whom I didn't know, but I had been invited through a mutual friend. I had only recently returned to this fantastic town called Hollywood, which is not a town at all but only a certain area within the corporate limits of the city of Los Angeles.

The room was crowded with motion-picture people—stars, directors, writers, extras, and various hangers-on. Clarence Brown, one of Metro Goldwyn Mayer's better directors, clawed his way through the mob to where I was standing. We shook hands and he said, "Frank, I want to talk to you. Let's find a corner in another room where we can at least hear each other."

I had met Clarence Brown in New York just prior to my departure for South America. He was, I believe, at that time Garbo's exclusive director. Clarence had been a World War I pilot and now piloted his own airplane. We found a secluded corner in a room away from the cocktail mob and sat down.

Clarence said, "I have just returned from Paris, where I purchased a book titled *Night Flight,* which I consider the most beautiful writing about aviation I have ever read. I'm going to try to get M.G.M. to produce it. By the way, have you read the book?"

"No, I haven't," I replied. "Never even heard of it."

"Well," Clarence continued, "the author is Antoine de Saint Exupery, a French airmail pilot flying for Aeropostale [now Air France] in South America. As you have flown a lot in South America, I thought you may have run across him."

"No, I never met Exupery, Clarence, but I did meet a couple of other Aeropostale pilots. They were all based in Buenos Aires at the time I was there."

"Well, what do you know about Aeropostale's operation?"

"Quite a good deal," I replied. "My company had a reciprocal agreement with Aeropostale whereby we, in an emergency, could use their airfields and facilities and they in turn would, also in an emergency, have the use of our facilities, including our communications system.

"In addition," I continued, "I have landed in all their fields from Recife, Brazil, to Buenos Aires. After flying for hours over dense jungle, it was a welcome sight to look ahead and see a well-laid-out flying field, boundary-lighted, with hangars, shops, radio tower, and refueling facilities."

After a long conversation consisting mostly of Clarence questioning me about the French airmail—their pilots, routes, facilities, et cetera—it was time to leave the party. Clarence thanked me for the information I had given him and departed. He had made no further reference to M.G.M. making a motion picture from the novel *Night Flight.*

This was the year 1933, probably the worst year of the worst depression this country had ever experienced. There were, of course, no jobs to be had, not even flying jobs. I became a free-lance pilot, hanging around the airports trying to pick up an occasional charter, instructing, ferrying aircraft, sometimes flight-testing new production aircraft. But it was a poor way to make a living, and the living was not very good. Thelma and I managed to eat fairly well, feed Marilyn, and pay the rent (sometimes belatedly), but it wasn't much fun.

About six months after my talk with Clarence Brown at the Hollywood cocktail party, I received a frantic call from M.G.M. It was Clarence on the phone. He had had trouble reaching me, for I had moved a couple of times during the six months.

"Listen, Frank," he said. "I want you to come out to the studio tomorrow and have lunch with me at the commissary. We are going to produce *Night Flight,* and I may need your help. Make it twelve-thirty; there'll be a pass at the gate for you."

This call came at a time when I was most depressed. I was despairing of ever getting anywhere in this world of economic chaos. It was becoming more difficult each day to eke out even a bare living.

Once one passed through the gates and entered the vast Metro Goldwyn Mayer studio in Culver City, one was aware that here was an entirely different world. There was no sign of a depression, no indication of a national financial crisis. The atmosphere was that of affluence, with actors and actresses, some elegantly dressed, rushing from set to shooting set in the huge, high-ceilinged stage buildings. Then there were the outdoor sets, streets with only the facade of storefronts, which were known as whatever name the shooting script called for but were used over and over again. It was a scene of wild, confused activity.

The commissary was crowded that noon hour as Clarence and I sat down to lunch. The conversation began with the same old litany—questions and more questions about the French airmail in South America. Almost all of them had been answered by me at that Sunday-afternoon cocktail party. Finally lunch was over and Clarence said, "Let's go up to Dave Selznick's office." Now this somewhat startled me. So far Clarence had said not a word about hiring me as a technical advisor (they called them technical directors in those days) or anything else. So why were we going up to the office of Dave Selznick, who at that time was a producer at M.G.M.?

Entering Selznick's office, I observed a somewhat corpulent young man with rimless spectacles sitting behind a huge desk. Clarence introduced me to this seemingly mild-mannered, affable person, who shook my hand and said he was glad to meet me.

Clarence then said, "Mr. Selznick, I would like to hire Mr. Jerdone here as technical director on *Night Flight*." He then proceeded to tell Selznick some of my background, emphasizing my South American experience.

Selznick merely nodded, mentioned a salary that seemed astronomical (I learned that I could have gotten more), and then picked up the phone and said, "Get me Ollie Garrett." Oliver H. P. Garrett was one of Hollywood's finest screenwriters. He was much in demand by all of the studios; in fact, Selznick had borrowed him from Paramount to adapt the novel *Night Flight* to scenario form.

In response to Selznick's demand, there appeared, in a very few minutes, a tall, handsome man probably in his early forties. Selznick introduced us and, nodding to me, said, "I want you to work with Mr. Garrett on the script; he will need some technical assistance in developing the novel to scenario form."

Garrett turned to me and said, "Come on over to my office. I want to talk to you."

The interview was over. I shook hands with Selznick, said, "Thanks" to Clarence, and followed Garrett out of the office.

At that time, the writers' building on the M.G.M. lot was a two-story barrack-like wooden building divided into little cubicles, euphemistically called offices—a disgrace to anyone even remotely qualified to be called a writer.

When we arrived at one of these cubicles located on the second floor, Garrett said, "Listen, Frank. [He started calling me Frank immediately, it was easier than Jerdone.] I can't write here; this place depresses me. I am going to work from my Santa Monica Beach home, which you will find much more cheerful than this dismal rat's nest. I would like for you to get down to my place about 10 o'clock; we will work a couple of hours, have lunch, and probably call it a day around 4:00 P.M." With those instructions, he said, "Let's get out of this dump. I'll see you tomorrow at my place."

My first impression of Ollie Garrett was that of an affable and extremely intelligent man. He possessed a world of experience as a scenarist, with a background of a journalist on the old *New York World*. We had seemed to hit it off immediately, and I felt that it would be a pleasure to work with him and not only would there be mutual cooperation, but I would learn a lot.

I was living at this time in North Hollywood, occupying a house situated near Laurel Canyon and Ventura Boulevard. J. B. and Ruth Alexander had rented the place, but having gone away on some business, had sublet it to Thelma and me. It was a small, but well-furnished house, and Thelma and I considered ourselves fortunate to get it even on a temporary basis.

To get to Ollie Garrett's estate, I started out the morning after our interview and drove through Laurel Canyon to Santa Monica Boulevard, west on Santa Monica, until reaching the ocean, I turned right into Malibu to the address Garrett had given me. The house was even more elegant than I had imagined. I approached the front door and rang the bell, and almost immediately the door was opened by a butler who bade me enter. He escorted me into a huge living room beautifully furnished with long davenports along opposite walls. I was just taking in the splendor of the room with its superb furnishings when suddenly Garrett appeared. He was most cordial, greeting me warmly and asking if I had had trouble finding his place.

There then appeared a most attractive woman, probably in her late twenties, whom Garrett introduced me to as Miss Laura Ingalls, his secretary. Carrying notebook and pencils, Miss Ingalls seated herself in a comfortable chair placed between the two davenports.

Ollie, motioning toward the davenport across from the one he had already sat down and was making himself comfortable on, said, "Take off your shoes and stretch out, Frank. Make yourself comfortable."

Now this seemed to me to be a very unorthodox way to start the first day of one's job, but I did as I was bid, noting that already Garrett was stretched out comfortably with his shoes off.

While Ollie knew nothing about aviation, his questions were somehow quite intelligent and to the point. And as I knew nothing about the motion-picture business, I had a few questions of my own. I remember asking Garrett why M.G.M. didn't send a camera crew to Argentina and film the entire episode on location.

Ollie's reply was, "You don't know the motion picture business; we

130

can do *anything* right on the lot." He then explained to me "process" shots, "Basevi" shots, and shooting on miniatures. I might add that production methods have changed radically from those of the days of which I write. Indeed, today the studios would do exactly what I proposed to Garrett: send a camera crew to Argentina to shoot the entire sequence on location. Today the stress is on realism and the producers would think nothing of sending an entire company—actors, directors, technicians, and camera crew—to any part of the world to ensure that the end product is indeed realistic.

To me, mine and Ollie's "conversation" was most interesting. For that was what it was, a *conversation* rather than a question-and-answer period. Due to Oliver Garrett's intelligent questioning, he was getting the technical knowledge he needed in order to write the screenplay. And I in turn was learning something of the technology of motion-picture production. This made for a more comprehensive understanding of each other's speciality.

Now the butler appeared with a tray of cocktails. It was almost lunch time, and the morning, like our conversation, had flown by with the speed of sound.

We had our drinks and then entered the huge dining room. After a delightful lunch, we again returned to our respective couches. The lunch and cocktails had taken just a little over an hour. The pace had been leisurely. I was to learn that with Ollie Garrett there was never a sense of haste and the mood was always relaxed.

It was now 4 o'clock, and Ollie said, "Let's call it a day. See you tomorrow, the same time."

I drove slowly home wondering if this was for real. Somehow I had been catapulted into a world of fantasy. Would I awaken tomorrow to the realization that all this was only a pleasant dream?

The days passed routinely until one day Ollie handed me the finished screenplay. A month had gone by, and I had not realized the passing of time. As I read the script from "Fade In" to "Fade Out," I slowly came to understand the subtlety with which Garrett had done his job. I now realized that all this time Miss Ingalls had been taking down in shorthand everything that Ollie and I had said and at the end of the day she had transcribed her notes and neatly typed them so that Ollie had before him all the information he needed to write the screenplay.

Oliver Garrett had done a good job. The script was approved by Clarence Brown and Dave Selznick, the producer. The final approval came from the "front office": Louis B. Mayer.

In a few days, shooting would begin. In the meantime, the assistant director started scheduling the production—so many days allotted to various locations, so many on the home lot. Aerial camera crews would be alerted—one at Burbank, one at San Francisco, and one at Denver—for the purpose of shooting cloud backgrounds. Paul Mantz would be in charge of all air work, hiring pilots, procuring different-type aircraft, et cetera. The assistant director's overall planning would necessarily be guided by budgetary considerations.

I was frankly amazed when Clarence showed me the cast of actors. John Barrymore was to play the lead. The other actors making up the all-star cast included Lionel Barrymore, Clark Gable, Bob Montgomery, William Gargan, Myrna Loy, C. Henry Gordon, and that celebrated actress Helen Hayes. M.G.M. had really "shot the works" on this one.

I was hoping to do a little flying on this picture. I particularly wanted to go to Dallas and ferry one of the airplanes back to Burbank. But Clarence would have none of it. He wanted me on the set with him at all times.

Playing a part, although a very minor one, in making a major motion picture was a fascinating experience. My job consisted mostly in answering questions, advising an actor how to pronounce "Bahia Blanca," and instructing various actors in using correct technical jargon in their dialogue. Also, I was constantly working with the research department, having them cable Buenos Aires for such detailed information as what the 1930 license plates for their automobiles looked like, the names of various streets, rules and regulations pertaining to civil aviation in the Argentine, and many other details that I had forgotten.

In the many months it took to complete the picture, I, of course, came to know the principal actors and technicians rather well. They were all very fine people. Gable seemed possessed of a pervading humility. He remarked several times to me that he was afraid that he would wake one morning and find all this just a dream. He at times seemed to think that his superstardom was just a colossal mistake. Bob Montgomery was a fun-loving guy with a fine sense of humor. He also was fond of the ladies. John Barrymore was just entering his final round in his fight with John Barleycorn. He was unable to remember his simplest lines. As a consequence, we had to do hundreds of retakes in his every scene. One day he appeared on the set carrying too much of a load. To sober him up, somebody ordered a huge steak. That proved to be a mistake. Barrymore just passed out. Clarence Brown, a teetotaler, was very tolerant of others' drinking, but when his leading actor passed out on the set, that was a little too much. He had to call off shooting for the day. The assistant director and I accompanied Clarence back to his office. He picked up the phone and called Dave

Selznick. In answer to whatever Selznick was saying, Clarence yelled, "I don't give a damn who you get; get me anybody—get an extra, for all I care." That was the first and only time I ever saw Clarence really mad.

One morning I appeared late on the set. Clarence confronted me as I walked through the door. "Have you read the additional dialogue I had Garrett write for Helen Hayes?"

"No," I replied.

"Here's a copy for you," he said, handing me a couple of sheets of paper.

I walked over to my chair, sat down, and read the script. The scene outlined by Garrett was as follows: Helen Hayes was playing the part of the wife of the pilot bringing the airmail from the far south to Buenos Aires. Her husband being long overdue, Miss Hayes had gone downtown to the office of the airline to inquire of the operations manager (Barrymore) why her husband was so long overdue. Barrymore had explained to her that her husband had long since run out of fuel and was down at sea somewhere between San Antonio and Bahia Blanca. He told her as gently as he could that there was no possible chance of his survival.

Now here comes the "additional dialogue" Clarence had dreamed up.

The scene was Miss Hayes's apartment in downtown Buenos Aires. The maid was preparing dinner. Miss Hayes had instructed the maid to set an extra plate at the table opposite her. The maid would serve a seven-course dinner, and with each serving to Miss Hayes, she would also serve that empty plate, along with appropriate wines. As I recall, there was some *dialogue* addressed to that empty plate, just as if the pilot were sitting there in person.

Now, having finished reading the script, I thought, *How in the hell could Clarence Brown, a veteran director and an airplane pilot himself, dream up such hokum as this?* So between takes I walked over to him and said, "Clarence, I'm surprised at you. This additional dialogue you had written for Miss Hayes has no place in this picture. You, being a pilot, should certainly realize that it is pure hokum and actually detracts from the picture."

Clarence replied, "Ah, but you don't know Miss Hayes. She can play this part with such dramatic effect that it will overwhelm the audience."

"I may not know Helen Hayes," I replied, "but in my opinion it's still a lot of hokum and has no place in the picture."

Now, being an outsider with no particular knowledge of the motion-picture business, I was being very brash indeed criticizing the judgment of this veteran director. But I had grown to know Clarence very well; we had long since been on a first-name basis, and in addition to our business relations we had become friends as well. Therefore I felt that I could talk plainly with him when the occasion called for plain talk.

I was sitting next to Helen Hayes when Clarence called, "Cut" and the crew started leaving for lunch.

"Miss Hayes," I asked, "what do you think of that additional scene that Clarence had written for you?"

"Well," she replied, "I think it's simply hokum, it has no place in this picture, and," she added, "I don't want to play the part, but being under contract to M.G.M. I suppose I'll have to."

"I'm glad to hear you say that, Miss Hayes, for only an hour ago I said those very words to Clarence Brown. You have quoted me almost verbatim."

Having this famous actress corroborate my judgment as to what should *not* be part of the screenplay made me feel pretty good, especially so as I was an outsider with practically no experience in the motion-picture industry.

We were on location at Mines Field (the present location of Los Angeles International Airport). It was night and a cold wind was blowing in off the Pacific. The scene called for Myrna Loy to kiss her husband (Bill Gargan) good-bye. Gargan was sitting in the cockpit of a Douglas M-1 mail plane wearing a fur-lined suit and helmet and goggles. In addition to the cold Pacific wind, the engine was turning over, causing the slipstream to blow back over Gargan and Miss Loy, who was reaching up to kiss her husband good-bye. Unfortunately, this scene required many retakes, and after each "take" we would all run into the hangar, where there was a fire going in an old wood stove. After a few minutes by the fire, we would dash out for another "take." This was particularly hard on Miss Loy, for she was not heavily dressed, wearing only a light coat over her dress. I remarked as much to her in one of the warming intervals in the hangar. She said, "Yes, this reminds me of the time I was on location in the Arizona desert. The desert, you know, can, at night, get very cold indeed, and the scene called for me to crawl on my stomach over the sand all the while I was supposed to be perishing with the heat. Actually my teeth were chattering with the cold; I was simply freezing."

During my tenure with M.G.M., there occurred two events of national importance; Roosevelt closed the banks and Prohibition was repealed. Somehow Ollie Garrett had gotten wind of the banks closing and he warned all of us to draw out sufficient funds to last awhile. I was thankful for his warning, for I never had much cash on me anyway. Of course the repeal of Prohibition was most welcome to all of us, and when that day after shooting was over we duly celebrated the occasion.

Inevitably the day arrived when Clarence announced the end of the picture. The final scene had been shot, and "Now," he said, "it's in the can."

"There'll be a preview one week from today," Clarence announced. He named an obscure theatre in Ontario, a suburb of Los Angeles. We were invited to bring our wives and girl friends. Reluctantly, I said good-bye to the technicians whose expertise had helped to create the finished product and the cast—John Barrymore, Helen Hayes, Clark Gable, Lionel Barrymore, Robert Montgomery, Myrna Loy, William Gargan, C. Henry Gordon, and others, all of whom I had enjoyed working with. I had developed a deep respect for not only actors' ability, but for their being very fine human beings.

The preview in Ontario was disappointing. The audience's reaction was apathetic, and despite that great cast, the picture somehow just didn't come off as we had all hoped it would. I learned later that it was definitely not a box-office success.

Chapter 17   Honduras

A friend of mine, a Lockheed test pilot, told me that Earl Halliburton was looking for someone to become his personal pilot. Halliburton was the founder of the Halliburton Oil Well Cementing Company with headquarters in Duncan, Oklahoma. (The Halliburton Company is now a huge conglomerate comprising many companies, including the huge construction company Brown and Root.) Halliburton owned a Lockheed Vega, which he used as his personal plane. He had previously ventured into the airline business, forming a company called Safeway based in Oklahoma and extending into other midwestern states. However, the airline had run into financial difficulties and was no longer in operation.

Upon learning of Halliburton's need of a pilot, I lost no time in arriving at his downtown Los Angeles office. I found Halliburton to be a man of short stature (about five feet, five inches) and a rather dark complexion, with black, bushy eyebrows. However, he greeted me cordially, asked me to be seated while he read my resumé. After about thirty minutes of conversation about pilots, airlines, and airplanes, he said, "Frank, I want to see you again on Friday," naming a specific time. This was Wednesday and I knew that he wanted a couple of days in which to consult my references.

At the appointed time, I again appeared at his office. This time he went into detail as to my duties as his personal pilot. After his interview, during which he said nothing about actually hiring me, he said, "Come back Monday at 9 o'clock." Now I needed this job in the worst way and I knew there was a lot of competition and in both interviews Halliburton had talked as if I had the job. But he had not committed himself. So the suspense of waiting over the weekend for what I hoped would be a final verdict on Monday was making a nervous wreck of me.

As I entered Halliburton's office promptly at nine on Monday morning, his first words were, "Frank, you've got the job." This good news almost overwhelmed me. I knew that my airline experience both in

South America and with Eastern had probably tipped the scales in my favor—also that I had considerable experience on both the Lockheed Vega and Ford trimotor.

Until now, Halliburton had been talking to me about my duties as his personal pilot, which would involve for the most part flying the Vega. However, this morning he surprised me with some startling news. "Frank," he said, "I have purchased a mining property (gold) in Honduras. It is very inaccessible, located in mountainous country, no roads, no railroads. We will have to develop this mine by air. I have bulldozers now working at the mine site leveling out a landing strip that will be adequate for a Ford.

"Now," he continued, "I have decided that you will be of more value to me flying equipment and supplies into this mine than just being my personal pilot."

This new development took me so by surprise that I hardly knew if I were being promoted or demoted even before I was on the payroll. While I had never heard of developing a gold mine by air in Central America or any other part of the world, for that matter, it did hold promise of some exciting adventure.

Halliburton explained that he had a Ford in the hangar at Glendale Airport. "One from the Safeway fleet I kept for my own use." He went on to say that the airplane would have to be modified for carrying freight. He enumerated certain changes. The floor of the cabin would have to be reinforced. Some sort of track with a dolly had to be installed for moving heavy freight over the center of gravity. A device for loading heavy equipment with a derrick and probably a hatch cut in the top of the fuselage would also be required.

The interview, for the time being, was over. Halliburton stood up, shook my hand, and said, "Frank, you will be in complete charge of all flying activity, including the modification of the airplane. I want you to be ready to leave for the Honduras by August 1. This will give you a little over a month to get the Ford ready. So go to work, and good luck."

I wanted very much to get out of that office into the outdoors, where I could breathe some fresh air and try to assimilate this sudden turn of events. I walked around the block a couple of times, trying to plan my first move. I got in my car and drove to Glendale and parked at the Timm hangar. The Timm brothers conducted an aircraft-repair depot and specialized in remodeling and converting aircraft for various purposes.

I found Wally Timm in his tiny office and told him of my plans for converting the Halliburton Ford to a freighter. Wally said that he had heard of such an operation (developing a gold mine by air) in New

Guinea, the first time such an undertaking had been successfully accomplished. This mining company, Wally informed me, used trimotored Junkers powered by the three Pratt and Whitney Hornet engines. It seems that a San Francisco mining-equipment company had asked the Timms to bid on some airplane parts needed for this particular operation and had forwarded him blueprints of the modification of the Junkers.

This was indeed a break for us, for Wally could practically copy the blueprints of the Junkers modification in converting the Ford. The Junkers, too, had a removable hatch about six feet long cut in the top of the fuselage and also a track and dolly installed on the reinforced floor.

I told Wally of our deadline of August first. He said that he could start immediately and probably finish the job by the required date. I thanked him for offering us the data obtained from the San Francisco company and told him I would drop by each day to assist him in any way I could.

Halliburton called and said that he had an application from a man named Clark who had been an airplane mechanic for United Airlines. "He seems to have the right qualifications for the job as your flight mechanic," he said. "He has had some flying time and could also act as your copilot. He will be in my office tomorrow morning at 10 o'clock, so come down and interview him. If his background and personality meets with your approval, we'll hire him."

When I arrived at the office promptly at 10 o'clock, Halliburton said, "Frank, meet 'Baldy' Clark." I shook hands with a ruddy-faced man of medium height who was indeed bald. What little hair he had left was blond. I do not remember his first name (if indeed I ever knew it), for he was known to everyone only as Baldy.

I looked over his application and was impressed with his quite considerable experience as an airline mechanic. Baldy seemed to be an affable young man, and I felt that we would get along well together. So I said to Halliburton, "I think he's the guy we've been looking for."

Turning to Baldy, I asked, "When can you go to work?"

"Right away," he said. "Today if you want me."

"Okay. Baldy, meet me at the Timm hangar in about an hour." I explained to him what we were doing on the Ford and said to him, "I want you to work with Wally Timm, and if you have any suggestions regarding this modification, feel free to consult with Wally or me. After all, it's now your airplane as well as mine. You will be responsible for maintaining it, and you will have to fly with it."

The days went by quickly and the work on the airplane progressed

138

on schedule. Two days before our departure date, Wally announced the work finished and the plane ready for test flight. On the morning of July 30, I arrived early at the Timm hangar. The plane was on the flight line, Baldy sitting in the cockpit warming up the engine. I climbed aboard, motioned Baldy to take the copilot's seat, and after checking the engines taxied out on the runway and took off. After about thirty minutes' flying, I was satisfied with the plane's performance. She handled beautifully. I looked at Baldy. "She's okay," I said, with a smile. Baldy, too, looked pleased. I landed, taxied to the flight line, and shut off the engines.

"Well, Baldy, it looks as if we're all set to leave the day after tomorrow. We will have to get out here early, meet our passengers, and load some freight, mostly spare parts and the passengers' baggage. Have the plane refueled, full tanks, and be ready for a 9 o'clock takeoff."

About a month before I landed this job with Halliburton, Thelma and Marilyn had left for Seattle. Thelma would stay with her mother until such time as I could once again establish myself financially. This was, I suppose, a trial separation. Our marriage had over the past few months been deteriorating. Why had our marriage begun to fail? Probably for several reasons. In the first place, we were both young and inexperienced as far as matrimony was concerned. There was quite a bit of incompatibility. Then, too, I had for the past couple of years been making a precarious living as a free-lance pilot. Our standard of living was by no means as high as it had been the first few years of our marriage. In retrospect, I realized that my personal life-style was not conducive to a successful marriage. I was an adventuresome, undisciplined young man—willing to take all sorts of chances, not only in flying but with life itself. Anyway, this job would not permit taking my wife and child with me. I would be living in a native village in the jungles of Honduras. It would be a rough life, even for me alone.

Arriving at the Glendale Airport early on the morning of August 1, I was greeted by Halliburton, who proceeded to introduce me to my passengers. There was Ross Prouty, a mining engineer, now general manager of the Agua Fria Mining Company. As such, he would be my immediate boss. Prouty, a man in his early forties, rather stockily built, with a graying mustache, had recently returned from the Soviet Union, where he had supervised the installation of mining machinery at a remote area of northern Siberia. He was accompanied by his wife, who would, upon arriving in Tegucigalpa return to their home in Burbank, via Pan American Airways. Hollister, who would be the mine's metallurgist, and two construction foremen, completed the passenger list.

We took off from Glendale and headed for Mexicali, which lies across the border from Calexico, a small town in California's Imperial Valley. Here we would clear customs into Mexico. I had planned our stops after leaving Mexicali; Mazatlan, where we would remain overnight, Guadalajara for refueling, and thence to Mexico City, another overnight stop. We were delayed at Mexicali for over two hours; the Mexican customs and immigration took their own sweet time clearing us into their country. This was a forewarning of many frustrating incidents to come involving Mexican and Central American customs officials.

Our flight down to Mazatlan was without incident. After a good night's rest at the Bieramar Hotel, we were off early the following morning for Guadalajara, where we landed briefly for fuel, thence on to Mexico City, arriving at 2 o'clock. After checking into the Regis Hotel, we still had time for some sightseeing, followed by an excellent dinner and then early to bed.

What aerial maps I had been able to obtain in Los Angeles were hardly adequate for pinpoint navigation. The Central American portions were really pages cut from a school geography book. At the airport the following morning, I talked with some Pan American pilots regarding the course to Tegucigalpa via Tapachula and Guatemala City. These pilots who flew this route (Brownsville, Texas, to Panama) knew, of course, the terrain as well as the palm of their hand. "The field at Tegucigalpa," one said, "is situated on a high plateau, and there is only one way to land, from the south. There is a banana patch adjacent to the field, and in your landing approach, if your wheels don't touch the banana plants, you had better go around and try it again, for this field is small and except for the south is surrounded by mountains."

I thanked the Pan Am boys and climbed aboard for our takeoff for Tapachula. We were obliged to land at this little village near the Guatemalan border in order to clear customs *out* of Mexico.

The airport of Mexico City lies at an altitude of 7,200 feet. Because of this altitude, the takeoff would require a much longer distance than taking off at sea level. Even in those days, the government of Mexico had provided a 5,000-foot runway. I taxied out to the edge of the runway and shoved the throttles full out. We were heavily loaded and there was practically no wind, so I expected a long roll before becoming airborne.

The airplane seemed sluggish; it simply would not pick up speed. I checked the instrument panel. Everything seemed normal. The tachometers indicated maximum RPMs. All instruments showed normal readings. But still the airplane was moving at a snail's pace.

Finally the tail came up; our speed increased a little, but far from sufficient for lift-off. We were using up that 5,000-foot runway at an alarming rate. At the end of the runway, I could see a concrete abutment about five feet high. At the same instant I realized that I had gone too far; I hadn't sufficient room to brake the aircraft to a stop. I was committed to a takeoff—or else. At this moment, without conscious thought, I reached down and opened the mixture controls and shoved them from full rich to lean. Immediately the airplane surged ahead. We had power, plenty of it. At the last possible moment, I pulled back on the control column, the plane responded, and we were airborne and climbing. We cleared the concrete wall by what seemed like two feet. I glanced at Baldy; beads of perspiration stood on his forehead, and I, from the waist up, was soaking wet.

Just why my subconscious mind started functioning at that last moment I'll never understand. Extra Sensory Perception? Perhaps. The reason for what today would be called a "near miss" was of course "pilot error." The only reason for this "pilot error" is the fact that I had never before flown from high-altitude airfields. Even so, I should have known better, for had I not always, upon reaching cruise altitude, leaned out the mixture to both save fuel and increase power? Anyway, I had learned a never-to-be-forgotten lesson, at the cost of near disaster.

We were now climbing through the overcast, for the ceiling was only 2,500 feet and we would have to cruise at 10,000 to clear the mountains of southern Mexico. Breaking out on top at 9,000 feet, we passed close to Popocatepetl (called Sleeping Lady) and Mount Orizaba, two extinct volcanos, towering some 18,000 feet through the cloud layer. I continued my climb to 10,000 feet and headed on a course of 140 degrees to Tapachula.

After about two hours, we were still over a solid undercast. Not knowing how far south these clouds extended, I decided to change course for Vera Cruz, situated on the edge of the Gulf of Mexico. Vera Cruz, I thought, might be open, as it was on the water, and I would have cleared the higher mountains and been over fairly flat terrain. Keeping careful track of time and estimated ground speed and hoping the wind had not drifted me off course, I figured that we should now be over Vera Cruz. I turned to Baldy. "We should be well clear of these mountains and over Vera Cruz, so I'm going down through this stuff." Baldy nodded his approval, so I throttled back and at 8,000 feet entered the cloud layer. The altimeter started unwinding: 7,000, 6,000, 5,000, and still no break. Had we cleared the mountains? We must have, for the map showed 5,000-foot elevation just north of Vera Cruz. Four thousand, three thousand, and still no break. I was really getting worried. Was the ceiling zero at Vera Cruz? I glanced at the altimeter; the needle was creeping up on 2,000. I caught a brief glimpse of ground. The clouds were breaking up. Down to 1,500 and now directly below us was a circle in the middle of a field: the airport of Vera Cruz.

From here to Tapachula we had sufficient ceiling to stay under the clouds. Refueling and clearing customs took only about an hour (it was easier getting out of Mexico than getting in) and then on to Guatemala City, another city on our route, over 5,000 feet above sea level.

We took off the following morning for Tegucigalpa, the final leg of our journey. (This time I was careful to properly adjust the mixture controls.) From the army communications system, I was able to get a weather report from San Salvador, indicating scattered thunderstorms along the route. However, about thirty minutes out of Guatemala City, we ran into heavy squalls and lowering ceiling, the clouds completely obscuring the mountains ahead. We couldn't possibly continue on our course to Tegucigalpa.

I told Baldy to take over while I studied the map. San Lorenzo, a small village on the Gulf of Fonseca, situated on the Pacific Coast of Honduras, seemed a possible alternative. The weather behind us had closed in, so there was no turning back to Guatamala City. Anyway, I knew that there was a good airfield at San Lorenzo, formerly used by Pan American before they moved their operations to Tegucigalpa. Besides, San Lorenzo was our ultimate destination, my base of operations for flying freight into the mine.

"Okay, Baldy, let's head for San Lorenzo." I gave him a heading of 167 degrees.

"It does look a little brighter that way," he replied.

We continued on for another half-hour; San Lorenzo could only be a few more minutes' flying. Visibility was decreasing rapidly and to my alarm there appeared directly ahead a well-defined line squall that extended from the Pacific Ocean as far inland as I could see—so close to a safe landing, yet so far. It would be foolhardy to try to fly through this line squall.

I said to Baldy, "Our only hope now is to head for the coast and turn north, hoping we can get into San Salvador; if we can't, we can always land on the beach, but from the looks of this map we will probably crack up."

Baldy nodded; he looked plenty serious. The beach looked very narrow. If we did have to land, one wheel would be in the water, the other in soft sand. Now we were flying under 500-foot ceiling through intermittent squalls. The mountains on our right were completely obscured by dark nimbus clouds. Our position was so remote that we seemed to be navigating on another planet.

Continuing on north, I now estimated our position to be near the boundary of Honduras and El Salvador. Another thirty minutes elapsed, and there seemed to be a break in the clouds. Approaching closer to the mountain range, I could see a pass that, from the map, I knew would lead into a wide valley in which both the airport and the capitol, San Salvador, was situated. I glanced at the gas gauges; the pointers were indicating zero. But I knew we had a few minutes' more fuel left. We were now opposite the pass. There seemed to be sufficient ceiling at the entrance, but farther ahead the clouds dropped again. If this pass continued on into the valley, all well and good. If this was a blind alley and a mountain peak was sticking up into the cloud layer— but again the map indicated that this pass should be clear. And I was confident that once into the valley, we would have sufficient ceiling to continue on to the airport.

I banked the airplane to the right and entered the pass. "Hold tight, Baldy; we're going through." Baldy looked unhappy, but said nothing. We were in the clouds for perhaps two minutes, and then the valley opened below us. There were only scattered clouds above, and visibility was at least ten miles. Lake Illapango, near which the airport was situated, lay directly ahead. I made a straight-in approach, and before I quite reached the hangar at the end of the field, the engines started sputtering. We were out of gas!

"You sure took a chance going through that pass blind," Baldy said with a grin.

"Yeah, but isn't this better than spending the night on that lonely beach in a cracked-up airplane?" I replied.

It was only a short hop the following morning to Tegucigalpa. Approaching the airfield, I understood very well what the Pan Am pilot had meant when he said to "roll your wheels in the banana patch or go around again." The field was surrounded by mountains except the only approach from the south. The city itself was situated on the north edge of the field. I circled over town, careful to miss a tall radio tower protruding from a hill to the north side of the field, and made a wide circle to the south, turned, and started my approach, not forgetting to touch my wheels in the proverbial banana patch, and landed on the rather rough turf field.

Well, we had finally made it. The last part of the flight had been rough—and not without a lot of tension on mine and Baldy's part. The passengers, too, were at times very apprehensive. Several times Prouty had come forward and peered into the cockpit with a worried expression.

I couldn't blame him. These people were flying with a crew they had never even heard of before, over rugged territory with which all of us were totally unfamiliar. Over the years I had had passengers who had caused me a lot of trouble, so I very much appreciated these people's exemplary behavior.

This airfield of Tegucigalpa, known as Toncontin, was the operating base for TACA (Transportes Aeros Centro Americanos) as well as the Honduran air force. Waiting to greet us were some TACA pilots, the American consul, Pan Am's resident manager, and Emilio LeFebvre, the manager of the Palace Hotel. Emilio took us in tow and drove us over narrow cobblestone streets to the hotel where we were assigned our respective rooms. The Palace Hotel (I was to find a Palace Hotel in almost every city in Central America) was very primitive indeed. As one entered the lobby, a very large room with a few chairs and lounges, a high ceiling fan gently stirred the stale tropical air.

Along the right side of the lobby were the guest rooms, including a "community" bath. On the left was the dining room and at the far end of the lobby a tiny bar. Only on special occasions, such as a dance or party, was there a bartender on duty. The established custom was for a guest who wanted a drink to go into the bar (it was never locked), help himself to whatever he wanted, and sign a chit for the proper amount and leave it in a receptacle on the back bar. To my surprise, there was never a record of anyone cheating this "honor system."

It so happened that on this, my first evening in Tegucigalpa, a dance was being held at the Palace Hotel. Soon after dinner, the lobby became crowded with young couples. The girls , some of whom were very pretty, were in their best dresses. I was introduced to a very attractive Italian girl and had the pleasure of dancing with her a couple of times. Later in the evening, I was sitting at the bar having a drink with Carlos Callejos, the local Pan Am manager, when a tall, rather ugly Honduran leaned over my shoulder and said, "Remember, you're in Honduras now."

"What's the matter with that guy?" I asked Carlos.

"Oh, don't pay any attention to him; he's just mad because you danced with his girl."

"Who is he anyway?"

"His name is Gonzales, he's a local attorney, and incidentally, he is Pan American's representative to the Honduran government." Carlos also informed me that Gonzales's girl friend was a person of some affluence: she owned a brick yard. Now I could better understand why Gonzales so jealously guarded what he considered his personal territory. I certainly hadn't gotten off to a very good start—my first day in

Honduras and already I had made an enemy of, of all people, a Honduran attorney.

Harold White, a TACA, pilot volunteered to lead me onto the airstrip at the Agua Fria Mine. So early the next morning I followed White, who was flying a Stinson monoplane, across the mountains to Agua Fria. It was only a twenty-minute flight, and as we circled over the area, I thought, *This field is laid out wrong,* but as it was the only open area in this mountainous region, I realized that it was probably the best they could do. A turf landing strip some 1,500 feet long extended from the mouth of a canyon north to the foot of a wooded hill about 500 feet high. You could make your approach for a landing either through the canyon from the south or come in over the mountain from the north. However, the approach over the hill would, with a heavily loaded airplane, bring me in so high that I would have used up too much of the field by the time my wheels touched to effect a safe landing.

Following White in his little Stinson, I saw that he was circling to the north for an approach over the mountain. Being unfamiliar with the whole area, I decided it best to follow White, who was familiar with the field. Of course, White, flying a small single-engine airplane, could land almost any way he wanted to. But even though my Ford was practically empty, it was going to be a close-shave landing over that hill. White had landed and taxied over to the side of the field as I throttled back for my approach. I was coming in as low as possible over the mountain when I heard a banging noise underneath the plane. My landing gear was brushing the treetops. I landed all right, but used every foot of the strip before bringing the airplane to a stop. I knew now that there was only one way to land on that strip; through the canyon from Danli.

Baldy and I flew back to Teguc, gathered up our luggage, and headed for San Lorenzo. San Lorenzo was a small native village some seventy miles south of Teguc, situated on the banks of a jungle river that emptied into the Gulf of Fonseca. The island port of Amapola served the Pacific coast of Honduras, referred to by most Hondurans as the South Coast due to the curvature of Central America.

The airfield, a mile out of the village, was owned by Pan American Airways. Pan Am had abandoned the field in favor of the airport of Toncontin to better serve the capital city, thereby eliminating a five-hour drive over a mountainous road to Teguc. If their passengers were not nervous from flying over these mountainous jungles, they would really be "shook up" driving over the road to Teguc.

The field at San Lorenzo proved quite adequate, a turf strip 2,500 feet long, and as it was at sea level, there would be no problem taking off with heavy loads. We were met by George Gray, a Pan Am radio operator; Pastora, a native woman who informed me that she was the cook; and another woman Pastora introduced as her assistant. Also there was a little, short native of indeterminate age whose name was Nunius, who with his wife, lived in a little shack adjacent to the flying field.

George Gray had been stationed at San Lorenzo for some time, sending weather reports to company planes in flight. The mining company had negotiated an agreement with Pan Am to pay half of George's salary, for we would need him to handle our traffic with the mine and Pan Am wanted him to continue providing weather reports for their aircraft flying over Honduras.

After the greetings were over, Nunius approached me and asked if there was any work he could do. He seemed like a nice, little guy, always smiling, and I took an immediate liking to him.

"All right, Nunius," I said, "you will be 'Jefe de Avion.' That means you are to keep this airplane clean at all times; also you'll help Señor Clark with any little jobs he needs you for."

Nunius just beamed; my giving him the title of "Jefe" (Chief) made him feel really important. And from that day on he kept that airplane immaculate and willingly did anything Baldy asked of him.

Pan Am had provided excellent accommodations on the field for their personnel. The buildings were all of concrete-block construction with red tile roofs. The group consisted of an office building with a radio room, a room for desk space and storage, and another room in which the radio operator slept. Another building consisting of two bedrooms provided Baldy and me each with a separate room. Across from our quarters were the dining room, kitchen, and sleeping quarters for Pastora and her helper. A few dozen yards down from our quarters was another building comprising a shower room and toilets. While our living quarters were more than adequate, the almost unbearable tropic heat, together with the atrocious food (fried black beans, rice, and tortillas), made life somewhat less than comfortable.

The operating procedure for the development of the mine started in San Pedro, California, where machinery and supplies were loaded aboard a Grace Line freighter, which, after several days' voyage, dropped anchor in the roadstead off the island of Amapola, the Pacific-coast port of Honduras. The freight was unloaded onto lighters and towed across the Gulf of Fonseca and thence up a winding jungle river to the mainland village of San Lorenzo. It was then transferred to ox carts and hauled out to the airfield and again unloaded into a *bodega* (warehouse).

146

Ford Trimotor loaded with freight for Agua Fria Mine

Ford Trimotor alongside oxcart in San Lorenzo, Honduras

In this manner, every conceivable piece of equipment needed to get a gold mine in operation, plus food and incidentals (also shipped down from the States), finally reached the mine site by airborne freight. Some of the machinery flown into the mine was fabricated in sections small enough to fit into the airplane. We transported a fifty-ton ball mill, a complete hydroelectric plant, a sawmill, and thousands of pounds of dynamite. I, at first, felt a little uncomfortable, sitting in the pilot's seat with 3,000 pounds of dynamite behind me, but it soon became routine.

My first flight with a heavy load (a sawmill) went very well. This time I entered the canyon from the south at Danli. Once you entered the canyon, you were committed to a landing. There was not sufficient room to make a 180-degree turn and go back in the event you encountered bad weather halfway through the canyon. Also, the mountains were too high to climb on top. I passed over the mill under construction on the west slope of the mountain, throttled back for my approach, although I could not see the landing strip for the canyon, and made a sharp curve to the right. Following this bend to the east with my right wing close by the pine trees, I suddenly saw the landing area, which was now on my left. Turning on final approach, we came in low over a *barranca* (steep cliff) and landed uphill, then rolled downhill for several hundred feet before coming to a stop. I turned and taxied up to a loading derrick that had been installed on the edge of the field. Baldy got out and removed the fuselage hatch; the derrick boom swung over the opening and in a few minutes the airplane was unloaded.

I elected to take off to the north over this low mountain, which I could easily clear with an empty airplane. In twenty minutes we were back on the ground at San Lorenzo. I would repeat this performance daily (except Sunday) for many months to come, until eventually the mine would start producing gold and then we would be flying concentrates from the mill to San Lorenzo. The concentrates would travel by ship to a smelter at Selby, California, where they would be reduced to gold bullion.

Honduras, at the time of which I write, was the most backward of all the Central America republics. The country has a long history of revolutions, some, it is said, instigated by United Fruit Company in order to obtain long-term land concessions for growing their bananas. Samuel Zemurray, a Russian Jew whose real name was Samuel Zmuri, founded a banana empire. Known as Sam, the Banana Man, he formed the Cuyamel Company, which he later sold to United Fruit for $31,500,000 thereby becoming United Fruit's largest single stockholder.

A tale I often heard told while I was flying for the Agua Fria Mine in Honduras was the story of Zemurray's conquest of Honduras. While in New Orleans, Zemurray enlisted the aid of Gen. Lee Christmas and Machine Gun Guy Molony, both soldiers of fortune.

Zemurray met with the two adventurers and, escaping from the watchful eye of the secret service, boarded his yacht, anchored off New Orleans, and set sail for Puerto Cortes, Honduras. From Puerto Cortes, Lee Christmas and Guy Molony, equipped with one machine gun, several cases of rifles, and three thousand rounds of ammunition, together with several thousand "Indians," marched over the mountains to Tegucigalpa. Upon the arrival of this formidable "army," the incumbent president was forced to resign. A new election was held and Manuel Bonilla (Zemurray's man) won an overwhelming victory. Zemurray won the concession he was after, duly approved by the new congress. Bonilla made Lee Christmas general of the Honduran army, and Guy Molony was appointed chief of police of Tegucigalpa. Molony took up residence in the Palace Hotel. Across the park from the hotel the church bells would start ringing every morning at 5 o'clock. This greatly annoyed Molony, so he would start shooting through the window at the church bells. However, there is no record that this procedure ever stopped the bells from ringing.

Honduras, at the time of my arrival, was the headquarters for some very colorful characters. Foremost among them was Lowell Yerex, a native of New Zealand who had established TACA Airlines and was running the airline with a remarkable degree of efficiency. Yerex had been flying for a local airline out of Mexico City when he met up with an American dentist who owned an old Stinson monoplane. The dentist, who was not a pilot, persuaded Yerex to accept his offer of a half-interest in the airplane, and together they would head for Central America.

Yerex and the dentist eventually arrived in Tegucigalpa with their decrepit, old Stinson just at the time that a revolution of sorts was taking place. In those days, there was always some sort of so-called revolution going on in Honduras. There were two political parties, the Reds were in power and of course the Blues were fighting to get in. The leader of the Blue party was a tough, old Indian from the backcountry by the name of Tiburcio Carios Andina. Yerex met Carios at the Palace Hotel bar one evening, and Carios, having heard that Yerex had flown his own airplane in to Toncontin, offered him any government position he wanted if Yerex would only drop some bombs on the Reds. Carios was convinced that with the aid of Yerex's bombing, his side would win and he would take over as president.

It so happened that Yerex met that same evening Guy Molony,

and over drinks Molony offered to act as Yerex's bombardier. The next day, they fashioned some makeshift bombs out of dynamite, glass, scraps of tin cans, and whatever else they could find that might do some damage. Carios informed Yerex that a contingent of armed Reds was assembled near the Nicaraguan border, preparing to march on Tegucigalpa, and asked him to fly over there and drop some bombs. It was only about thirty minutes' flying from Toncontin, so Yerex and Molony loaded some of the homemade bombs into the Stinson and took off. Molony still had his machine gun, with which, he said, if the occasion arose, they would "ground strafe" the "enemy."

Yerex found the Red encampment with no trouble and dropped some bombs from a very low altitude. The Reds started firing from the ground, and a bullet hit one of the metal longerons (an aluminum section of the airframe), ricocheted, and hit Yerex in his right eye. Fortunately, he did not lose consciousness, and with Molony holding a handkerchief over his eye to stop the blood flow, he was able to fly back to Teguc and land safely on the airfield.

Yerex lost his eye, the Blues won, and Carios was installed as president. True to his word, Carios offered Yerex any position he wanted. He told Carios that he was not interested in a government job, but wanted to start an air service and needed money to purchase airplanes and other equipment. Yerex had by this time become quite a hero, at least to the Blue party, which was now firmly entrenched as the governing power. So Carios without hesitation had congress appropriate the necessary funds requested by Yerex. Thus the airline known as TACA was born.

Yerex, the Aviator of Fortune did not look like an adventurer. His appearance, always immaculate in business suit and wearing spectacles, was more that of a banker. But he ran his airline with a firm hand and demanded the utmost from his pilots. On several occasions when a pilot canceled his flight on account of weather, Yerex would climb into the airplane and take off, always completing his schedule. This of course did not endear him to his pilots. He established a "staff house" and required all of his personnel to live there. On several occasions when I was invited to dinner, we would all march into the dining room and everyone stand behind their chair until Yerex entered and was seated.

In spite of Yerex's dictatorial method of operation, his pilots and, in fact, all other personnel were quite loyal to him and I heard of few complaints. This was all the more astonishing to me, for the pilots who flew for TACA were a swashbuckling, independent, and determined lot. All of the pilots were American except one Honduran by the name of Fiaras. There was Charlie Mathews, whose chief duty was that of maintenance superintendent, Fred Young, Ken Mathewson, Harold White, and Ed Brice. Ed and I were to become good friends in later years when he was flying out of Miami. His untimely death several years ago was a deep shock not only to his wife, Dorothy, but to all of us who knew him. He was a great guy.

Eric Holmberg, chief of communications for TACA, was a native of Sweden, another adventurer who had somehow found his way to Honduras. Eric was living at the Palace Hotel; he had somehow managed to evade Yerex's edict that all personnel live at the staff house. Eric, who liked to drink (so did we all), was a very likable chap. And on the occasions when I would spend a night in Tegucigalpa, we would procure a bottle of Scotch from the bar (leaving our signed chit) and retire to his room or mine and, with the aid of the Scotch, try to settle the affairs of the world.

Another character living at the hotel whom I must mention was a woman with the unusual name of Astrid Dam. A native of Denmark, she had been working her way around Central and South America. Miss Dam had arrived in Honduras about a year before from Santiago, Chile, and was presently employed by the Banco Atlantido in Tegucigalpa. Although of Scandinavian ancestry, she was a tall, dark-haired, strikingly pretty girl. Needless to say a beautiful Danish woman living alone in Tegucigalpa did not lack for male companionship. Astrid and I became good friends, and when I flew into Teguc for a weekend, we would often have dinner together. Sometimes there was a party at the hotel, and then I would be lucky to have one dance with her. She would give me magazines and newspapers that she had saved up and usually came out to the airport to see me off for San Lorenzo. I have often wondered whatever became of that beautiful, intelligent woman who was the female counterpart of the male soldier of fortune.

Living in San Lorenzo could drive one mad. In fact, it had done just that to a couple of Americans, Pan Am employees living there before our arrival. The heat was almost unbearable, and the food, fried beans and rice, was hardly of gourmet quality. There was absolutely nothing to do but drink. Of course, due to our work schedule, there had to be a limit to this sort of thing. We couldn't fly freight into this mine every day with a continuous hangover.

Poor George Gray, the radio operator, finally was fired by Pan Am for drinking too much and was replaced by a young man named Billy Begg. Billy was another of those implausible people one meets in the tropics. He was a tall, handsome young man with dark-brown hair and pale complexion. Billy, in spite of the tropical sun, never seemed to even get a tan. He was a very meticulous guy. He always appeared as if he had just stepped out of the shower, his white linen shirt and slacks immaculately clean and well pressed. He slept in silk pajamas. Billy's tastes seemed more in consonance with a New Orleans drawing room than this dirty tropical dump called San Lorenzo. Billy drank as much as George Gray, but he handled it better. He never appeared intoxicated and he never missed a weather schedule with either a Pan Am aircraft or traffic with the mine.

The native Honduran, an admixture of Indian and Spanish, was, when sober, an amiable friendly person. But when drunk on *guaro,* a drink distilled from sugarcane and I don't know what else, they thought nothing of cutting each other up with a machete or blowing each other's heads off with a handgun. Because of this, most of us gringos carried a pistol. I, for one, was not about to get my head chopped off with a machete, so I always carried a .38 long-barreled special in a holster slung low from the belt around my waist.

There was a building called the Hotel Marina situated on the river front, built on stilts because of the high tides. It was a terrible shack with a few rooms and a bar. One could get a meal there, if one could stand the horrible food. The bar was tended by an American-Mexican whose name was McAllister. It was my, Bill's, and Baldy's custom, after landing from the last flight from the mine for that day, to get into the station wagon (courtesy Pan American Airways) and drive the mile to the village and the Hotel Marina.

One day the three of us, Bill, Baldy, and I, arrived at the bar late in the afternoon, sat down at a table, and ordered a drink. I was sitting with my back to the railing overlooking the river, Baldy sitting on my left and Billy on my right, when a short, stocky Indian walked over to our table and demanded that we buy him a beer. I had never seen this guy before. In fact, I hadn't even seen him when we walked into the bar. But now he really attracted my attention, for the native was a walking arsenal. On his right hip hung a .38 long-barreled special, on his left a Colt .45 automatic. From his left shoulder hung a machete encased in a leather scabbard. To add to all this weaponry, across his chest were two bandoliers of ammunition.

Baldy turned to me and asked, "Do you want to buy him a beer?" I shook my head, and Baldy asked Billy the same question. Billy, too, shook his head in the negative. Now this "walking arsenal" was standing opposite me across the table not four feet away and I suddenly realized that we were unarmed; the three of us had somehow forgotten our guns. The native just stood there patting the butt of the .38, drawing it half out of the holster, all the while glaring at me. Suddenly he jerked the gun out of the holster and raised it high in the air, cocking the hammer as it went up. He then started lowering the gun slowly, its muzzle pointed directly at me, and when the barrel reached down to where I thought my feet were, he started firing. By reflex action, I drew my feet up as high as I could while he shot the floor full of holes. This all happened so abruptly I really hadn't time to become frightened. I remember, though, glancing at Baldy and Bill and noting that they both were very pale, and I also remember thinking that I perhaps was paler than either of them.

As the native started to reload his gun, McAllister arrived with our drinks. I said to Mac, "Get this guy a beer; get him a case of beer if he wants it." While Mac was back at the bar retrieving a beer from the icebox (he seemed awfully slow about this), our erstwhile nemesis proceeded to pull out his machete and took a swipe at us, missing our throats by short inches. I was thinking, *Mac, bring the beer, quick!* I would much rather get shot than cut up with a machete. Mac finally arrived with an opened bottle of beer. The native took the bottle and shoved it down the front of his pants, turned, and said, "I go now." Without conscious effort, I heard myself say, "*Con mucho gusto* [with much pleasure]."

As I said before, none of us had ever seen this chap before, but I later learned that he was one of a few natives whom the government of Honduras had commissioned to go into the hills and shoot the bandits. These men were given just enough money to buy weapons and ammunition, but instead of shooting bandits, they would raid the villages, robbing the local merchants and otherwise creating havoc among the village inhabitants.

Whenever we visited the Marina bar, we almost always encountered a small, nondescript native by the name of Igapita Salgado. His clothes, what there were of them, were dirty, and he was invariably drunk. However, he did speak fairly good English, and I had been told that he was a good friend of President Carios. This I couldn't believe. But one day, Igapita appeared at our quarters at the airfield, immaculately dressed in a business suit, complete with white shirt and tie, and he was sober.

Now, as I pointed out earlier, the Honduran air force was also based at Toncontin. At that time, their aircraft consisted of four Stinson biplanes especially built for the air force. Their armament consisted of two Browning machine guns operated by the pilot firing through the propellor. The rear seat was equipped with a rotating gun turret with a Lewis machine gun operated by a gunner or observer.

There being one or two Honduran pilots (and they were hardly qualified as fighter pilots), it was the custom that TACA pilots would fly what missions were necessary. And the few missions consisted of flying over the countryside, usually near the Nicaraguan border, ground strafing some Reds.

Igapita proceeded to tell me that he had just come from Tegucigalpa, where he had visited the president at his office in the presidential palace. It seems that, according to Igapita, Carios was dissatisfied with the way Yerex was handling his air force. (Yerex was of course the commanding officer, for it was his pilots who actually flew these military airplanes.) Carios thought that Yerex was devoting all his time to his airline, thereby neglecting the military operations. To sum up, he wanted to fire Yerex and find someone else to head up his air force.

For some reason, I had made quite an impression on Igapita Salgado. So he now informed me that he had recommended to the president that I be appointed chief of the Honduran air force. He said that he had told Carios that I would not hesitate to shoot up the whole republic if it became necessary. I had unwittingly assumed the role of "soldier of fortune."

Igapita said, "I am going back to Teguc. The next time you land at Toncontin, call me at this number," handing me a slip of paper, "and we will meet with El Presidente."

"Okay, Igapita. I'll call you, but this sounds to me like a Richard Harding Davis chronicle."

Thinking over these bizarre events of the past week, I came to the conclusion that: 1) Lowell Yerex was not about to relinquish control of military aviation in Honduras; after all, the Honduran air force was *his* security, too. 2) Carios would certainly not *force* the ouster of Yerex as commander of the air force: he owed Yerex too much. But what the hell? I might as well play along with Igapita; it would be a lot of fun, and anyway, I would get to talk with a president of a republic.

In the meantime, Prouty and I had come to an understanding: If a replacement pilot was available, I would be released from my job, which I had gotten fed up with anyway. I was tired of living under such lousy conditions, and my pay was meager indeed. It appeared that a guy named Morgan, an American living in Honduras who professed to have considerable time on Ford trimotors, was available and had been recommended to Prouty. I was asked to check Morgan out landing at the mine. This procedure proved a near disaster. I had put Morgan in the pilot's seat at San Lorenzo and told him to go ahead and fly to the mine just as if I weren't aboard. After all, he was supposed to be a Ford pilot. I had deliberately lightened the load to 2,000 pounds. We came in through the canyon, and Morgan started his approach much too high, but I decided he had enough room to make it. We hit the ground hard, bounced about six feet in the air, and hit again, this time with the airplane headed across the field toward a swamp. Fortunately, it turned away from the loading derrick, or we both would have been killed. The worst of it was that Morgan did nothing to correct his mistake. I grabbed the brake, shoved open the left throttle, and managed to straighten the airplane out and taxi it up to the loading derrick. I was so angry I could have hit Morgan over the head with a spanner wrench. I saw Prouty standing near the derrick and knew he had witnessed the whole thing.

I got out of the airplane, walked over to Prouty, and just looked at him. I was too angry to talk.

He looked at me and said, "Bad landing, wasn't it?"

"What do you think?" I replied.

"Okay. Take Morgan back to Tegucigalpa. I'm afraid you'll have to stay on a while longer," he said.

"Okay Prouty, I'll give you two more weeks to get a pilot down from the States. And," I added, "that's going to be it."

On the flight back to Tocontin, neither Morgan nor I said one word. Immediately after landing, I called Igapita. He said, "Meet me at the palace in half an hour."

"Wait a minute, Igapita. I'm hardly dressed to meet with a president. Give me a chance to go to the hotel and clean up and change clothes."

"Okay," he said. "Make it an hour."

I met Igapita outside the palace gates. There was a uniformed guard on duty, but Igapita and I just brushed right past him into the austere-looking building. We went up the stairs to the second floor, and another uniformed guard ushered us into the president's office. Carios was a rather burly man with a clipped mustache. He had the coloring and facial lines of an Indian, which he predominantly was. He greeted Igapita warmly (I still couldn't believe this, to me, strange relationship, having known Igapita at his worst) and shook hands with me cordially.

The conversation was mostly in Spanish, and my Spanish was so limited that very frequently Igapita had to interpret for me. Carios's questions were brief and to the point. He wanted to know what military experience I had, how much time in military aviation, and would I be willing to defend his regime by using armed force, in other words bombing and strafing the Reds. The interview lasted about thirty minutes. Carios rose from behind his desk, shook my hand, and said, "The next time you are in Teguc, come see me. Igapita will arrange it." As Igapita and I were walking down the stairs, Igapita said, "You did all right; he wants you."

Walking through the gates of the palace grounds, we were confronted by a tall young Honduran who was just about to enter. He greeted Igapita warmly and was introduced as the minister of war. Igapita explained to him our interview with Carios. This young man (I have forgotten his name) suddenly showed great interest in me. It seems he, too, wanted a new chief of the air force. He insisted that I return soon for a second interview with Carios.

In the meantime, one of the TACA pilots told me of an opportunity in Nicaragua. He said that someone had flown an old Ford with Wright J-5 engines in to Managua and had apparently abandoned it. A local businessman by the name of Don Luis Palazio had expressed a desire for an experienced pilot to come over and start an airline with this one piece of equipment. I was further told that this could be a great opportunity for me, as Palazio was very wealthy and also had the confidence of the government. He offered to fly me over to Managua for an interview.

From my talk with Ken Matheson, the TACA pilot, and realizing the vast potential for aviation in Central America, I decided that Nicaragua was the place for me.

About a week later, my two weeks' notice to Prouty was nearing an end. I flew back into Toncontin and repaired to the Palace Hotel. At breakfast the next morning, I was introduced to a big six-foot Texan who had just arrived on Pan Am as my replacement. I told Brown, or whatever his name was, that I was glad to meet him, but as far as flying the Ford into the mine, he was entirely on his own. I explained my near-disaster with Morgan and told him I was taking no chances on sticking my neck out again. I said, "The airplane is on the ground at Toncontin. Baldy here knows the mine and its approaches as well as I do. So he will show you the way in. It's nice to have met you. Good luck and may your stay in San Lorenzo be a pleasant one." This last of course was pure sarcasm.

I called Igapita and he came by the hotel. We had an appointment at the palace in an hour. The minister of war also wanted to see me.

On our walk over to the palace, Igapita said, "You know that SOB Gonzales told me he was going to kill you. I said, 'You kill Jerdone; I kill you.' That ended the matter." So Gonzales never got over his hatred of me, incurred that first night of my arrival.

We entered the palace and sat down in what passed for a reception room on the first floor. Igapita said, "You wait here while I first speak with the president."

While I was waiting for Igapita, Lowell Yerex appeared and hastily mounted the stairs to the president's office. I thought, *Now they will learn that they simply cannot make me minister of aviation or whatever.*

After about twenty minutes, Yerex left and Igapita and the war minister returned. They both wore long faces.

The minister said, "Yerex won't agree on this deal, but you wait a few days; we'll arrange everything."

I said, "Listen. I told you both that Yerex would never consent to this arrangement, so I'm leaving for Managua."

The minister said, "Please don't go to Managua; just wait a few days."

"My plane leaves for Managua tomorrow morning, and I'm going to be on it."

This seemed to shake up the minister badly. I knew what he was thinking; Jerdone would go to Nicaragua and organize the Reds on the border and start an invasion of Tegucigalpa. Preposterous, of course. But I had learned how these Indians think.

Igapita didn't want me to go either, but he was more philosophical about it. That night, my last in Honduras, we had a big party at the hotel. Igapita acted as host. Some of my friends from TACA—Emilio LeFebvre, the manager, and many others—attended. We drank heartily, for tomorrow I would embark on another adventure in Central America.

Chapter 18   Nicaragua

Ken Mathews was the pilot of that little Stinson Reliant that flew me to Managua on that early December morning of 1934. We were met at the airport by a former Hungarian citizen whose name, he informed us, was Pataky. Pataky, a nervous type who seemed the walking definition of perpetual motion, drove me promptly to the office of Don Luis Palazio, who had arrived in Nicaragua from Italy only a few years before. Don Luis had, in these few short years, acquired considerable wealth and was now one of the leading businessmen of Managua.

Don Luis, a heavyset, dark-haired man in his late forties, greeted me affably and introduced me to his brother, Carlos, a somewhat effeminate man, and a Bob Ewalt, who, I learned was a former enlisted marine-corps pilot. Don Luis pulled a bottle of whiskey from his desk drawer and offered us a drink, which at first we all refused—after all, it was only 11 o'clock in the morning.

Don Luis explained that there was an old Ford trimotor out at the airport as well as a Waco cabin plane owned by the Guardia Nacional, but with the compliments of Gen. Anastasio Somoza, it was at my disposal. Don Luis also indicated that should our initial efforts in running an airline prove successful, he would furnish the financial backing necessary for further expansion. In other words, more and better airplanes and additional personnel were required to operate an expanded airline.

Finally Palazio turned to Pataky and said, "Take Jerdone out to the field and let him fly the Ford." He seemed satisfied that I was the guy to run an airline in Nigaragua, although he had not asked me one question as to my experience or background. I'm sure he knew all about me long before my arrival in Managua.

We arrived at the airfield and pulled up alongside the Ford, which was parked in front of an old wooden hangar. We got out of the car and were greeted by a smiling, rather tall Nicaraguan whom Pataky introduced as Salvo. Salvo, it appeared, was the mechanic in charge of the Ford and would act also as my copilot and perform any other duties attendant to operating the two-plane airline. I immediately learned that Salvo spoke not a word of English. This, I thought, was going to be interesting, what with my meager knowledge of Spanish. I had hoped that Ewalt, an experienced pilot who knew the country, would be of some help to me, but Ewalt had simply disappeared. In fact, I was to see very little of Ewalt in the months to come.

Palazio had asked me to fly the Ford, so I thought I might as well get it over with. If this pile of junk held together long enough for me to circle the field and land, I would be lucky. I climbed aboard, motioning Salvo to follow me. I sat down in the pilot's seat with Salvo in the right-hand seat. He explained to me that the throttles would not stay open, as a set screw that, when triggered, held the throttles open, was missing. He also stated that the left engine was rough, but he thought it safe to fly. He explained all this in Spanish with the aid of hand motions. I was able to understand.

I started the left engine, with short exhaust stacks; it made an awful racket and poured out clouds of blue smoke. The center and right engines acted the same way. I ran up the engines, checked the magnetos, and deciding that they would function long enough for a short flight, motioned Salvo that I was ready for takeoff. Looking back into the cabin, I was horrified to see that the airplane was full of women. I yelled to Salvo to, "Get these women out of here. Where in hell did they come from anyway?" Sitting in the front seat to my right was a buxom rather pretty young woman with dark hair with whom Salvo was engaged in animated conversation. He returned presently to the cockpit and said that the woman he was talking to was the wife of General Somoza and she refused to leave the airplane. It seems that she had gotten word that I was going to fly the Ford and had invited her friends along for an airplane ride.

It was bad enough that I had to fly this old crate that should have long ago been relegated to the dump pile, but carrying a load of women, the upper crust of Nicaraguan society, was a risk I was very reluctant to take. We took off, Salvo holding the throttles open for me. I climbed to 1,500 feet, circled the field, and landed—one of the shortest flights I ever made. Actually, the airplane handled very well; the engines ran smoothly in spite of the racket they made. The ladies seemed to enjoy the flight, even though it lasted only about five minutes. They left the airplane all smiles and chattering away in rapid Spanish.

It was Christmas Eve and tomorrow I had a flight to Puerto Cabezas. Why it should be so important that I fly some freight to Puerto

Cabezas on Christmas Day I don't recall. Of course there was no celebrating Christmas for me, but my companion that evening was a Mexican-American by the name of "Machete" Rivas. Rivas sold machetes throughout Central America from Mexico to Panama. Tourists used to buy them for souvenirs, not realizing that they were actually made in Hartford, Connecticut.

There were a few horse-drawn vehicles in Managua at that time, so Rivas and I hired one and proceeded to drive around the city. Rivas, who had been drinking all afternoon, would hail a policeman and proceed to bawl him out in impeccable Spanish. This made me nervous, for I had no wish to spend Christmas Eve in a Nicaraguan jail. We ended up at the Azotea Club, a rather prestigious social club, and after a couple of dances with a pretty senorita, I called it a night and went back to the hotel and to bed.

I arrived at the airport early Christmas morning. The airplane was loaded and Salvo had run up the engines and we were ready to take off. Salvo said he knew the route, as he had been over it several times before. We would fly due east to Bluefields and thence north, following the coast of Puerto Cabezas, via Prinzapolka. Salvo informed me that our landing at Bluefields would be on the beach.

"What if the tide's in?" I asked.

Salvo grinned. "We land anyway," he said.

Sure enough, the tide was in. This was going to be a hairy landing, what with one wheel in the water and the other in soft sand. I turned to Salvo. "Here we go," I said as I throttled back for the approach to the beach. We landed okay, using both the Atlantic Ocean and the soft sand of what was left of the beach at high tide.

We continued flying up the coast, passing over the thatch-hut village of Prinzapolka, situated at the mouth of the Prinzapolka River. This village would be a stop on our regular scheduled run from Managua to Puerto Cabezas, which we would inaugurate later. Arriving over Puerto Cabezas, I circled the turf airfield, formerly used by the marines during their occupation of Nicaragua, and landed with plenty of room to spare. (What a relief after that hairy landing on the beach at Bluefields.)

At the time of which I write, Puerto Cabezas was a Standard Fruit town. It was also a port of call for the company's steamships that, in addition to bananas and miscellaneous freight, brought many tourists for a day's layover in this tropical setting. There were many frame houses occupied by the officials of the fruit company. Also, there was a huge clubhouse used for social gatherings, including a dining room open daily serving breakfast, lunch, and dinner.

The marines had landed in Nicaragua in 1927 and occupied the country through 1933, at which time they were ordered by President Hoover to evacuate the country. This was only two years before my arrival. The purpose of the marines' presence in Nicaragua was to put down a rebellion against the government of Nicaragua led by a Gen. Agustus C. Sandino. To the marines and the United States government, Sandino was a bandit who threatened the peace and stability of the government of Nicaragua. To most of the natives, especially those living in the rural areas, Sandino was a patriot who would overthrow the incumbent officials of the present government and provide a better life for the Sandinistas, who were able to eke out only a bare subsistence from the land that they did not own.

Most other Latin American nations were also *simpatico* to Sandino, and he had the backing and goodwill of many high-placed officials of these other Spanish-speaking countries. But in all their six-year campaign through the jungles of Nicaragua, with ample manpower and equipped with modern weaponry, including machine guns and automatic rifles and with adequate air support, the marines failed in their effort to capture Sandino or to inflict sufficient casualties to defeat his army. Actually, the marines were inexperienced in guerrilla warfare. Sandino's knowledge of the terrain and the support of the natives, most of whom were loyal to him, gave him the advantage; he would only fight when the odds were in his favor. He would strike and then vanish into the jungle.

It was only after the marines had left that Sandino offered to negotiate with the government of Nicaragua. At that time, Juan Batista Sacasa had become president and General Anastasio "Tacho" Somoza had been appointed commandant of the Guardia Nacional. The national guard, marine-corps trained and equipped, was by far the most formidable military force in all of Central America. Sandino made several journeys to Managua to confer with President Sacasa and General Somoza until the final one, when he was assassinated.

There were varied accounts of the assassination of Sandino that were told to me while I was in Nicaragua. However, I will relate the one that came to me from what I consider a reliable source and which also seems most plausible. It seems that what Sandino wanted was that the government of Nicaragua (in other words, Sacasa) grant him outright the Nueva Segovia territory for him to govern as he saw fit. Now Sacasa was amenable to Sandino's demand, but Tacho Somoza was violently opposed to any such action on the part of the government. In fact, Somoza was opposed to any concession to Sandino per se.

On this, which was to prove to be his last night on earth, Sandino had been invited to dine with Sacasa at the presidential palace. Also in attendance were other government officials, as well as General Somoza and some of his staff. After much after dinner talk, Sandino wished to call it a night and requested that he be driven back to his temporary place of residence. The presidential palace was situated on a hill overlooking the city of Managua. The road to the airport led down the hill toward the city and then made a right turn directly to the airport. At this junction, Sandino's car was stopped by a government vehicle from which there emerged three or four national guardsmen, led by Captain Guiterrez. The captain and one of his men got in Sandino's car and ordered the driver to proceed to the airport, the government vehicle following.

At the airport, Sandino and an aide were bound and stood up against a tree. A machine gun manned by a couple of guardsmen was set up, and with Sandino protesting vehemently, the captain gave the order to fire. At this time, Arthur Bliss Lane, our chargé d'affaires in Nicaragua, was entertaining company at the legation, situated on a hill overlooking the airport.

At the burst of machine-gun fire, Lane exclaimed, "My God, they've killed Sandino!" He jumped in his car and drove at top speed to Somoza's house, running a roadblock on the way.

Lane greeted Somoza with the same words; "They've killed Sandino."

Before Somoza could reply, there was a knock on the door and Captain Guiterrez entered and said, "General, I have killed Sandino."

Somoza replied, "The Guardia Nacional has killed Sandino."

Now as I have said, this is the version of Sandino's assassination as told to me. I cannot, of course, substantiate the validity of this account, but no doubt at least part of it is true.

Upon my return to Managua from Puerto Cabezas, Don Luis handed me a letter from Mr. Wolf who was in charge of United Airlines surplus-equipment sales. The letter stated that the airline was now receiving delivery of the new DC-3s and there were four Ford trimotors for sale. He also advised that if we were interested, they would sell one or all four of the planes and suggested that I come to Chicago to negotiate the purchase.

Don Luis suggested that I leave immediately for Chicago and, if the price and condition of the airplane was satisfactory, purchase one of the Fords and fly it back to Managua. We both realized that we could not operate an airline with one broken-down Ford airplane. Two days later, I left for Chicago on Pan American's flight to Brownsville, Texas, and thence via United to Chicago.

162

Shortly after checking into the Sherman Hotel, I received a call from Frank Ambrose, whom I had known some years before in New York. Frank was a dealer in surplus aircraft and had been extremely successful. Over the phone he said, "Frank, I understand you want to purchase one of United's Fords." I admitted that that was my intention. (How he learned of this and of the almost exact time of my arrival at the Sherman I never found out.) "I'm at the Stevens [now the Conrad Hilton], Room 1104. Come over here right away; I want to talk to you."

About forty minutes later, I was knocking on Frank's door. He greeted me warmly, asked me to be seated, and offered me a drink, which I refused. In dealing with Frank Ambrose, I needed to be as mentally alert as possible. Frank got right down to business. "As you know, United has only four Ford trimotors left and they are anxious to get rid of the lot. Now my client has authorized me to negotiate for two of them, and if you could take the other two, we would really be in a good bargaining position."

"What do you think we could get them for?" I asked.

"These airplanes are the latest type Ford built. I have seen the logs on all of them, and they have very little time on both aircraft and engines. If you will let me do the negotiating, I think we can get them for $5,000.00 each."

"Well, that's quite a bargain, Frank, considering they cost about $90,000.00 new."

"But," I added, "I will have to cable Managua for authorization to purchase the second airplane. I will send it off immediately and should have a reply by tomorrow afternoon."

"Okay," Frank replied. "I'll wait another day, but time is important. I can't hold my client off more than a couple of days."

I went back to my hotel and wrote out a long cable to Palazio, explaining that we really needed the two aircraft and mentioning the low price Frank had estimated we could close for. The following afternoon, I received a cable from Don Luis: "Go ahead with the second airplane. Cabling National City Bank to honor United's draft for ten thousand dollars. Good luck, Palazio."

I called Frank. "We're in business. What's the next move?"

"E. P. Lott is in charge of sales here in Chicago. I'll phone for an appointment for tomorrow morning. Stand by. I'll call you right back." So "Everything Perfect" Lott whom I had known in Kansas City when he was operations manager for old National Air Transport, which was now a part of United Airlines, was the guy with whom we would have to bargain.

In a few minutes the phone rang. "It's all set for tomorrow morning at 9 o'clock. Meet me in Lott's office at Midway Airport." Frank's voice sounded jubilant; I could tell he would be waiting impatiently for tomorrow to come so that he could start doing what he did best—negotiating a business deal.

Frank was already waiting when I arrived at Lott's office. After the amenities were over, Lott and I shook hands, each making a passing remark about the old days at Kansas City. I sat back and, as I had promised, let Frank take charge of the business at hand.

It was a fascinating experience to watch Frank's masterful display of negotiating ability and his superb salesmanship. Lott was no slouch himself, but he was no match for Frank, who on every issue maneuvered him into the proverbial corner. At the end of the session, which lasted nearly two hours, we had closed the deal or, rather, Frank had, not only for the four airplanes but what sounded like a carload of spare parts. In addition, I was to get a free engine overhaul at United's Cheyenne shops on one of the airplanes that had the most time. Also we were to get free passage over United's system. This amounted to a lot of free airfare, as one of Frank's airplanes was located in Seattle and one of mine in Portland, Oregon. My other airplane was located in Oakland, California. I would hire a pilot to fly this one to Cheyenne for the free engine overhaul.

Frank and I found ourselves sitting across the aisle from each other on the flight from Chicago to Seattle. I had wired Thelma my time of arrival in Seattle and asked her to meet me. I was looking forward to a visit with her and Marilyn. Clearing the Cascades, we dropped down for a low approach to Boeing Field. The weather at Seattle had deteriorated, and the ceiling was now less than 500 feet. The pilot on his approach to the field was just clearing the apartment houses by only a few feet. We could almost reach out and grab the clothes drying on lines stretched from the rooftops. There was a roar of power as the pilot shoved the throttles full out. He had missed his approach and was going around again. Frank and I looked at each other. This procedure was not at all to our liking. To say that we both were on "pins and needles" was an understatement. Now we were on our second approach, again just missing those clotheslines. We passengers could not, of course, see the field ahead, only those buildings directly below us. There was another surge of power, another miss. Frank and I with white knuckles clutched our seats, belts tight around our waists.

Once again we were scraping the roofs of the buildings, our third attempt to land. I could now see the end of the runway. I thought, *We're too high; surely we will overshoot the field.* The ground kept rushing beneath us. "Damn it," I muttered to myself, "get this airplane on the ground." We hit, hard, and were rolling down the runway. I could feel the pilot braking frantically. At last, the airplane came to a stop. As the pilot turned to taxi back to the terminal, I saw that we had used every foot of runway. For Frank and me it was a hairy experience. Being pilots, we understood the situation only too well. The other passengers were better off. There's a case of ignorance being bliss.

Thelma, with Marilyn clutching her hand, greeted me warmly. She had watched these attempts at landing with considerable apprehension, for she knew enough about flying to understand the hazards involved in trying to land in this kind of weather. It was good to be with them again. Marilyn was now five years old—a pretty child and quite intelligent. It was a joy to be with her.

One night at dinner, I discussed with Thelma the possibility of our resuming our married life. I told her of my situation in Nicaragua, explaining that I thought it to be a great opportunity to develop a viable airline that would provide a sorely needed service to a country whose only form of surface transportation was a railroad running from Managua to Corinto, a distance of some 100 miles. I also explained to her the disadvantages of living in such a primitive country, a life-style so vastly different from that to which she was accustomed. She seemed somewhat amenable to my suggestion, but said she would think about it and let me know the following day.

Over a delightful seafood luncheon at a picturesque restaurant overlooking Puget Sound, she informed me that she had thought it over seriously and decided that we should try again. She would accompany me back to Nicaragua.

I told her I would take the night train to Portland and give the airplane a flight test and she and Marilyn could follow me in a day or two. I arrived at Swan Island Airport the following morning and hired a couple of mechanics to roll my airplane out of the hangar and run through a preflight routine. The airplane was in excellent condition; the engines were smooth and turned up their maximum RPMs. I took off and flew around for about an hour, enjoying the beautiful scenery. I landed on the 7,000-foot runway using only about a fourth of the distance; I was so accustomed to landing in unbelievably short fields in Honduras and Nicaragua that I instinctively landed short here at Swan Island; consequently I had to taxi about a mile to get to the terminal.

I met Thelma and Marilyn on the early-morning train from Seattle, and we took a taxi directly to the airport. The mechanics had the airplane ready for flight, so we climbed aboard and I took off, climbed to cruise altitude, and headed on a course for Oakland, California. I had said to Thelma, "We'll remain overnight in Oakland and continue on to Los Angeles tomorrow."

The flight down to Los Angeles was very pleasant, the weather clear, with brilliant sunshine and blue skies, with occasional white cumulus clouds. Landing at Burbank, we taxied to the Hollywood Plaza Hotel where I had lived so many months as a bachelor. This was to be our headquarters for at least a month, for I would be busy purchasing parts and equipment and hiring pilots and mechanics. I was fortunate in encountering Harry Downs, a former Lockheed test pilot and former marine-corps pilot in Nicaragua. Harry was temporarily unemployed and accepted my offer with not much hesitation. I asked Harry to fly to Oakland, pick up my Ford there, fly it to Cheyenne, wait there until the engine overhaul was completed, and then bring it back to Los Angeles. United had promised a two-week delivery date, which I thought was a remarkably short time.

I gave Charlie Babb, out at Glendale, an order for spare parts that amounted to quite a substantial dollar value, probably the biggest order Charlie had received in a long time.

I was now very much in need of a chief mechanic, and by inquiring around I was able to obtain the services of a man named Garrison, a former United mechanic who came highly recommended. And Gary did indeed prove to be a very valuable asset to the company. I couldn't have gotten along without him.

Harry arrived from Cheyenne with the newly overhauled engines and was enthusiastic with their performance. Things now were approaching the final stage. We started loading Harry's plane with all the freight, for he would be flying alone and I would have passengers.

When last in Chicago, I had visited my old friend Bob Wood, a reporter for the *Chicago Tribune.* I was telling Bob about my impending flight back to Nicaragua with the Fords when Peggy, his wife, exclaimed, "Gee, I'd like to go with you!"

I laughed; her statement was so sudden it somewhat startled me. I said, "Okay Peggy, if it's all right with Bob, I'll be glad to take you."

Much to my surprise, Bob said, "It's okay with me, Peggy. Go ahead. It'll be quite an adventure for you."

So upon my arrival in Los Angeles I wired Peggy my estimated time of departure from Los Angeles and told her if she still wanted to go along, she should be in LA not later than a date I gave her. Frankly, I had little doubt that she would change her mind in the meantime. However, much to my surprise she appeared one day at the hotel, eager to embark upon the flight south.

166

Another surprise was in store for me. Suddenly Pataky appeared upon the scene. He was still the perpetual-motion machine—dancing around, asking all sorts of questions. He said that both he and Palazio thought I had done a good job purchasing the airplanes at such a phenomenal price. I wondered whether Palazio had sent him to check up on me or he just wanted an excuse to get to the States and a free ride back to Managua. Perhaps both.

So bright and early one morning in March, we took off from Glendale, heading south for Nicaragua—Harry alone with his freight load and me with my passengers, the list now including Thelma and Marilyn, Peggy, and Pataky. We would fly the same old route; Mexicali, Mazatlan, Mexico City, and Tapachula.

The flight was uneventful until after we cleared out of Mexico at Tapachula. We left rather late in the afternoon for Managua, and that is where I used poor judgment. That time of year, the farmers burn their fields. From Mexico to Panama exists a smoke condition that very much restricts visibility. I was leading the flight and expected to check my position on Lake Illapango in El Salvador. Now my flying time indicated that I should have the lake off my right wing. But there was no lake Illapango to be seen. Well, I thought I'd continue on a few more minutes and surely I'd pick up the lake. After another ten minutes' flying, I knew I was in trouble. Having missed my checkpoint, I wasn't sure of my position. In those days, airports were few and far apart. Also, none was lighted, and there were no aids to navigation. In this latitude there was practically no twilight; from daylight there was sudden darkness. And as suddenly as darkness would descend, I found myself on the horns of a dilemma. The overwhelming truth that confronted me was that somehow both Harry and I had to get on the ground safely. But we were over rough country, treacherous jungle country, and there were few, if any, "safe" places to land. With only straight-down visibility, it was going to be difficult to find *any* place to try a landing.

I decided that Harry, who was carrying only freight, should be the first to try for a forced landing. After all, I was responsible for the lives of four passengers, not to mention my own wife and child. Also, I knew that Harry was a very capable pilot. (He later became Lord Beaverbrook's personal pilot.) But we had no radio in either plane. How would I communicate with him? I flew close alongside Harry's plane so the he could see me through his window. I wiggled my wings at the same time pointing downward. He waved and broke away, motioning me to follow. He had understood my message.

Almost immediately, Harry throttled back and started losing altitude. I followed him down until we were below a thousand feet. I now saw that we were over a small river and Harry was circling a postage-stamp-sized strip of sandy beach strewn with what looked like small boulders. Still circling, now below 500 feet, I watched Harry start his landing approach. He went in low, dragging the tops of some trees, and landed. he rolled about a hundred feet, and I thought, *God, he's gotten away with it.* But just at that moment I saw his airplane go up on its nose, the tail seemed to rise in slow motion, and the airplane came to a stop.

Now it was my turn. And I didn't have much time; it was getting dark and I could hardly see the trees as I came in nose high in a stall landing, pumping the throttles to keep her from falling off. I was determined not to nose up on *this* landing. I hit the sand, fortunately missing the boulders, and I rolled what seemed like only a hundred feet. And the airplane remained in an upright position—the shortest landing I would ever make! The passengers looked pale and of course nervous (so was I), but they took it as the good sports they were.

Night was fast approaching, but we still had just light enough to inspect Harry's plane. I rushed over to where he was standing. "Thanks for saving the day for us both," I said.

"Thanks for the compliment, but you made a magnificent landing. Thank God you didn't go on your nose. We've only got *one* spare prop," he added.

"Maybe that's why I got away with this landing," I replied. "My unconscious mind reminded me of that fact."

We checked our charts and found that we were about fifty miles south of San Salvador, the capital, on the Lempa River. Now visitors began to appear. All told, there seemed to be over 150 Indians—that is, mestizos, a mixture of Indian and Spanish. They kept jabbering away in Spanish, excited by our appearance from the sky, a scene they would talk about for the rest of their lives. I might add that they remained our overnight guests, sleeping under the wings of the airplane.

There was nothing to do now but prepare for the long night by making ourselves as comfortable as possible for sleeping in the airplane or else on the sandy beach. Garry and I removed the four seats and tried to make some sort of bed for Thelma and Marilyn. Garry and I elected to sleep in the cockpit, which meant sitting upright all night. Needless to say, we didn't get much sleep. Peggy, Pataky, and Harry took seats behind us. We had some emergency rations aboard, but nobody cared to eat. We were all too nervous.

About midnight, there was a knock on the cabin door. A barefoot Indian handed us a telegram. It was from the president of the republic, offering us any aid the government of El Salvador could extend us. Talk about jungle grapevine; we were fifty miles from the capital and there was no form of transportation except one's feet. From the time of our landing until the receipt of the president's telegram was a matter of approximately six hours. This act of jungle magic puzzles me to this day.

After an endless, sleepless night, finally came the dawn. The Indians, still with us, began to stir. Garry and I left our cramped seats and walked along the river's edge, surveying the terrain, estimating our chances of ever getting off the ground against such formidable obstacles as soft sand, huge rocks, and an unbelievably short run for the takeoff. We had landed just short of where the river made a right-angle bend and then extended in a straight line for a distance of only about 600 feet before making another right-angle turn. Even this area was strewn with rocks, which had to be cleared before any attempt to take off.

I said to Garry, "The first thing on the agenda is to change the center prop of Harry's plane. While you and Harry are doing that, I will try to put these native guests of ours to work clearing a runway for our takeoff attempt."

Garry nodded his agreement. "Changing props will offer no problem; there is no other damage to the airplane," he said.

It was now 7 o'clock, and already the heat under the tropical sun was stifling. I was still nervous as a cat, and this intense heat didn't help any. I helped Harry and Garry get the airplane back to level by throwing a line around the tail wheel and the three of us pulling the tail down to the ground. This was accomplished with no difficulty, and Harry and Garry were now ready to pull the bent prop and install the spare. I found a native who spoke a little English and explained to him we would have to clear the rocks off the available takeoff area and would he get his friends (over a hundred of them) to do this job for me. "Si, si," he answered with a wide grin. He seemed only too willing to oblige. My singling him out and sort of appointing him the leader enhanced his own self-importance immensely. So the Indians, under the command of Luis (he had told me his name when I first approached him), went to work clearing the rocks.

Harry and Garry were just finishing installing the new propellor when a man and a woman, each riding a beautiful bay horse, arrived, followed by a retinue of servants carrying huge hampers of food and lugging two wooden horses and several long boards. I never did learn the names of this aristocratic couple, or if I did I have forgotten them. But they were apparently Salvordorean ranchers and indeed of the country's aristocracy. The señor or *patron* came over and introduced himself as Don Something or other and then presented us to his very lovely señora. He asked a few questions as to our well-being and the nature of our "accident" and seemed genuinely interested in our welfare. In the meantime, the servants were setting up the table (the boards across the horses) and there appeared as if by magic huge stacks of food—eggs, ham, bacon, steaks, potatoes, rice, beans, and every conceivable vegetable. Unfortunately, due to my nervousness and the intense heat, I could eat hardly any of this delightful food. Harry felt more or less like I did, but the rest of my friends accounted for themselves in great fashion.

To me, these kind people taking the trouble to bring all this food and equipment from their hacienda to this isolated place on the banks of a jungle river in order to see that we strangers were properly fed was not only a most kind act of hospitality, but almost incredible. (When I read of the fighting and bloodshed that occurs in this little Central American country today, I think back on those calm, peaceful days and those hospitable, peaceful people of that time. It does indeed seem incredible that such a change has taken place.)

Luis and his boys had done a good job of clearing the beach, and the time had come to attempt a takeoff from this remote spot. I conferred with Harry: I would be the first to try to get off and, if successful, would fly to San Salvador. (After all, I had gotten us into this mess, so it was up to me to try to get us out.) I told Harry, "If I get off, you shouldn't have any trouble, so just follow me on to San Salvador."

I got the passengers aboard, tried to give them a reassuring smile, and took my seat in the cockpit. Garry took his place in the copilot's seat. I taxied to the very edge of the turn of the beach and headed toward the far end of the so-called runway. The natives had cleared away most of the rocks, but there was nothing they could do about the soft sand. There was about a ten-knot breeze, which I was headed into. This would be a help, and believe me, I needed all the help I could get. Garry held the brakes and I shoved the throttles full out. Checking the tachometers, I saw that all three engines were turning up their maximum RPMs. I yelled to Garry, "Okay here we go," and as Garry released the brakes, the plane started to move, but ever so slowly. I was just mushing along, the wheels deep in sand. Slowly, very slowly, our speed increased, but we were using the runway too quickly. Finally the tail came up and our speed increased a bit more. I glanced at the air-speed instrument; we were traveling at a sad fifty miles per hour. Only a hundred feet more to go now and we'd either be airborne or crash into the jungle ahead. I waited until the last possible moment, then pulled back on the control column. The plane seemed to hesitate briefly; then the wheels left the ground. We were airborne, but would she stay there or settle back to earth? She stayed in the air, and after picking up a little more speed, I started to climb. We had made it! But what a close one!

In about twenty minutes, we were over the airport at Lake Illapango. We landed and taxied up to a hangar in front of which stood a crowd of people. The word had gotten out. (Jungle grapevine?) We all piled out of the airplane and embraced each other. Our throats were very dry, so we all had a cold drink, and in ten minutes we sighted Harry approaching the field. We greeted him boisterously, yelling and cheering. He was all smiles.

Harry said, "Boy, I didn't think you'd make it. When you were a few feet off the ground, she started to settle and I thought *Oh my God, there she goes,* but then you picked up speed and hauled away."

"How'd you make it, Harry?"

"No trouble, but I tried to stay in your tracks, so that made it easier for me. But it was still hairy."

Even today as I look back on that incident of the Lempa River landing, it seems incredible that we should have landed in such a seemingly impossible place with two three-engine airplanes the size of the Fords and with capacity loads were able to take off from there and land at the airport of San Salvador—all with no damage to the airplanes except the bent center prop on Harry's aircraft.

After an hour's rest, we departed from San Salvador for the comparatively short flight to Managua. Palazio had arranged a welcoming party, and we were greeted warmly after touching down on the smooth turf field that was the Managua Airport.

We all moved into the Palace Hotel, as the house Palazio had arranged for us in the Dumbach Colony, a newly developed suburb of Managua, was not yet ready for occupancy. The next few days, Garry was busy checking the two Fords and Thelma and Peggy were getting acquainted with Managua. On my first flight to the Bonanza Mine via Bluefields, Prinzapolka, and Puerto Cabazes, which was to become a regular run, I took Peggy along as far as Puerto Cabazes and deposited her aboard a Standard Fruit steamship bound for New Orleans. Peggy had had quite an adventure—more, I am sure, than she had bargained for. Anyway, she was bubbling over with excitement as she told me good-bye with repeated thanks for a wonderful trip. I am sure that the events of that flight from Los Angeles will last in her memory always.

It was evident that this airline that we called Lineas Aeras Nicaraguense and, which a few years later, was to become officially Lanica, the national airline of Nicaragua, was to be a profitable operation. We soon obtained contracts to supply the two leading gold mines, Bonanza and La Luz, with all their supplies and equipment. In the case of Bonanza, we occasionally flew out gold bullion and ferried some of their personnel from the mine to Managua and back. For these and for an occasional charter, I usually used the little Waco.

Some weeks after I had been operating from our base in Managua, there arrived on the field a Boeing 39B single-engine mail plane piloted by Bill Kingsley, a former American Airlines pilot. Bill started his one-man operation almost immediately and very soon obtained sufficient business to keep him busy. He was a friendly competitor. Bill and I got along well, and he actually did us no competitive harm, for we had all the business we could take care of anyway.

One day on a flight from Bonanza Mine to Managua, Bill failed to arrive on schedule. We waited until dark and still no Bill. He had simply disappeared, down somewhere in that dense jungle, over which we all flew on the course to Bonanza. For days after Bill was reported missing, both Harry and I flew low over the jungle, searching for the wreckage of an airplane but knowing full well that our chances of spotting it were slim indeed. Some of those trees were nearly 200 feet tall, and when an airplane crashes, the tops of the trees open up and the plane dives into the ground. However, the treetops close in and the airplane becomes invisible from the air. A ground search would be an exercise in futility, for to make any progress walking in the jungle, one would have to cut his way through the thick underbrush with machetes.

Some eighteen years after this incident, while in business in Miami, I had occasion to fly to Nicaragua with my friend Bill Quick, who at that time was operating an airline from Miami to Managua via Puerto Cabezes and the Bonanza Mine. In the meantime, Puerto Cabezes had ceased to be a Standard Fruit town and had become a center for the timber industry. We learned upon landing at Puerto Cabezes that a couple of "timber cruisers," in their search for suitable timber, had stumbled across Bill Kingley's skeleton, propped against a tree less than two miles from the airstrip at Bonanza. He had apparently not been killed in the crash, but had tried to walk out of the jungle, for the timber men found no trace of the airplane. The only articles found with Bill were his wristwatch and machete. This anomaly only proves the tragic fact that when a pilot crashes in the jungle, he usually stays there.

For some time, Lowell Yerex had on various occasions approached me with a proposition to purchase our airline. Lowell was expanding his operations, and eventually he did acquire all of the local airlines in all of the Central American countries. However, when Yerex first approached me, I was not interested in selling the airline. But as time went by, I realized that I would have to leave Nicaragua and return to the States. Thelma was becoming more and more disenchanted with our life in this tropical country, and I really couldn't blame her. There were few American women of her age with whom she could socialize. Then, too, I was away almost every day, flying to some remote corner of the republic. If there was a possibility of saving our marriage, I would have to leave the operation of the airline to someone else and take Thelma and Marilyn back to California.

I recommended to Palazio that we accept Yerex's offer, explaining to him my problems and why I had to leave Nicaragua.

Carlos Palazio accompanied us to Corinto, where we boarded a coastal steamer for La Libertad, the Pacific port of El Salvador. At San Salvador we checked into the Nueva Mundo Hotel, where we would wait a week for the Grace Line's *Santa Paula* for the voyage to San Pedro, California. One afternoon while I was sitting in the lobby of the hotel talking with Billy Begg, my former radio operator in Honduras, Larry Calloway, the local manager for Pan American, came into the hotel escorting a tall, handsome young man whom he introduced to us as James Saxon Childers, the author.

Larry informed Billy and me that Jim Childers was a columnist on a Birmingham, Alabama, paper and also the author of several books, one of which I remember was titled *Through Oriental Gates*. Larry and Childers spent the afternoon in the bar playing a dice game for drinks. Bill and I joined them for dinner, and later, while we were sitting in the lobby drinking coffee, Jim looked at me and asked, "What have *you* been doing in Central America?"

He took me rather by surprise, for, during the entire afternoon and throughout dinner, we had not exchanged a word. So somewhat facetiously I said, "I have been flying for gold." With this statement, Jim Childer's attention immediately became riveted on me. He wanted to hear about some of the experiences I had had flying for gold mines in Honduras and Nicaragua. For the rest of the evening the conversation focused on Childers and me, and I, warming to the subject, did most of the narrating. Finally when we bid each other goodnight, Jim said, "Frank, you've got to write this."

The next morning as I entered the dining room, I saw Childers sitting at a table alone. He motioned me over and invited me to have breakfast with him. The first thing he said was, "Frank, I've got a title for your book, *I Flew for Gold*."

"The title sounds good, Jim, but I am not a writer; I am only an airline pilot."

"You can do it all right. Just write the story as you would tell it to me, and I will edit it for you."

"Thanks, Jim. Maybe someday I'll try it."

The *Santa Paula* finally arrived, and Thelma and I, with Marilyn in tow, boarded the vessel at La Libertad. Four days later, after sailing off the coasts of Guatemala and Mexico, we docked at San Pedro. I had wired ahead reserving a suite at the Hollywood Plaza Hotel. (I always seemed to be coming back to the Hollywood Plaza.)

We had been only two days ensconced in our hotel suite when Thelma decided to leave for Seattle, taking Marilyn with her. The following day I bought a new car and drove to Reno. This time our marriage was definitely over.

My destination was the home of Judge Bartlett, who at that time was a famous divorce judge. In fact, someone had written a Broadway play based on the judge's career on the bench. It was ironic that I should now be seeking to retain the judge as my attorney in the divorce proceedings when on that April day seven years before, his daughter, Margaret, had been one of my passengers on mine and Thelma's honeymoon flight from Los Angeles to Detroit. I had been told by a friend of mine, True Vencill, who was also a friend of the Bartlett family, that Margaret had become a recluse, that she never left her bedroom and would see no one. This was certainly a contrast to the girl I had flown across the continent years before. At that time she was a vivacious, outgoing person. So upon my arrival at the Bartlett home and after introducing myself to the judge, his wife, and Margaret's sisters, Dorothy and Jean, I was quite surprised when Dorothy said, "Frank, Margaret would like for you to come up to her room and say hello."

When I entered her room, I said to myself, *This is not the Margaret Bartlett I used to know.* She seemed to have aged so many years that she looked almost like an old woman. Deep lines furrowed her formerly beautiful face, and her eyes were circled by dark shadows. She greeted me warmly and talked of that flight of long ago. She remembered all of the details and seemed to thoroughly enjoy reminiscing about those days when aviation was very young and flying across the continent was not a routine affair. As far as I could tell, Margaret seemed mentally alert and quite in command of herself. But this was the first and last time I was to see her during my six weeks' tenure in Reno.

I am not going to dwell on my six weeks' residence in Reno. I will only say that it was indeed an interesting, if traumatic, experience. The most important event of my days in Reno was meeting Helen Kittridge, a tall, statuesque blonde who was destined to later become my wife. Helen and I were immediately attracted to each other, and throughout our stay in Nevada we were together most of the time. We would drive up to the Pyramid Lake Dude Ranch some thirty miles north of Reno. There we would spend a few days riding horseback over the desert. Sometimes at night we would get a group together and ride out into the moonlight and broil steaks over a fire built of mesquite brush, and sometimes we would drive up to Glenbrook, a village on the Nevada side of Lake Tahoe, and visit with Boyce Hart, my old friend of Buenos Aires days. Boyce was now in Reno for the same reason I was, and I had accidentally run across him while riding in the desert from Pyramid Lake Dude Ranch. Boyce was trying to write a book; he had had a colorful life while working for the National City Bank, having been stationed at such outposts as Shanghai and old Petrograd, as well as Moscow and Peking.

Our six weeks' mandatory residence finally came to an end. Helen and her friend Zelda left for San Francisco, where they planned to take an apartment and look for a job. Due to a legal technicality, I was held over for another week. Then I drove down to San Francisco, where I visited with Helen and Zelda for a few days before returning to Los Angeles to once again take up residence at the Hollywood Plaza Hotel.

Chapter 19   London

Shortly after my arrival back in Los Angeles, I received a call from Jerry Vultee: president of the Vultee Aircraft Corporation. I had previously for a brief period been Vultee's sales manager and had sold a few of the Vultee transports to American Airlines and Pan American. This was a very fast airplane (200 MPH cruising) for those days. It was an all-metal, single-engine aircraft, its configuration quite large for a single-engine job. As I recall, it carried twelve passengers.

Jerry greeted me pleasantly and proceeded to tell me of his plans, which involved my very active participation. It seems that one of his airplanes was parked in a hangar at the Hanworth Airdrome outside of London. For some reason, which he didn't make clear, he had fired the pilot and the mission had to be aborted, at least for the time being.

At that time there resided in London a British oil promoter by the name of Francis Ricket. Ricket had received considerable publicity in the United States as having obtained a large oil concession from the Abyssinian government. But according to an article in *Time* magazine, our State Department had somehow invalidated the deal. Now the mission that I mentioned previously was to fly Francis Ricket to Baghdad and Addis Ababa, as he had to go to these two cities in connection with his oil business. Somehow Jerry had gotten in the act and he very much wanted his airplane used on this mission, as he shrewdly foresaw that the attendant publicity would enhance the sale of Vultee airplanes in both Europe and the Middle East.

Of course, all this boiled down to the fact that Jerry wanted me to go to London and fly Ricket to Baghdad and Addis Ababa, thereby resuming the mission that my predecessor pilot had aborted. While I really had other plans, Jerry offered me such a good salary and expense account that I could hardly turn him down. However, my acceptance of what appeared to be a simple procedure was to prove complicated indeed. My first project was to get my pilot's license renewed. For this

I had to go to CAA headquarters at the Burbank airport. There was a Vultee on the line at the Glendale Airport, where the factory was located, and Jerry very graciously offered me the plane to fly over to Burbank. I accepted a little reluctantly, for while I had *sold* these airplanes, I had never actually flown one. At the time of my tenure as sales manager, we had a demonstration pilot on the payroll. Anyway, this being the noon hour, there was no one around to even give me a cockpit check. So I climbed into the pilot's seat, carefully scrutinized the instrument panel, found that I was familiar with most of the instruments, and relaxed a little. There were three things, however, that were new to me: prop pitch control, flaps, and retractable landing gear. (Remember, I had been flying in the jungles of Central America with airplanes almost as old as I was.)

I observed the position of all controls, practiced simulating their operation, started the engine, and took off. Approaching Burbank, I dropped the gear, set the flaps at fifteen degrees, and made a respectable landing. Well, so far so good. I still had to get the airplane back to Glendale.

The inspector renewed my license, a mere formality, as I had taken a recent physical and of course he knew me and knew of my flying ability.

Again I got in the airplane and took off for Glendale. Of course, the two airports are almost adjacent to one another; it was only a matter of getting airborne before you had to throttle back for your landing at Glendale. Now that I had the use of Jerry's airplane, I decided I might as well fly around a bit and get familiar with the characteristics of this particular craft. After about a half-hour, I decided that I liked the airplane, as it handled well. I prepared to land. This time as I approached Glendale at about a hundred feet, I seemed to have forgotten all about the flaps. I was too high and coming in too fast. At the last moment, I shoved the flap control lever to "full"; the airplane immediately slowed down, but by now I was almost halfway down the runway. However, I continued fighting the airplane to the ground and finally hit the runway with a hard jolt, braked hard, and managed to stop just before running off the end of the runway.

After lunch, I received some more instructions from Jerry. In the first place, there was little time in which to prepare for my departure for London. It was one of those "do it yesterday edicts," Jerry informed me. E. L. Cord, the automobile magnate, wanted to talk with me. Jerry said I had an appointment with him the following morning at ten at his Beverly Hills home. Jerry said that as Cord was a director of the company, it was necessary to play ball with him. Also, he personally was to pay my expenses while I was in Europe and the Middle East. In addition, there was a third party, one Ben Smith, who was known in financial circles as "Sell 'em Short Ben." It seems that he had made a fortune selling the market short when everyone else was losing his shirt. Jerry further informed me that Ben Smith would pay my expenses across the Atlantic. I never did learn Smith's exact relationship with Vultee Aircraft. "Of course," Jerry continued, "Vultee Aircraft will pay your salary." I was glad to learn that the company was going to pay something. After all, I was under the impression that I would be representing Vultee Aircraft, rather than E. L. Cord and Ben Smith.

The next morning promptly at ten, I arrived at the Beverly Hills home (a replica of Mount Vernon) of E. L. Cord. A butler met me at the door and escorted me into a huge living room and bade me be seated. In a few minutes, Cord appeared, a short man with a Napoleonic bearing. He was, of course, expecting me, so formalities were dispensed with. He questioned me briefly regarding my experience, which of course he knew all about anyway. Also, he emphasized to me the importance of my journey in that I was representing Vultee Aircraft and, naturally, the primary objective was the sale of aircraft.

The interview lasted only about twenty minutes. Cord shook my hand and wished me a good trip and a successful one. Driving down the hill toward Glendale, I thought, *What a screwy deal I've gotten mixed up in. Cord, Ben Smith, Jerry Vultee, Vultee Aircraft—all having a finger in my pie.*

The next few days were hectic—rushing here and there, obtaining passports, visas, and a lot of photographic equipment which Jerry insisted on, and finally packing, not only my clothes and personal belongings, but a ton of photographic paraphernalia. So at last, one evening at 6 o'clock, I boarded a plane for New York. We went through on schedule as far as Washington. There a tractor towing the DC-3 somehow pulled the tail wheel out of the fuselage. As the airline had no spare plane at Hoover Field, we had to take the train for New York. At that time, all sailings for Europe left at midnight from the North River piers. These midnight departures had confused me into thinking I had a day in New York. In fact, I had planned on seeing some old friends and really enjoying myself.

However, when my train arrived at Penn Station, I was paged. The train official so mispronounced my name that I hardly recognized it. It turned out to be Ben Smith who had had me paged, and as I came forward, he greeted me with, "I've held the *Bremen* for a half an hour, but I couldn't hold it any longer. She has sailed, but we can still catch it down the bay aways." I thought, *This must have cost him a fortune.*

The *Bremen* at that time was the fastest and most deluxe liner plying the North Atlantic. So to hold up its departure for a half-hour, to say nothing of the mails, must indeed have cost him a bundle.

We dashed madly toward the North River pier, Smith's limousine breaking all speed records along those icy streets. It was plenty cold that night—it was the end of January—but we finally arrived at the North German Lloyd Pier in one piece. A tug covered with ice came alongside the pier, and my baggage was thrown aboard. In the meantime, Smith said, "I'm supposed to pay your way across to Southampton. Here's a thousand-dollar bill. Think that'll be enough?" I had never seen a thousand-dollar bill, and in fact, I have never seen one since, but I thanked him and assured him it would indeed be adequate. I thought to myself, *What in hell am I going to spend a thousand dollars on?* Strangely, I thought, he asked for no receipt, just casually handed me the bill as if he were tipping a maitre d' or a dining room steward.

As I climbed aboard the tug, Smith shook my hand and wished me a bon voyage. The tug charged down New York harbor past the Statue of Liberty and finally caught up with the *Bremen*. The ship hove to as we came alongside, a rope ladder was thrown from the hold of the vessel, the crew of the tug threw my baggage up into the hold, and I climbed up an icy rope ladder. Remember, this was 1 o'clock in the morning on a damn cold January night. As I stepped aboard, my room steward met me. "I'm sorry, sir; the bar is closed, but I'll bring you some hot tea to your stateroom." I thought, *Well, here I am aboard the Bremen, but what a peculiar way to sail for England.*

The next morning, somewhere off the Newfoundland banks, I was called to the radio office, the steward saying that someone wanted to talk with me over ship-to-shore radio telephone. It was Ben Smith wanting to know if I had warmed up from my exposure to the elements the night before. That, too, cost him plenty, for in those days talking over ship-to-shore to a vessel at sea was not cheap.

The voyage over was very pleasant. It was made more so by my good fortune in meeting Marjorie and Mel Waddington from Toronto. I had accidentally literally bumped into Marjorie walking down a companionway, and we immediately struck up a conversation. She and her husband took me under their wing, and we were inseparable from then on through the rest of the voyage and also all the time I was in London. The accommodations on the *Bremen* were superb, the food excellent, and everywhere one looked there was luxury. Even the decor of our staterooms was most eye-appealing.

As we docked in Southampton and I stepped off the gangplank, the first thing I saw anchored in a section of the harbor that seemed to be a graveyard of ships was the old *Van Dyke*, the ship I had sailed on to Buenos Aires so long ago.

The Waddingtons and I sat together on the boat train to Waterloo Station. They had insisted that I accompany them to the Waldorf Hotel on the Strand, where they had reservations. They assured me that it was a reasonable hotel where I too should stay. Frankly, I was only too glad to stick close to them, for I knew no one in London and they were delightful company.

My first order of the day was going out to Hanworth and checking the Vultee. I went over the plane thoroughly, running up the engine, which sounded fine, with maximum RPMs. The airplane was in good condition and ready for flight.

Returning to my hotel, I called Ricket and made an appointment to see him in his downtown London office at ten the following morning. I had already heard a lot about Francis Ricket. It seems that he was quite a man about town and owned a large estate about twenty miles out of London, where he played polo, hunted foxes, and entertained extensively. He was also, I learned, a somewhat mysterious character. No one apparently had any idea from where his obvious wealth was derived.

Promptly at 10 o'clock the following morning I was ushered into the elaborate office of one Francis Ricket, oil promoter. Ricket arose from his desk, greeted me cordially, and offered me a seat at his right. He was a good-looking man, probably in his early forties, of medium height, with dark hair and deep-brown eyes, clean-shaven and immaculately dressed. *The typical London sportsman,* I thought.

Ricket proceeded to inform me of his plans for the forthcoming flight to Baghdad and Addis Ababa. However, he stressed that these plans were tentative. He emphasized that the flight itself could be canceled. Certain events had taken place even while I was crossing the ocean. Finally, when I got up to leave he said, "I'll call you at the Waldorf as soon as I have something definite. In the meantime, enjoy yourself in London. If you wish to do some flying, go ahead, but it's not much fun flying in our horrible English weather, is it?" I decided that I liked this guy and we would get along just fine.

The Waddingtons seemed to know just about everybody worth knowing in London. They introduced me to a great many of their friends, not the least of whom was Sandy McPherson. Sandy was a tall and, as his name implied, good-looking Nova Scotian, and of all things, he played the organ at London's Empire Theatre. (Sandy was later to become very famous as a performer on the BBC, and even to this day, I often, in my travels, meet many residents of London who either knew

Sandy personally or knew of him through his performances on the BBC.) Sandy and I hit it off right away, and we had many good times together. He was a two-fisted Scotch drinker, but one of those rare people who never showed it. The pubs as I recall at that time closed at a ridiculous early hour. However, Sandy knew all of the after-hours places frequented by the theatrical crowd.

One day when the weather gave us a break, I visited several of the aerodromes—Heston, Croyden, and all those active in that day. I met some Royal Flying Corps officers, and they entertained me royally at their Royal Flying Club in London. Then, too, Marjorie and Mel were constantly inviting me to cocktail parties and "afternoon teas" where there was more spirits drunk than tea.

This went on for about three weeks until finally Ricket called and asked me to come to his office. He looked kind of glum as I entered, and I knew instinctively this trip was off, at least for the time being. Ricket got right to the point. "Sorry to tell you the bad news," he said. *Or maybe it's good news,* I mused. After all, the weather all over Europe was very bad indeed and I really did not relish flying over the Alps in February.

"You might as well return to the States," Ricket said. "I have no idea if or when my business affairs will necessitate my going to these cities."

"Okay, Mr. Ricket. I'll book passage right away. Good-bye and thanks for everything." At that moment I experienced real regret that I would not get to know this chap better.

I returned to the hotel, found Marjorie and Mel in the lounge, and told them of the new development—that I would now be returning to the States. They understood, they said, but were very sorry to see me go. And I knew they meant it. They called Sandy and arranged a party for me that evening. In the meantime, I booked passage on the *Manhattan* of the United States Line, to leave Southampton on February twenty-eighth. Marjorie, Mel, and Sandy had arranged for a dinner at a private club to which Sandy belonged. It was a gala event, with good food and excellent wines, and after dinner we carried on over many drinks until a very late hour. The three of them wanted to escort me to Waterloo Station the following morning and see me off on the boat train for Southampton. But I said no to their kind offer. I would take a cab to the station. No sad good-byes! I wanted to leave these fine people on a joyous note.

It was a rough crossing that February of 1936. When the *Manhattan* entered the English Channel, she began to roll and pitch, and by the time we approached the Irish Sea, it was difficult even to walk aboard the vessel. We did, however, manage to pick up the pilot to guide us into the harbor of Cobh. We sailed from Cobh at midnight, and as we approached the sea buoy at harbor's entrance, it was obviously too rough for the pilot to board the pilot boat. So the pilot had a free, if unscheduled, passage to New York.

For the rest of the voyage, I saw little of my fellow passengers. Not until we fetched Ambrose light did some begin to emerge from their staterooms. After a few days visiting friends on Long Island, I took a bus for Detroit, where I would pick up a new car I had ordered before leaving for England. It was a cold, uncomfortable, and altogether miserable trip to Detroit. I swore off buses for good, and to this day, I have not been on a long-distance bus.

My car was ready for me, and after a good night's rest at the Book Cadillac Hotel, I started driving westward to California. Five days of hard driving and once again I was home in my quarters at the Hollywood Plaza Hotel.

Chapter 20

Costa Rica

My first act after settling into my hotel was to call Helen in San Francisco. She seemed in unusually good spirits, informing me she had a job as a photographic model.

"That's fine," I said. "Being a statuesque blonde, you should make a good model."

"When are you coming up here?" she asked.

"Well, today is Thursday. I'll see you tomorrow, Friday. I'll be on the 5 o'clock flight. Will you meet me?"

"Sure thing. I'll be at the airport waiting."

For the next month or so, Helen and I commuted between Los Angeles and San Francisco. One week I would fly north, and the next week she would fly south. Steve Stimson, United's San Francisco manager, got to know us well; he said we were his best commuter passengers.

One late afternoon, I returned to my room feeling particularly depressed. I picked up the phone and called Helen at her San Francisco apartment.

I said, "Call Steve and get a seat on the next flight down here."

"What for?" she asked.

"To get married, of course," I replied. "We're spending too much money on United Airlines."

"Are you serious?" she asked. "You sound as if you're sober enough."

"Of course I'm serious.

"And quite sober," I added.

In a few minutes, she called me back. "I'll arrive at Burbank at twelve midnight. Don't forget to meet me."

"I'll try to remember. Hope the plane is on time. I just might fall asleep."

The following morning, I called a friend of mine at the Glendale Airport who was in the airplane-charter business. "Jim, how soon can you have a plane and pilot ready for a flight to Las Vegas? There will be four of us—me, my bride-to-be, and Ralph and Ada Carter."

"Will a Stinson Relient do?" he asked.

"That'll be just fine."

"Okay, Frank. She'll be ready in an hour."

"We'll be there, Jim."

Helen insisted that we be married in Nevada. She said that as I had been divorced in Nevada, we wanted to be sure to make our marriage legal, therefore we should be married in Nevada. I had asked Ralph and Ada Carter to accompany us on this marital flight as we needed their presence at the ceremony. Ralph was the manager of the hotel, and we had become good friends.

When we arrived at the airport, Jim escorted us to the waiting airplane. I merely glanced at the pilot sitting at the controls waiting for us to get aboard. I looked at him again and did a double take. For the pilot was none other than Sam Taylor with whom I had barnstormed in Savannah, Georgia, back in 1922. And we hadn't seen each other since!

This would indeed be a day to remember. In addition to my marriage, my reunion with an old flying buddy after so many years was another excuse for celebrating.

After the ceremony, performed by a Methodist minister, we repaired to the hotel for lunch. It was late in the afternoon when we finished lunch, and as Sam didn't want to arrive back at Glendale after dark, we all checked into the hotel. That evening we celebrated in great fashion, a gala dinner with plenty of champagne and everyone in a festive mood.

When Helen and I arrived back in Los Angeles, the first thing on our agenda was to look for an apartment. We found a small efficiency in Hollywood and rented it immediately. It was nearing the holiday season, and we seemed to be on a continuous party through New Year's. Many of my friends from the East showed up in Hollywood that winter of 1936. So there was always an excuse to celebrate. It was also a winter of extreme bad weather. Tragically, three United Airlines flights approaching Burbank flew into the Tehachapi Mountains.

It was now a new year, 1937, and I was still unemployed and had no particular plans for the future. But I knew this couldn't go on much longer. I had, after all, to make a living especially since I had acquired a new wife. One day I said to Helen, "Let's take a boat to Panama. I can always get a job as a pilot in those countries, and besides, it will be a wonderful honeymoon voyage."

For some reason, my "itchy feet" kept taking me back to Central America. So we booked passage on a Japanese vessel, the Something

(?) *Maru,* and sailed from San Pedro the latter part of June 1937.

The voyage down the coast of Mexico and Central America was without incident with one exception. And what an exception it was! Off the Isthmus of Tehuantepec, we ran into a hurricane. Shortly after breakfast that morning, the wind started to howl through the rigging and the seas became violent wind-streaked walls of water, which had turned a bilious green in color. The stern of the ship was rising out of the water and settling back with a dull thud. Helen, always curious about everything, went back on the stern to watch the propellers come out of the water, causing the ship to vibrate violently until she fell back into the water. By this time, it was evident that Helen was going to have trouble getting back to the safety of the smoking salon. I grabbed a passing sailor and yelled, "Get a line and follow me." He grabbed a line coiled on a stanchion nearby, and together we crawled aft to where Helen was hanging onto a stanchion. The sailor made the line fast to the nearest upright and with the end of the line crawled to within a few feet of Helen. He motioned for her to grab the end of the line and hold on tight. Then together we hauled on the line, dragging Helen across the deck to where we were standing. We helped her back to the salon, where she collapsed breathlessly onto a sofa.

After a few minutes' rest, she said, "I guess that wasn't so smart, was it?"

"The next time, young lady, when the seas get rough, you stay put in the stateroom or the salon. Don't even go on deck," I said.

She looked at me and grinned. But I knew that she wouldn't ever repeat such a performance.

The wind blew ninety miles per hour for about fourteen hours. There was considerable damage to the superstructure, the waves breaking over the bridge, smashing most of the lifeboats to splinters. I had been in some rough seas before, but nothing like this. I learned firsthand what a hurricane at sea could do to a vessel of such size as 10,000 tons and more.

Finally we were out of the hurricane and proceeded under clear skies to Panama, where our battered vessel docked at Balboa in the Canal Zone.

Helen and I checked into a small hotel on the Avenida Central in downtown Panama City and immediately proceeded to look for an apartment. We found a suitable, if not too elegant, place on Fourth of July Avenue. This street is the dividing line between Panama City and the Canal Zone. Coincidentally, we moved into our apartment on Fourth of July Avenue—you guessed it—on the Fourth of July.

I had been told by a mutual friend to look up a chap by the name of Ralph Sexton, who was also a pilot and had operated his own airline across the isthmus from Colon to Balboa. However, Ralph had offered too much competition to Pan American, and they had, with their political influence, according to Ralph, put him out of business. I called Ralph and explained who I was, and while he sounded rather gruff over the phone, he invited Helen and me out to his Bella Vista (a suburb of Panama City) home for cocktails. Ralph and his charming wife greeted us cordially. He was a short, rather heavyset man with sandy hair and deep-blue eyes. I sensed immediately that here was a real "diamond in the rough" type who, if he liked you, would go to great lengths to be of help, but if he didn't, you might as well forget you had ever met Ralph Sexton.

Ralph and I discussed aviation while the women talked of other things. I learned later that Ralph had made a fortune constructing oil-storage tanks in Colombia. He had sold his fleet of Hamilton airplanes (all-metal planes built of corrugated aluminum). He now owned a Beechcraft on floats, which he flew all over the republic, where he had built fishing camps and duck blinds on the various rivers of Panama. Helen and I were invited along on many of these trips, and we had a great time, for the four of us soon became very good friends.

One day, Ralph phoned and asked me to meet him at the El Panama club for lunch. After lunch, we moved into the lounge for some coffee, and while waiting to be served, Ralph said, "I was talking yesterday with Narcissus Garay, the minister of communications. He said he was looking for someone to establish a licensing and inspection department of the government for the commercial aircraft—in other words, a CAA of Panama. I immediately thought of you, especially since you helped organize the old Aeronautics Branch of the U.S. Department of Commerce.

"Now," he continued, "you can have this job if you want it. I know you have been anxious to get on a payroll here in Panama, and while this job won't amount to much to begin with, it could develop into something of importance as commercial aviation here develops."

"Okay, Ralph. It sounds like a challenge, and I'd like to give it a try. And thanks very much for your help." I appeared a few days later (Ralph having set up an appointment for 11 o'clock with Garay) at the office of the minister of communications. I was ushered into a huge room, and at the far end sat a diminutive man behind a large desk that almost obscured him from view. The distance from the door to Garay's desk seemed as long as a football field as I proceeded to walk forward.

Garay was a somewhat surly, arrogant little man of few words.

The conversation lasted all of five minutes, in which time he explained that I would be stationed at Patilla Point, the commercial airport of Panama. A salary was mentioned, which I considered very modest indeed, but better than nothing. I had purchased an old Buick, which I now drove out to Patilla Point, to survey the scene of my future labors.

The only operator on the field was a Panamanian by the name of Gelabert, who ran an airline to David, a city about 150 miles north, near the border of Costa Rica. Gelabert's fleet consisted of one Hamilton (which he had purchased from Sexton) and an old Lockheed Vega and one pilot, an Indian named Honcho. Incidentally, both Gelabert and the Indian were excellent pilots. This, I thought, was going to be one hell-of-a-job—two pilots and two airplanes to ride herd on. Licensing the pilots and the airplane was no problem, but what was I going to do for an encore? Go fishing?

The days dragged on with utter boredom. One day, Gelabert asked me to fly up to David with him and then take the motor-rail tram up the mountain to Boquete, a resort nestled in the Chiriqui Mountains. "We'll stay overnight at a lodge run by two former nurses from Gorgas Hospital," he said. "We need to cool off a bit from this humid heat of Panama City," he continued.

Gelabert's invitation was rather surprising, for he had never been particularly friendly toward me and consequently we had not developed any rapport between us. Anyway, I thanked him and said I would be delighted to go—anything to break this monotony—and the thought of cool mountain breezes was very enticing.

It was indeed delightfully cool in the mountains; we even had to sleep under a blanket at night. And the two nurses (originally from Los Angeles) were most hospitable, so we relaxed under their efficient care and enjoyed the excellent food they served. What a contrast a hundred or so miles could make—from the steaming jungle heat of Panama City to this refreshingly cool climate. After a lazy night and day, we flew back to Patilla Point, to stifling tropical heat and everlasting boredom.

I soon decided that I wanted no more of this silly job, an exercise in futility. I also decided that I wanted no part in Latin American politics, in which I was very much involved, whether I liked it or not. I had heard through some sort of grapevine that a man named Ross who operated an airline based in San Jose, Costa Rica, needed a pilot. I wired Ross that if he needed a pilot, I was available and stated briefly my qualifications. After all, I couldn't really wire him a full résumé. I couldn't afford it. I received a wire from Ross the following day saying to come on up—I had the job.

In the meantime, I advised Ralph of my decision. I thanked him for his kind help, but I just couldn't hack it in that job. "Anyway," I said, "I really want to get back to flying."

"I understand," he said. "I can't blame you a bit. Anyway, Costa Rica is a nice place to live, and," he added, "you and Helen will join Jane and me for dinner tonight at the El Panama Club."

I will always remember that farewell dinner. It was, for me, a memorable occasion—and a rather sad one, for I hated to take leave of this delightful couple with whom Helen and I had done so many interesting things. Together we had flown over most of the Republic of Panama. We had fished in the rivers, hunted wild pig on the savannahs, and flown up the Santa Maria River for duck hunting. I would miss all that, surely, but now it was time to change directions, and my direction was north to Costa Rica.

Arriving in San José, I was met at the airport by a young man, in his early twenties, who introduced himself as Ross. I had not expected to meet such a young person, and I was surprised to learn that he was half American. He carried two passports, a Costa Rican and American. This could be a great convenience in his travels; he could switch from being a citizen of one country to another, if the occasion warranted it.

There were three local airlines operating from the San José Airport in addition to the international carrier, Pan American. Ross drove me over to his hangar and showed me his two airplanes, a Travel Air 6000, a high-wing monoplane powered by a 225 H.P. Wright Whirlwind engine. Also there was a Hamilton, that ubiquitous corrugated aluminum airplane that looked like a Ford trimotor without the outboard engines. This was equipped with a Pratt and Whitney 550 H.P. Hornet engine. Ralph had done well peddling his airplanes throughout Central America.

While we were talking, a car drove up and out stepped a short, stocky young man with blond hair and a ruddy complexion. He looked as if he just came off a farm in Ohio, which indeed he had. Ross introduced him to me as Rupke, his *other* pilot. Rupke proved to be an unusual pilot. Most of us were rather devil-may-care adventurers, sort of soldier-of-fortune types. But Rupke was of the ultraconservative type. He didn't drink or smoke and saved almost every penny of his salary. (I understand that when he finally left Costa Rica, he went back to Ohio and bought two apartment houses.)

Ross then drove me to a downtown hotel where I would hole up until Helen joined me. I wanted to get settled in my new job before she joined me in San José.

Ross asked me to be at the airport early the next morning, and I would fly with Rupke to familiarize myself with the route. And, as some of the airstrips were not very long, I would learn the tricks of landing on them and remaining in one piece. So at 7 o'clock with Rupke flying and me sitting in the right seat, we took off for Puerto Limon. We would fly from there to La Questa and thence to Punta Arenas and, after landing at several airports in the Guana-Costa area, back to San José.

The following morning, I took off alone in the Travel Air with a cargo of freight, including a crate of chickens, a few sacks of beans, and one small pig—also, two male passengers going to La Questa for farm work. All local airlines in Central America tried to do most of their flying in the mornings. Usually cumulus clouds started building up early, and by afternoon, they invariably turned to cumulonimbus, producing heavy rain in sometimes violent thunder squalls. Therefore, we avoided afternoon flying like the plague, except for an occasional charter.

I experienced no trouble with the route or the airfields, and the next day I took the Hamilton on the run. The Hamilton was a good airplane. It carried a 3,000-pound payload and landed fairly short for such a big airplane. Again, I had no trouble, and from that time on, it was merely routine flying.

I soon met all the other pilots flying out of San José. There was Snarky Wilson of ENTA Airlines, also Slim Perret of ENTA, Carl Overly, and Pete Crawford of Aerovias Nacionales—all good guys who liked a good time together. After a couple of weeks, I sent word to Helen to take a coastwise steamer to Punta Arenas and I would meet her there and fly her into San José. So early one morning, I removed all the seats in the Travel Air, making room for Helen's baggage, and flew down to Punta Arenas. Helen's boat arrived on schedule, and after getting her baggage aboard the airplane, we took off for San José with Helen sitting in the copilot's seat. The engine was pouring out blue smoke, and Helen, somewhat disconcerted, asked what was wrong with it. "Think nothing of it," I replied. "This airplane burns coal." Maintenance on our two airplanes amounted to less than nothing. The one lone native mechanic was totally lacking in any expertise concerning both the airplanes and engines; Rupke and I had abandoned any effort to write up any malfunctions of the aircraft. We simply continued to fly the airplanes until one or the other developed some problem we considered dangerous. Then we just refused to fly the plane until the offending part was repaired or replaced.

I hadn't been with Ross very long before I decided that my services were going to be of a very temporary nature. In the first place, Ross's

Stinson trimotor, formerly owned by Marion Davies. We called this plane the "flying boudoir."

behavior was that of a petulant child. Whenever he was confronted with a problem demanding an immediate decision, he would jump in his car, dash madly home, and barricade himself in the house and not show up for sometimes two or three days. This left Rupke and me to fend for ourselves as best as we could.

This ridiculous situation continued for about a month; then Aerovias Nacionales surprised me by an offer of a job. Aerovias was owned by the Macaya brothers, headed by Roman, a pilot, and assisted by Alfonso and Hernando. The Macayas were a very prominent Costa Rican family, of aristocratic Spanish heritage. Alfonso and I soon became good friends, and our friendship lasted over the years until his death about three years ago. He was an extremely intelligent person, and unfortunately he had suffered severe injuries in an airplane crash in Oakland, California. At the time of the accident, he was not expected to live and his face bore scars of the crash.

I, of course, lost no time in accepting this offer and immediately notified Ross that I was leaving his employ. I found that I was replacing "Penny" Rogers, who, I understood, had a drinking problem that had progressed to the point where he had to be discharged. I had, of course, met Penny and found him a very likable fellow. Penny was from Ok-

190

lahoma, part Cherokee Indian, and claimed to be a cousin of Will Rogers.

I had observed Aerovias's operation and considered it to be a well-run airline. Their fleet of airplanes, all in excellent condition, consisted of a Curtiss Kingbird (the same airplane I had flown on Eastern), a Travel Air powered by a Pratt and Whitney Wasp engine, a Ford trimotor and a trimotored Stinson, formerly owned by a Marion Davies. This Stinson, whose interior resembled a lady's boudoir, was the bane of my existence. In the first place, the airplane was very much under-powered, with its three 200 H.P. Jacobs engines.

The airport of San José at that time was adjacent to the downtown area, partially surrounded by high-tension wires, and a rather small field at that. Taking off from this field with the Stinson fully loaded was a hazardous bit of business. If we had lost a hundred or more RPM on any of the three engines, we would have "bought the farm." Another peculiarity of this aircraft was that it was equipped with "heel" brakes. On a conventional braking system, to apply brakes, one merely presses forward with the ball of the foot. However, on this aircraft, you applied brake by pressing down with the *heel* of your foot. Now, to me this was very awkward indeed. My feet were just not attached to my ankles in a manner permitting me to operate the brake system efficiently.

Carl Overly spent most of one afternoon trying to teach me to taxi the Stinson. Taxiing down the field, instead of going straight, I was scribing the letter "S." Finally Carl decided that I could possibly get the plane off the ground and back in one piece, so he changed over to the pilot's seat and proceeded to taxi the plane towards the hangar. As we approached close to the hangar door, I saw a mechanic standing facing the right outboard engine, which, of course, put him directly in front of me. Suddenly, to my horror, the man started walking toward the rapidly turning propellor. *What's the matter with this guy?* I thought. *Surely he's going to stop before he gets any closer.* But he didn't stop; he just walked into the propellor. There was a sharp metalic thud as if someone had thrown a crowbar into the propellor. The propellor had cut off most of the back of the man's head, and the force had knocked him flat on his back. Of course, Carl couldn't see this tragic drama from his pilot's seat. And there was no time to warn him to cut the engines. Carl and I stuffed a handkerchief in the back of the man's head and laid him in the back seat of a car and drove frantically to the hospital. But the mechanic was dead before we arrived.

By this time, 1938–1939, United Fruit had begun a $50 million expansion program. Of course, 50 million would not be considered much these days for such an undertaking. However, the company (United

Fruit) was developing banana plantations all along the Pacific Coast of Costa Rica. Such villages and towns as Quepos, Puerto Jiminez, Parrita, and Golfito formed the nucleus of these developing plantations. Our fleet of airplanes was kept busy supplying these projects with all sorts of freight, including tractor and bulldozer parts, foodstuffs, such as beans and rice, and hogs, both live and dressed. All this was in addition to our regularly scheduled runs to various towns in the republic.

We also had an international run to Managua, Nicaragua, which we flew three times a week. Only Carl and I flew this schedule, as we were the only pilots qualified on the Ford, which airplane was used exclusively on this run. One day on my return flight from Managua to San José, I had as a passenger a representative of the McGraw-Hill Publishing Company. I have forgotten his name, but he was a very likable chap and I suggested that he come home with me for dinner. During the course of the evening, he expressed a desire to see something of the country away from the capitol, San José. I told him that I had a flight out the following morning for Parrita, a United Fruit town on the Pacific coast, and suggested he come along for the ride. I was to fly this same Ford trimotor that I had flown on the Managua run the previous day.

When we arrived at the airport, I found my plane fully loaded with freight and the passengers sitting in their seats waiting to be airlifted to Parrita. It was a beautiful clear day with blue skies dotted with puffy cumulus clouds. I knew that upon our arrival at Parrita, the tropical heat (this being at sea level) would be stifling, in contrast to the air-conditioned climate of San José, situated at an altitude of 3,500 feet.

The turf airstrip at Parrita was quite long, but narrow, with an eight-foot irrigation ditch paralleling each side of the field. My landing was smooth, and as we were rolling along at sixty miles an hour, the plane started a turn to the left. I immediately applied the right brake to correct this start of a ground loop, but nothing happened. This beast I was riding herd on seemed to have a mind of its own, determined to swing 180 degrees into this eight-foot–deep ditch. Realizing that something was mechanically wrong with the left brake, I shoved the left throttle wide open, still applying hard the right brake. If this had been a large airfield, the airplane would have simply ground looped and the most damage done would have been a blown tire.

But the ditch, even while we were rolling straight down the field, was only about fifty feet off my left wing. There was no chance whatsoever of avoiding a crash. We hit with a dull thud and the sound of ripping metal. The left wing had sheared off, and the center engine had broken off from its mount and came to rest under my feet. The gas tanks had ruptured and high-octane gasoline was pouring down on three hot engines. To this day, I can't understand why the plane didn't catch fire. I grabbed the handle of the emergency hatch, which was directly over my head, but it had jammed. I yelled to Perez, the copilot, to get the main door open and get the passengers out, quick! As I turned toward the copilot, I saw my friend from McGraw-Hill standing behind my seat (he had stood throughout the flight, as all seats were occupied when he got aboard) with his left ear almost severed from his head and blood pouring from the wound. Fortunately, Perez was able to get the door open and all passengers were safely evacuated. Perez and I helped my friend up the hill to the United Fruit hospital where a surgeon sewed the man's ear back on. The surgeon did a superb job of stitching and promised that once the wound had healed, there would be no sign of the injury. My friend's cavalier disregard of his injury impressed me greatly. He was even smiling and joking about it as he emerged from the operating room. I decided that this guy was something special—he would do to ride the range with.

It seems that my guess that there was a malfunction of the left brake was right. The official investigation of the accident revealed that indeed that left brake had locked and the wheel had not turned one revolution, as the skid marks showed plainly. The Macayas completely exonerated me from any blame. (There was no "pilot error" verdict in this case.)

There is a sequel to this incident, which I think worthy of telling. About eighteen years later, I was conducting my own business in Miami, Florida. I had occasion to take one of my airline customers to lunch at a restaurant across the street from the Miami International Airport. Sitting at the bar, I heard a chap a couple of seats away telling his friend of an airplane crash he was involved in at Parrita, Costa Rica. He was a Costa Rican, but was speaking perfect English. "You know," he said to his friend, "this damn fool American pilot landed us in an irrigation ditch. The crazy fool damn near killed us."

I found his narration of the incident very amusing. The chap was really humorous. When he finished his spiel, I leaned over to him and said, "I was that pilot."

Well, the man was still full of humor. He looked at me with a wide grin and said, "No wonder you quit flying."

With a sense of déja vu, I continued to fly over the mountains, valleys, and jungles of Costa Rica. The landscape of all Central American countries seen from above had a common similarity. They all had their mountains and valleys and jungles. Yet there was a difference. Guatemala had its beautiful Lake Atitlan; the mountains of Honduras were drab and forbidding. And Nicaragua's thousands of square miles of jungle could prove dangerous for pilots in the event of emergency landings. But Nicaragua also had its Lake Managua, the volcano Momotombo, and of course the huge freshwater Lake Nicaragua. But Costa Rica was different from them all. This was indeed a beautiful country. The lush green mountains and the farm lands of the fertile valleys and banana plantations spread over thousands of acres of flat lands; all formed a pattern of color, illuminating the entire landscape. And everywhere flowers grew in profusion—orchids of all varieties and color, hibiscus, and night-blooming cereus.

Costa Rica was indeed a beautiful country in which to live. But I was born and raised a citizen of the United States, and for some time I felt that I should stop wandering around these Central American countries and return home to a more conventional way of life. Over the years I had dreamed of owning a cattle ranch somewhere in the West, and now I thought perhaps the time had come to try to realize that dream.

It was nearing the end of December 1939 when I approached Helen with my plan to leave the tropics for good. She heartily agreed, for she too was tiring of life in these banana republics. So I broke the news to Alfonso that I wanted to leave for the States around the last of December, about two weeks hence. I told him (truthfully) that I had enjoyed working for him and had been privileged to become his friend, but the time had come for me to leave Central America. Alfonso, I had long since learned, understood most things about life.

Carl Overly, piloting the Wasp Travel Air, flew Helen and me with our baggage to Punta Arenas, where we boarded the *Acajutla,* a small coastwise steamer, for Panama. I had cabled Ralph and Jane Sexton my and Helen's time of arrival at Balboa, and when we docked, they were there to greet us. We had a very enjoyable two days as their house guests in Bella Vista before boarding a Japanese freighter for New York. We were returning to the East Coast this time, for Helen wanted us to visit her mother and brother in Ohio. We were the only passengers aboard this Japanese freighter, which had accommodations for twelve. It was a new ship, and our stateroom was quite large and the decor was quite pleasing. However, the crew, from the captain down, were a surly lot. Only the boatswain spoke English, and I eventually conned him into arranging for me to visit the bridge. At that time, Japanese technology was far behind that of most western nations, especially that of the United States. (Today they have advanced to the point where they are ahead of these same nations.) I found their electronic equipment to be of Sperry manufacture. In retrospect, I can understand their surly behavior, for it was less than two years before Pearl Harbor.

It was a cold overcast morning when we docked in Brooklyn. Shivering, Helen and I disembarked and after clearing customs, we took a taxi to Manhattan, where we checked into the Commodore Hotel. That evening, we took my Aunt Ida to dinner, and the following day, Helen and I boarded a train for Ohio. Helen had been raised on a farm on the outskirts of a small town known as Belle Center.

After a week on the farm, I purchased a used automobile in Belle Center and Helen and I started driving west. The trip across the continent was monotonous and tiresome, and we were happy to finally arrive in the warm, sunny climate of Southern California.

I had always had Arizona in mind as a place to own a small ranch, having spent a week some years before on a 35,000 acre spread owned by my friend "Chuck" Orme. The country fascinated me and the climate was ideal at over 5,000 feet. I wanted no part of the desert heat of Phoenix and the Salt River Valley.

After driving to Prescott, Helen and I checked into the local hotel and straightaway sought the services of a real-estate broker. He drove us about fifteen miles out of Prescott into the Williamson Valley. Turning off the main road, we continued for about a mile, crossing a stream of water, on the far side of which were some buildings consisting of the main ranch house, a cottage, a large barn, and a machine shop that also served as a garage.

Helen and I both fell in love with the place immediately. The setting was beautiful, with Granite Mountain in the background and a magnificent view of Williamson Valley. We drove back to Prescott, and the real-estate man took us to see the owner of the ranch, who was the proprietor of an electrical service shop located on the main street of Prescott. It didn't take long for us to consummate a deal, and we walked out of his store the proud owners of Mint Valley Ranch.

It didn't take long for us to adapt to the ways of ranch life in Arizona. The five quarter horses that came with the ranch afforded us much pleasure, as we rode over the mountain behind our cottage viewing the magnificent landscape below. We soon made good friends with some of the residents of Prescott and the Stringfields, who owned a large ranch adjacent to ours.

Then at night we would lie in bed and by short-wave radio listen to Edward R. Murrow say, "This is London," describing the Nazi bombing and the battle of Britain.

And soon afterwards came Pearl Harbor, and early in 1942 I was

195

once again back in the uniform of an officer of the United States Army Air Corps, flying various types of military aircraft. I have no intention of telling the story of my military career during the Second World War, for really there is no story—nothing of interest or importance happened to me during those four years. I was only one of thousands of officers who, because of our age, were given staff duties and allowed to occasionally fly a ferry mission within the continental limits of the United States.

I am now retired from both flying and business, living in Daytona Beach, Florida. I have been around a long time, and, fortunately still in good health, I expect to be around for a while longer.